ALSO BY FALL RIVER HISTORICAL SOCIETY PRESS

Parallel Lives: A Social History of Lizzie A. Borden and Her Fall River (2011)

The Commonwealth of Massachussetts vs. Lizzie A. Borden: The Knowlton Papers, 1892-1893 (1994)

WOMEN AT WORK

AN ORAL HISTORY OF WORKING CLASS WOMEN IN FALL RIVER, MASSACHUSETTS 1920 TO 1970

Fall River Historical Society

Edited by Dennis A. Binette, Michael Martins, and Joyce B. Rodrigues

Fall River
Historical Society
Press

Fall River Historcal Society Press
451 Rock Street
Fall River, MA 02720
fallriverhistorical.org
(508) 679-1071

For information, write us at Fall River Historical Society, 451 Rock Street, Fall River, MA 02720.

LIBRARY OF CONGRESS CONTROL NUMBER: **2017935986**

ISBN-10: 0-9641248-4-X
ISBN-13: 978-0-96-412484-4

Printed in the United States of America on acid-free paper.

Book and cover design by Stefani Koorey, PearTree Press, Fall River, MA

Front and Back Covers: Fabric; Barnard Manufacturing Co., Fall River, MA; cotton, 1925-early 1930s. *Top image:* A stitcher in an unidentified garment factory in Fall River, MA, in the 1960s; *Middle image:* Workers at Gamma Leather Company, Inc., 228 Plymouth Avenue, Fall River, MA, 1966; *Bottom image:* Fall River garment workers on strike on South Main Street, Fall River, MA, during the 1970s.

Printed in the United States of America

WOMEN AT WORK

CONTENTS

LIST OF ILLUSTRATIONS

All illustrations are from personal collections, except those so designated. Images marked FRHS are from the collection of the Fall River Historical Society.

ILLUSTRATIONS

ILLUSTRATIONS

INTRODUCTION

Women at Work documents the lives of a group of working-class women in the city of Fall River during the middle decades of the twentieth century. Their stories provide a first-hand account of labor issues and everyday life during a tumultuous era in the city's history.

It was a time of change, hardship, and recovery, when the city and its residents faced the decline, and ultimate collapse, of the textile industry; the early depression years of the late 1920s; the Great Depression years of the 1930s; and the rise of the female-dominated manufacturing and needle-trade industries.

The women profiled in this volume are of Azorean Portuguese, English, French-Canadian, Lebanese, and Polish descent. The progeny of immigrant ancestors who were drawn to the "Spindle City" by the promise of work and betterment, they are interwoven through marriage to form the warp and weft of the fabric that is the city of Fall River.

The interviews provide an opportunity for participants to explore, evaluate, and interpret their individual lives through conversation and reflection. Interviewees address questions that focus on their childhood and adolescence; work life and leisure activities; marital status; roles as mothers, homemakers, and breadwinners; family relationships; religion; the impact of unions and strikes; health issues; and finally their old age.

None of these women knew each other socially, yet their stories reflect a collective commonality of civic, family, socio-economic, emotional, and generational experiences. They walked the same streets, worked in many of the same factories, and persevered through Fall River's economic transition from the world's largest producer of cotton cloth to a major garment and manufacturing center.

The oral histories of *Women at Work* tell a Fall River story unique to the time, events, and culture of a city determined to re-establish itself.

But memories fade, and life is fleeting. A glance at the obituary section of local newspapers makes one acutely aware of the loss of important history as this generation passes. *Women at Work* captures those voices and stories, preserving them as primary sources for the benefit of present and future generations.

To view the corresponding online exhibit, please visit fallriverhistorical.org/WomenatWork/.

FOREWORD

Informal extemporaneous remarks by President Franklin Delano Roosevelt at Fall River, Massachusetts, October 21, 1936:

> *I was glad to hear about the better conditions in Fall River for I know very well that the depression started here long before 1929. I am grateful to all of you men and women for the courage that you showed through all those difficult years and I am confident that in the future that courage will be rewarded by better conditions.*

Franklin Delano Roosevelt Papers, File 988
FDR Presidential Library and Museum

When President Franklin D. Roosevelt made this optimistic prediction during a New England campaign swing, the city of Fall River, Massachusetts, had lived through the worst effects from the collapse of the textile industry and had started the long road back to economic recovery.

The fifty years covered in this study begin with the deindustrialization of the textile industry in the 1920s or "the depression" as referred to by President Roosevelt. The stories tell of how Fall River reindustrialized in the 1930s led by the factory and garment sectors. This ended in the 1970s with a second period of deindustrialization as American factory and garment workers faced an uncertain economic future due to globalization and foreign competition.

The women interviewed for this oral history program were born between 1916 and 1937, and grew up in homes where unemployment was routine and sacrifice was expected. They came of age during the Great Depression and World War II, then prospered during the postwar period and into the 1970s. Now, through Women at Work, they are able to reflect on their lives and past experiences.

Deindustrialization (1920-1930)

In 1911, Fall River, the so-called "Spindle City", hosted the Cotton Centennial, a celebration of the city's textile industry, with President William Howard Taft in attendance. The city, with a population of over 120,000, was, at that time, home to 111 cotton manufacturing companies that employed nearly 40,000 wage earners. But storm clouds were on the horizon.

While the 1920s roared in the rest of the country, Fall River's textile mills confronted competition from southern factories and an uninterrupted decline in print cloth prices.[1]

The mills of Fall River had built their business primarily on one product — print cloth. In 1910, the city's largest employer, the American Printing Company, employed 6,000 workers and was the world leader in the production of print cotton cloth.

In 1923, the city witnessed the first wave of mill closures and mergers. The following year, the American Printing Company opened a new plant in Kingsport, Tennessee, moving much of its operation there, eliminating many Fall River jobs in the process.

With the collapse of print cloth prices, Fall River began a fifteen-year decline during which seventy-three mills and three-fourths of the city's industrial capacity was liquidated. The years 1928 and 1929 brought more crippling blows: a disastrous fire in the city's downtown, labor unrest, and the stock market crash.

Reindustrialization: Power Looms to Power-Stitching (1930-1940)

By the 1930s and the Great Depression, many more mills were out of business, and employment opportunities for Fall River's textile workforce shrunk by seventy percent, with only nine thousand jobs remaining.

In a devastating measure, Fall River declared bankruptcy in 1931 and was in state receivership for a decade. These years saw many of the city's mills occupied by numerous smaller companies, primarily garment manufacturers traditionally based in New York City. Investors were attracted to New England, and more specifically Fall River, by the lure of inexpensive factory space, often advertised by the Chamber of Commerce as free factory space. An additional lure was an eager workforce in dire need of jobs.

The growth of manufacturing during the 1930s in Fall River was abetted by the passage of New Deal labor legislation such as the National Labor Relations Act (aka the Wagner Act), which established the legal right of workers to organize, to join labor unions, and to bargain collectively with their employers. Furthermore, in a city with a long history of trade unionism emerged "new unionism": the establishment of the International Ladies Garment Workers Union (ILGWU) and the Amalgamated Clothing Workers of America (ACWA).

By 1940, there were only seventeen textile companies in operation in Fall River. The city's new bedrock industry was the factory and garment industry, employing twenty percent of the workforce, eighty percent of which were female.

Reindustrialization Continues (1941-1970)

State receivership ended in June 1941. Fall River had put its financial house in order and was ready to start again.

The new beginning coincided with World War II. A key industry during this period was the Firestone Rubber and Latex Company, Inc. Establishing their Fall River operation in 1937 on Water Street in former American Printing Company buildings, Firestone was a key defense industry, employing 2,600 of Fall River's workers.

The postwar years saw the continued supremacy of the factory and garment industry. The high point of ILGWU membership was in 1961, when there were more than 17,000 members in the Fall River area. Business was good with a thirty-five-hour work week, overtime pay, union health care, and union training and education programs.

Deindustrialization Again (1970-Present): Fall River Today – Lessons Learned

The last quarter of the 20th century would be marked by another bout with deindustrialization, and Fall River, like many other industrial sites in the United States, fell victim to globalization and foreign competition.

This time, the road back would take longer and would involve collaborative efforts by private, government, and education partners to diversify the economy, redesign and upgrade the city's infrastructure, and renovate area assets to cultivate existing and emerging industries. The goal today is to build on manufacturing, green technology, the life sciences, transportation, professional services, and a creative economy.

Examples of niche industries that are currently operating in Fall River and manufacturing products that are "MADE in the USA" are: John Matouk & Co., Inc. (luxury linens); Merida LLC (hand-finished rugs); and Frank Clegg Leatherworks (handcrafted leather bags).

Along with long-time industrial giants like Duro Textiles, LLC (textile fabric finishers) and Borden & Remington Corporation (chemical manufacturing and distribution), and the new innovative technology companies that are located in the Fall River Industrial Park and the SouthCoast Life Sciences and Technology Park, the city of Fall River is, once again, writing a new story to tell.

Joyce B. Rodrigues
Fall River, MA
September, 2016

---

[1]A decade noted for the passage of the Eighteenth (prohibition) and Nineteenth (women's suffrage) Amendments to the U.S. Constitution, and the Johnson-Reed Act establishing the immigration quota system (1924-1952).

ONE:

CONSTANCE JOAN ABDALLAH, NÉE WASKIEWICZ

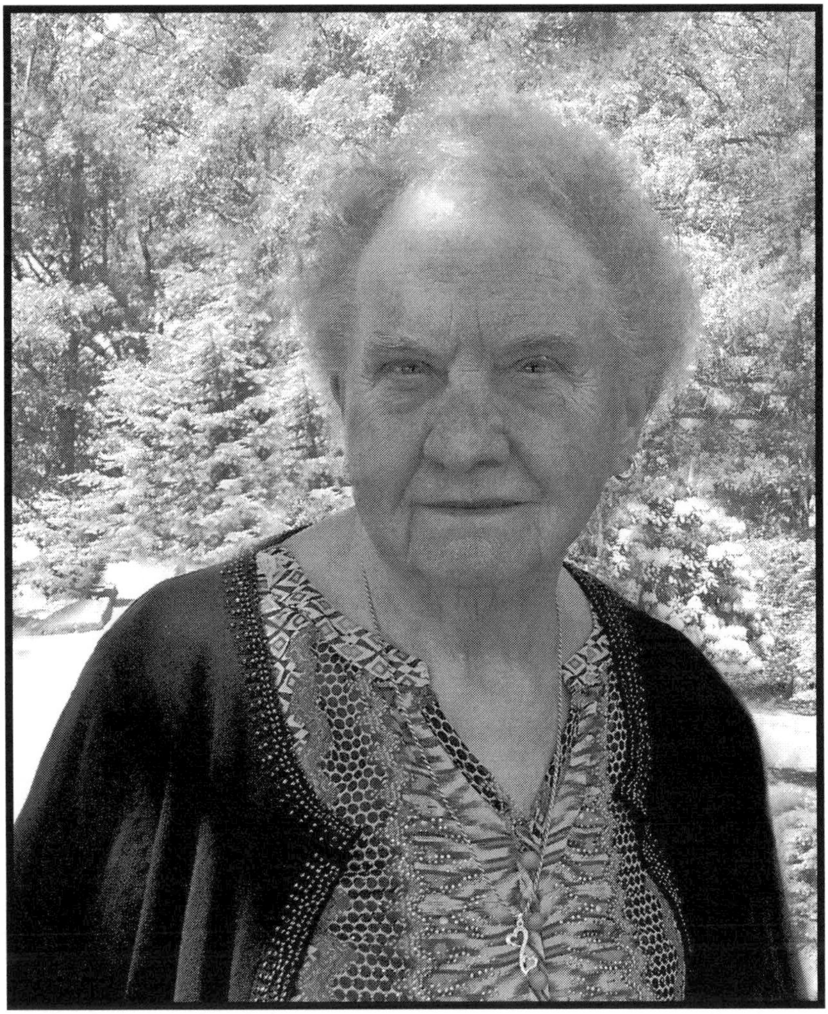

Personal Statistics

Name: Constance Joan Waskiewicz
(Mrs. Alphonse Kalil Abdallah)

Date of Birth: February 11, 1932

Place of Birth: Fall River, Massachusetts

Father: Wacław Waszkiewicz (1891-1952)

Mother: Stefania "Stella" Bukowska (1891-1974)

Siblings: Anna "Ann" Waskiewicz (1917-2010)
---(Mrs. Michael Kostka)
Theodore Joseph Waskiewicz (1919-2004)
Mecislaus "Mathew" Joseph Waskiewicz
(1923-1991)

Note: The children of Wacław & Stella Waszkiewicz dropped the 'z' in their surname, hence Waskiewicz

Spouse: Alphonse Kalil Abdallah (born 1920)

Date of Marriage: : April 1, 1959

Children: Alan Paul Abdallah
Robert Mark Abdallah

Employment history:
W.T. Grant Company, Fall River
Har-Lee Manufacturing Company, Fall River
Fall River Electric Light Company

EDITED TRANSCRIPT

Interview with Mrs. Alphonse Kalil Abdallah, née Constance Joan Waskiewicz

Interviewer: **(CM)** Constance C. Mendes

Interviewee: **(CA)** Constance Joan (Waskiewicz) Abdallah

(AA) Alphonse Kalil Abdallah

Additional Commentary: **(JR)** Joyce B. Rodrigues, Fall River Historical Society

Date of Interview: May 27, 2015

Location: Abdallah residence, Swansea, Massachusetts

Summary by Joyce B. Rodrigues:

Constance "Connie" Joan (Waskiewicz) Abdallah was born in Fall River on February 11, 1932.

Alphonse Kalil Abdallah was born in Fall River on September 9, 1920.

The Waskiewicz family

Connie's father, Wacław Waszkiewicz, and mother, Stefania Bukowska, emigrated from Poland to the United States in 1905. They met in Fall River and married in 1916 at St. Stanislaus Parish, a Polish-American Roman Catholic Church. The family lived in the South End, the Globe Village section of the city and worked in the textile mills. Connie was the youngest of four children, and had a sister and two brothers. She graduated from B.M.C. Durfee High School in 1949.

The Abdallah family

The Lebanese-Syrian communities in Fall River are predominately Lebanese and members of the Maronite Eastern Rite Catholic Church. Lebanese immigrated to the United States in the late 19th century to escape political and religious persecution by the Turks.

The first Lebanese immigrants to Fall River lived on lower Columbia Street and in the Globe Village section of the city and worked as shopkeepers. Later immigrants settled in the Flint Village particularly around the Quequechan Street area and found employment as mill operatives.

Alphonse's father and mother were in this second group of immigrants. Alphonse was the seventh of eight children, two daughters and six sons. The Abdallahs struggled through the Great Depression years. Alphonse, his brothers, and sisters, worked and brought their pay home to support the family. He graduated from B.M.C. Durfee High School in 1938.

Working for Har-Lee Manufacturing

Alphonse and Connie were interviewed as a couple because they both worked for the Har-Lee Manufacturing Company, the largest cotton dress manufacturer in the United States. Their narrative tells what it was like to work in the garment industry during the 1930s and 1940s and the obstacles they overcame to marry outside of their ethnic group.

Alphonse was a supervisor in the trimming department. Connie worked in the same department and managed the shop's inventory. At its peak, Har-Lee employed over 2,000 employees and was a union shop.[1]

Har-Lee Manufacturing Company

Har-Lee Manufacturing Company, a division of Wentworth Manufacturing, was founded in Chicago, Illinois, in 1901 by Russian immigrants. In 1934, the company moved from Chicago to Fall River.

The plant was located at 425 Pleasant Street in the former Durfee-Union mill complex. The Durfee-Union mills, founded in 1866, were one of the more successful of Fall River's textile corporations and had an impressive group of large mill structures in the city.

Har-Lee Manufacturing moved to South Carolina in 1957. The business was restructured by Gerhard Lowenstein, a supervisor for Har-Lee, as Lowenstein Dress Corporation.

---

[1]For information on working at Har-Lee Manufacturing see: *Excerpts from a Diary of an Operator at Har-Lee, Fall River, Mass.*, Hilda Tanner Papers, ca. 1930s, Kheel Center for Labor-Management Documentation and Archives, Martin P. Catherwood Library, Cornell University. at: rmc.library.cornell.edu/EAD/htmldocs/KCL05780pubs.html.

Note: This interview has been slightly edited for continuity and readability; in order to preserve the integrity of the conversation, the phraseology remains that of the interviewer and interviewee. Italicized information in square brackets has been added for the purposes of clarification and context.

This transcript begins with a conversation with Mrs. Abdallah's husband, Alphonse, who spent a number of years employed at Har-Lee Manufacturing Company in Fall River, Massachusetts; the firm was, at the time, the largest producer of inexpensive ladies dresses in the United States. His notes on the Har-Lee Manufacturing Process can be located online at: fallriverhistorical.org/WomenatWork/har-lee-manufacturing-process/.

CM: When did you start working at Har-Lee [*Manufacturing Company, 425 Pleasant Street, Fall River, Massachusetts*]?

AA: See, um … before I went into the service [*during World War II*]. I went into the service in 1942 [*United States Army, enlisted November 14*] but I was there about three years before that….

CM: '39?

AA: Yeah, '39.

CM: How big was the factory at that time?

AA: That was what it was, they had over twenty-two hundred girls. That was the worst thing to happen to Fall River, [*Har-Lee*] leaving [*in 1957*]. They'd never had left if the girls that learned had stayed. But you couldn't blame them, they wanted to go to a smaller shop that would grow around them. And they'd tell them, 'Go to Har-Lee and learn,' [*where*] they were learning and teaching them…. They modified, and the plant, you couldn't beat it, conveyor belts and all. And nobody bothered you, it was very, very, very nice. Um, all the years I worked there, I [*was*] never criticized, never. All I was told was make sure the floors are … suppl[*ied*] … and never [*get*] behind. All the, um, overtime you need, take it. You need more girls, get them from there, different places. Never, never being criticized.

JR: Let's go back to the beginning…. Was it Harrison Street that you came from?

AA: There was Harrison, Flint, Quequechan, [*and*] Barnard [*Streets*], all this was [*where*] the … people that came from Lebanon congregated….

JR: Tell me about your parents. They came from Lebanon?

AA: They came from Lebanon…. [*His father, Kalil Abdallah, was born in Beit ed-Dine, Lebanon, and immigrated to the United States in 1905; his mother, née Nazara Joseph Solomon was also born in Beit ed-Dine, and immigrated to the United States circa 1907.*]

JR: Did your parents work in the mills?

AA: My parents, in the cotton mills. I went only once, I carried a ...

CA: Dinners.

AA: Dinners for my Dad. Oh, this is not for me. You shout, you have to shout to see what is what. My dad, because of his health, didn't work too long, and in those days, I think all the family [*helped out*]. See, I made $10 a week, I gave them $8 to the family, $2 for me. And that is what they all did, they gave [*to*] the family. You had to do it in order to survive.

JR: You turned your pay over.

AA: Even though we [*his parents*] owned a six-tenement house [*at 322 Harrison Street, Fall River*], the people couldn't afford the rent, we were paying for them to live there. And I said, 'Gee, Dad, what are you going to do?'

JR: Do you remember the mill your father worked in?

AA: Oh, it was … Wampanoag [*Mills, 69 Alden Street, Fall River*]….

CM: Were they up near Harrison Street?

AA: Yeah.

CM: They would have walked.

AA: And I used to, my mom used to wake me up when I was in the first grade [*at James M. Aldrich Primary School, 295 Harrison Street, Fall River*], wake me up at five in the morning, [*to*] go to the local mills, wait for the engineer [*with*] the big wheelbarrow [*to*] empty the furnaces; we knew where he was going to empty them. And not only I, but other people, would be there with a digger, a potato sack, [*to*] fill it up, put it in the wagon, and come home. And in those cinders were coal … which … was still good to burn. And if we didn't have any wood – someone would be wrecking a house in the area – I would go there with a wagon. Whatever they didn't want, whatever the contractor [*said*] was broken, he would let us take them, and start a fire. And if there wasn't enough wood, we would get bobbins from the mill.

JR: So your mother was at home? Was she working in the mill, too?

AA: No … I was the seventh child.

CM: Out of how many?

AA: Eight children.

CM: Who owned Har-Lee … when you went to Har-Lee, who owned it?

AA: Oh my God, how can I forget it? What a wonderful man, what a wonderful man. All the years I was there, I never, never was criticized, 'Just make sure the floors are supplied. Take all the overtime you want.' [*The 'wonderul man' he is referring to is Alvin Abraham Sopkin, the general manager of Har-Lee; he was the son of the company's president, Benjamin Sopkin.*]

JR: I think that … someone else said … the name Har-Lee came from the family….

[*Har-Lee Manufacturing Company, was a division of Wentworth Manufacturing Company; its manufacturing plant was at 425 Pleasant Street, Fall River, and its corporate office and showroom was at 1350 Broadway, New York, New York. The Wentworth firm was founded in 1901 in Chicago, Illinois, by Russian immigrant Benjamin Sopkin, who served as its president. The Har-Lee division of the company was founded in Chicago by Sopkin and a business partner, Harry Lee, also a Russian immigrant, who served as its treasurer; Har-Lee was derived from the name of the latter. In 1934, the company was moved from Chicago to Fall River by Sopkin's sons, Alvin Abraham Sopkin, and Henry Sopkin, in order to take advantage of the city's abundant supply of labor and manufacturing space.*]

AA: I don't know. They came from Chicago. [*The company's president, Benjamin Sopkin, and its treasurer, Harry Lee, were former Chicago residents.*] And [*on*] each floor was a young floor manager, and when I got there, they all took a liking to me. They told the big boss, the manager [*of*] the whole plant [*Alvin A. Sopkin, general manager*], 'Put Alphonse in charge, put Alphonse in charge.' And ... what a wonderful man, [*he*] came up to me – I wanted to learn everything, wanted to know everything – let me know, 'I am putting you in charge [*as supervisor of the trimming department*].' At that time, they had two people running the department; one of them passed away in the war [*World War II*]. So, when I got there, there was one more [*man*] there, he wasn't too well, he used to be ... mostly watching the girls. I never, never had to do that. All I did, all I got was ... a lot of requisitions into the office; I had thousands of dozens. So that meant for me to go overtime [*and to*] go in the office, I go in his room, get the records and [*would*] be sitting down and taking care of all the work. And sometimes [*the manager*] would walk in at night [*and*] he would smile.

CA: Good memories.

AA: He would smile [*and*] look at me.

JR: I am going to go back a little bit to your family. Your family of eight. How many girls and how many boys?

AA: Two girls [*Josephine Kalil Abdallah, later Mrs. Thomas Joseph Moroon, and Izabel 'Isabel' Abdallah*] and six boys [*Joseph Kalil Abdallah, Michael Kalil Abdallah, Albert Kalil Abdallah, Abdallah Kalil Abdallah, Alphonse Kalil Abdallah, and George Kalil Abdallah*].

JR: What was their careers like?

AA: They all went to the shops.

JR: They worked in the shops? Tell me about that, where did they work?

AA: Shelburne [*Shirt Company, Inc., 111 Alden Street, Fall River*].

JR: Your sisters worked in Shelburne?

AA: Yes, my sister [*Josephine*] worked in Shelburne [*circa 1942 to 1945. From 1932 to circa 1940, she was employed as a sewer in an unidentified factory, and circa 1941 at Auerbach Bathrobe Company, 473 Pleasant Street, Fall River*], and one of my sisters [*Isabel*] went to Har-Lee, where I was working; she was there quite a few years [*from circa 1945 to 1956. She was also employed at: Stella Anne Frocks, 420 Quequechan Street, Fall River, circa 1957; K & G Manufacturing Company, Inc., 273 Pleasant Street, Fall River, from circa 1958 to 1978; and Tiffany Sportswear, 372 Kilburn Street, Fall River, circa 1979*]. When I was in the sixth grade at Davis [*Grammar*] School [*33 Quequechan Street, Fall River*], I used to go – my Mom would make a dinner for [*Josephine*] – I would go in the wagon, and go and do lunch hour, take it to her, and she would give me ten cents a week.

JR: To bring the lunch.... How about your brothers? What happened to them?

AA: One of them [*Michael*] worked for Nasiff Fruit [*395 South Main Street, Fall River*]. They had a store, and he would work for them before going into the army [*United States Army, enlisted April 13, 1942*]. Another one worked in Attleboro ... at a jewelry place [*Lloyd Garfield Balfour Company, Attleboro, Massachusetts*], I believe. [*In fact, two of his brothers, Joseph and Abdallah, were once employed at L.G. Balfour Co.*]

JR: Okay, that's well known.

AA: In fact, before going to the Har-Lee, [*Joseph*] got me a good job. My brother says, 'Go see ... so-and-so, who lives on Alden [*Street*]. Tell him I sent you.' I went ... and said, 'My brother Joe sent me to see you. I am looking for a job.' 'Go to the Flint Furniture [*Manufacuring Company, Inc., upholstered furniture manufacturers, 410 Quequechan Street*]; tell him I sent you.' Just then, I went to Flint Furniture; right away I started working, and it was a, I mean, doing that was a very good job, you know ... making furniture.

CM: Did you do that before Har-Lee?

AA: Yes. No, wait, I went to Har-Lee for a very short time, and they were very slack, and the boss said – I don't know who he was – said ... 'Alphonse, I'm sorry I have to lay you off.' But that is when my brother got me that other job [*at Flint Furniture Company, Inc.*]. But then, when I couldn't do [*it*] too well, a lady friend of mine that lived on Harrison [*Street*] knocked on my window before I went for breakfast, before I went to work. 'Har-Lee has been looking for you.' They came looking for me for a long while, because, in those days, we didn't have a telephone. Then she says, 'Alphonse, they have been looking for you for a long time. My sister didn't want to tell you, hoping to get it for one of our relations.' She told me the truth, she was a good friend. So, when I went to work, seeing I couldn't cut it, the Jew [*David Kass, president of Flint Furniture Manufacturing Company*] says, 'You are doing well.' 'How can I be doing well? I am not even penetrating the goods.' When I went to the Jew that was running the plant, I says, 'Well, I am leaving.' He said, 'You are leaving? You're doing fine,' and, 'How come you are leaving here? You are doing fine.' I said, 'I am not doing as well as others.' 'I hate to see you go.' A good thing I went to Har-Lee, and in a very short time, the manager came upstairs and said, 'Alphonse' – I was doing mostly stock work – he said, 'You won't be doing this all the time.' Then, they took a liking to me, they saw something in me I didn't see.

CA: You are reliable.

AA: I never cared to learn, never. I did well in high school [*B.M.C. Durfee High School, Fall River, Class of 1938*], but not as good as I should have.

CM: How about medical things? Did they have a first aid room there or a nurse?

JR: In the Har-Lee?

AA: Yes, yes. They had twenty-two hundred employees. A doctor would come once a week....

JR: So you had a doctor come to the factory?

AA: Once a week, if anybody needed anything.

JR: What happened if there was an accident on the job, or if someone needed medical attention?

AA: I guess they would have to contact him.

CA: Did they have a nurse in there all the time or a first aid person?

AA: I don't know.

JR: The other question I had ... was about the union. I don't know if Har-Lee was a union shop. Was it ever a union shop?

AA: Oh, yes.

JR: When did it start?

AA: I don't know, but it was. [*Following an election conducted by the National Labor Relations Board (NLRB) in 1941, the International Ladies Garment Workers Union (ILGWU) successfully unionized Har-Lee Manufacturing Company; eighty percent of the ballots cast were in favor.*] I know, I hated to see it go. All the years I was there, never, never criticized.

CM: When did it close?

AA: 1957 [*at which time the company moved to Lake City, South Carolina*] and the owner – how can I forget his name? What a wonderful man. Any time he came from New York, he had to pass my department; always says, 'Good morning, Al.'

CM: Was he Jewish?

AA: Oh, yeah.

JR: Many of the factories…

CA: Almost all of them.

JR: They...

CA: They worked hard, and their sons inherited. [*Three generations of the Sopkin family were involved in Wentworth Manufacturing Company.*]

JR: Yes, they did. A lot of the manufacturers came from New York. You said Chicago on this one. A lot of them come from New York.

AA: They [*Har-Lee Manufacturing Company*] had an office in New York [*Wentworth Manufacturing Company, 1350 Broadway, New York, New York*] and I visited that office once with my wife [*née Constance Joan Waskiewicz*].

JR: I am going to move up on to Connie ... because Mrs. Abdallah was also an employee of the Har-Lee. I want to ask some questions about that, because I heard this was a Har-Lee romance.

CA: Yeah.

JR: How did you get started there?

CA: My sister-in-law [*Mrs. Theodore Joseph Waskiewicz, née Mary Veronica Rys*] wanted me to have a better job, you know. I was working in Grant's [*W.T. Grant Company, department store, 149 South Main Street, Fall River*].

JR: In Grant's?

CA: For a year out of high school [*B.M.C. Durfee High School, Fall River, Class of 1949*].

JR: I remember Grant's on Main Street.

CA: And then, um.

AA: That was a blessing for her and me. This is the truth now.

CA: I went to the Har-Lee because my sister-in-law offered me a permanent job. So, full time.

AA: This was before eight o'clock [*a.m. that*] she and her sister-in-law would punch the clock, and my department was caged in.

CA: The romance began.

AA: I was outside the cage. So, as I am doing my work on requisitions, I look up and I saw her and her sister-in-law – her sister-in-law was an excellent worker – working; none of my workers were bad. I looked up and this girl is for me, okay?

JR: Just like that.

CM: How long did it take for you to hook her?

AA: Unfortunately, her mother took a liking to me.

CM: Unfortunately?

AA: Fortunately. Unfortunately, her brother [*Theodore*], for some unknown reason, he knew some Lebanese people.

CA: He worked in Flint Furniture.

AA: Didn't want me, you know, to go out with her. So, he'd bring his wife [*Mary*] and ... he'd be going up Pleasant [*Street*], and I'd be going down Pleasant [*Street, and*] he'd look the other way; I always looked to smile, he would look the other way. We had to elope.

JR: This is even getting better! This is a great story!

AA: We got married in [*Waterville,*] Maine [*on April 1, 1959*].

JR: You had to run away?

AA: In Maine; my sister [*Josephine*] had a nice cabin there. And the church [*St. Joseph's Church*] was, the ceremony was much, much better than if it was done on Rockland Street at the Polish church [*St. Stanislaus Church, 40 Rockland Street, Fall River*]. They had a choir, they sang the Ave Maria, she was dressed beautifully; you can see the picture. And she was kneeling at the altar while they sang. Very, very nice ceremony.

CA: The Polish priest [*in Fall River, Rev. Hugo Emanuel Dylla*] wasn't too happy because, you know, he wanted me to get married there.

JR: That brings up the question of this competition between the Polish and the Lebanese. So, are you saying your brother didn't care for a boyfriend that was not Polish?

CA: That's part of it. Because all of the members of my family married Polish, you know? He was an oddball.

AA: They all said, 'It's all Mary's fault.' And Mary was the one who, her sister-in-law, that worked for me.

JR: Now did your parents, Connie, come from Poland?

CA: Yes, they [*Wacław Waszkiewicz and his wife, née Stefania 'Stella' Bukowska*] came from Poland [*in 1905 and 1909, respectively*]. They worked [*for*] the textile mills. My mother was [*in*] a mill right across from me [*Berkshire Fine Spinning Associates, Inc., Plant E, 372 Kilburn Street, Fall River*], and my mother worked there for years and years, even when my two brothers [*Theodore J. Waskiewicz and Mecislaus 'Mathew' Joseph Waskiewicz*] were in the service. [*Theodore, United States Army Air Forces, enlisted April 20, 1942, and 'Mathew', United States Army, enlisted March 9, 1943.*] And then my father worked in the Kerr Mills [*American Thread Company, Martine Street, foot of Kerr Street, Fall River*] for a long time.

JR: Now, what area was this?

CA: South End. [*198*] Kilburn Street.

JR: Kilburn Street?

CA: When I was about six, seven years old, I wanted to go see Mom in the mill. So, I went with my neighbor, a little boy; we went to the mill. When they saw us coming in, they were screaming, 'Get out of here … there is stuff you can get hurt on. It's dangerous.' So, I saw my Mom and she says, 'Take off, go, go home.' But, that was it, I had to go see her that time.

JR: But she didn't want you to go to the mill.

CA: No way.

JR: She wanted you to go work somewhere else.

CA: I never, you know, that didn't come up. Because I wanted to, I had the regular course in [*B.M.C.*] Durfee [*High School*] and I didn't have a college course. But, I worked, after the Har-Lee I went to the Fall River Electric Light [*Company, 85 North Main Street*] for a while [*as a clerk, circa 1957 – 1960*] … until I got pregnant; I couldn't work anymore there.

JR: You got a smart lady, here.

CA: Yeah.

AA: I knew when I looked at her, I knew she looked smart. I knew she came from a good family, because Polish people are good religious people, just like the Lebanese. That is why I married her....

JR: So, how did you ... get to Maine? That is the question. If you are going to elope....

CA: His sister lived in Maine. It wasn't easy to do, you know. It was very hard.

CM: What did his mother think? What did your mother think?

CA: My mother was very upset but, as it turned out, my two brothers came to the wedding.

JR: I guess that Durfee class worked. You went into retail when you were at Grant's, so you weren't in the mill. Your mother must have been happy about that.

CA: I worked a long time, a few years part-time. And then they had nice prizes ... if you did so much in sales, they gave me prizes. That was something to look forward to.

JR: When you went to Har-Lee, who taught you how to sew those dresses?

CA: I didn't sew anything.

JR: Oh, you didn't sew anything?

CA: No, I was in the trimming department, I was perpetual inventory. I took care of that, and the buttons and stuff, and then I took care of the parts department. Belts, snaps, you know, whatever.

JR: Well, I am going to move on.... I am going to jump to more of the social side ... of living in Fall River ... going back to the Polish and the Lebanese holidays. What about holidays, how do you celebrate those? And Thanksgiving and Christmas?

CA: I always used to...

AA: It's multi-family with us.

CA: I used to love polka dancing in my teenage years and twenties. I'd go and they had a lot of Polish dances at the Polish [*National*] Home [*872 Globe Street, Fall River*].

JR: And that is where the teenagers would go?

CM: Would he go with you?

AA: No. We didn't know one another.

JR: What did the Lebanese do to meet girls? How did you meet girls when you were a teenager?

AA: A lot of us went to Lincoln Park [*State Road, Westport, Massachusetts*]. I didn't socialize too much. My social life was, this is true, was going to the dogs and the horses. I loved to gamble. Loved it.

JR: You did that when you were single and married?

AA: I loved to gamble. When they were running [*horses*] in Narragansett [*Park, Pawtucket, Rhode Island*], I was there. If the dogs [*greyhounds*] were running in Raynham [*Park, Raynham, Massachusetts*], I was there six nights a week.

CM: Where was she?

AA: She was taking care of the house and children, but I was holding my own; that is what counts.

JR: You mentioned the Depression. What was that ... like in Fall River when you were growing up, during the Depression? You couldn't get jobs during that time.

AA: No, all I did was play.... We had the schoolyard across the street [*James M. Aldrich School, 295 Harrison Street, Fall River*], the big schoolyard. We played baseball, horseshoes, football, instead of going to Lafayette Park.

JR: So, how did your parents make out during that time? They had eight children, and times were tough.

AA: Well, thanks to the fact that ... two of my sisters worked steady, and then my older brothers – like I told you – they'd give the money to the family.

JR: You all chipped in.

AA: And, uh, we ate good, I can say that. Depression, but we ate good. Anything we wanted, it was fresh. If we wanted steak, we'd go to the Polish Market [*Polish Co-operative Grocery Stores at 177*] Quequechan Street [*Fall River*], that they used to have. 'What do you want?' Whatever cut you want, they cut it. We never had anything ...

JR: No frozen. Because nobody had those refrigerators.

CM: You didn't know it was a Depression.

AA: We had an ice box.

JR: So, so up 'til that point, everything had to be fresh from the store.

AA: Yes.

CM: But you didn't know you didn't have a lot of money to do this. You didn't think there was a Depression ... I grew up during the Depression and I don't think I ever knew that there was a Depression. They do with what you have. You made do with what you had.

JR: Yeah, you just had to make ends meet. Oh, my goodness, [*we are*] going to have to stop [*at*] that.

PHOTO GALLERY

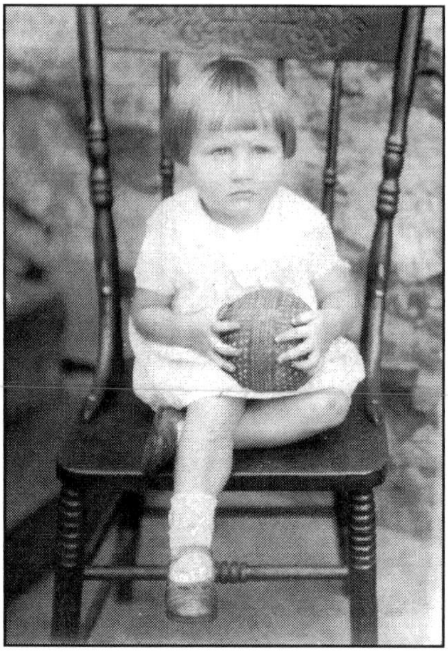

1.1 Constance, circa 1935.

1.2 Constance's father, Wacław Waszkiewicz, and her mother, née Stefania "Stella" Bukowska with their son, Theodore Joseph Waskiewicz, circa 1942. *"My two brothers were in the service."*

1.3 Alphonse Kalil Abdallah, circa 1943. *"I went into the service in 1942."*

1.4 Connie's B.M.C. Durfee High School portrait, Class of 1949. *"I had the regular course in Durfee and I didn't have a college course."*

1.5 An interior retail display in W. T. Grant Company, department store, 149 South Main Street, Fall River, Massachusetts, 1930s; the interior remained much the same when Constance was employed here circa 1949. *"They had nice prizes ... if you did so much in sales, they gave me prizes. That was something to look forward to."*

1.6 W. T. Grant Company, department store, first floor on left, 149 South Main Street, Fall River, Massachusetts, 1940s. *"I was working in Grant's ... for a year out of high school."*

1.7 A reception at the Polish National Home, 872 Globe Street, Fall River, Massachusetts, 1936. *"I used to love polka dancing in my teenage years and twenties. I'd go and they had a lot of Polish dances at the Polish Home."*

HAR-LEE MANUFACTURING CO.
Division of WENTWORTH MANUFACTURING COMPANY
Distinctive Wash Frocks
425 PLEASANT ST. Tel. OSborne 8-5226 FALL RIVER, MASS.
NEW YORK DISPLAY ROOMS: 1350 BROADWAY — TEL. LOngacre 3-2198

1.8 *Above:* Advertisement for Har-Lee Manufacturing Company, from the *Fall River City Directory*, 1957, the year the company relocated. *"I went to the Har-Lee because my sister-in-law offered me a permanent job."*

1.9 *Left:* Constance's mother Mrs. Wacław Waszkiewicz, née Stefania "Stella" Bukowska. *"When I was about six, seven years old, I wanted to go see mom in the mill ... When they saw us coming in they were screaming, 'Get out of here ... there is stuff you can get hurt on. It's dangerous.' So I saw my mom and she says, 'Take off, go, go home."*

1.10 Durfee Mills, Mill No. 1, Fall River, Massachusetts, early 1930s; the building housed Har-Lee Manufacturing Company from 1934–1957. *"They had over twenty-two hundred girls. That was the worst thing to happen to Fall River, it leaving."*

1.11 Mr. & Mrs. Alphonse Kalil Abdallah on their wedding day, April 1, 1959. *"I looked up, and, this girl is for me, okay?"*

1.12 Constance and Alphonse Abdallah.

TWO:

OLIVIA RAPOSO ABDOW, NÉE TERCEIRA

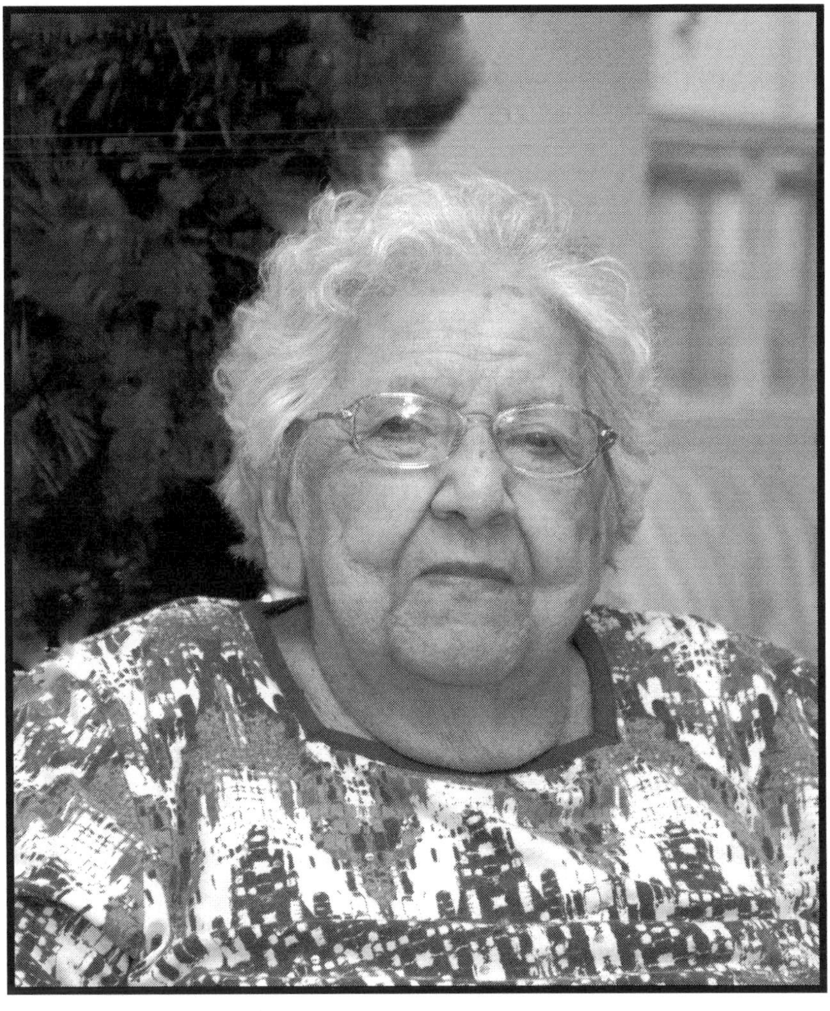

Personal Statistics

Name: Olivia Raposo Terceira
(Mrs. Dolar "Duke" Bernard Abdow)

Date of Birth: September 1, 1928

Place of Birth: Fall River, Massachusetts

Date of Death: October 12, 2015

Father: José (Joseph) Raposo Terceira, Sr. (1898-1979)

Mother: Rose Souza Farias (1901-1960)

Siblings: João (John) Raposo Terceira (1920-1969)
George Raposo Terçeira (1923-1986)
José (Joseph) Raposo Terceira, Jr. (1933-2008)

Spouse: Dolar "Duke" Bernard Abdow (1928-2000)

Date of Marriage: : June 18, 1949

Children: Steven Dolor Abdow
Keith Bernard Abdow

Employment history:
Kerr Thread Mills (American Thread Company), Fall River
Nancy Dress Company, Fall River
Rondo Knit Sportswear, Fall River

EDITED TRANSCRIPT

Interview with Mrs. Dolor "Duke" Bernard Abdow, née Olivia Raposo Terceira

Interviewer: (JC) Joseph J. Conforti, Jr.

Interviewee: (OA) Olivia Raposo (Terceira) Abdow

Additional Commentary: (JR) Joyce B. Rodrigues, Fall River Historical Society
(GK) George D. Kelly

Date of Interview: December 10, 2014

Location: Catholic Memorial Home, Fall River, Massachusetts

Summary by Joyce B. Rodrigues:

Olivia "Olive" Raposo (Terceira) Abdow was born in Fall River on October 26, 1928.

Olive's parents were married in Fall River in 1919. Her father was born in Fall River in 1898. His parents immigrated to the United States from the island of St. Michael in the Azores. They arrived in New Bedford, Massachusetts, where they met and were married, and later moved to Fall River. Olive's mother immigrated to the United States from St. Michael in 1915.

The Terceiras lived on Choate Street in a six-family triple-decker tenement house surrounded by an extended family of aunts, uncles, cousins, and grandparents. The neighborhood was primarily populated by first-generation Azorean-Portuguese.

There were four children in the family. Olive had two older and one younger brother. Both parents worked as weavers in a cotton mill.

Olive characterizes herself as a "Depression baby" and a "working girl." As a "Depression baby," she vividly describes everyday life during the Great Depression years of the 1930s: the food, movies, dating, favorite radio programs, the presidency of FDR, the March of Dimes Foundation, and later leaving school to care for her mother who had suffered a stroke.

Olive married Dolor "Duke" Bernard Abdow in 1948 and began a successful Fall River "mixed" marriage of a second-generation Portuguese-American and a second-generation Lebanese-American.

As a "working girl," Olive explains how she managed to work and care for her two sons with the help of her Lebanese in-laws. Her career took her to factories in Fall River:

the Kerr Thread Mills (American Thread Company), Rondo Knit Sportswear, Nancy Dress Company, where she worked for twenty-eight years expertly manufacturing better dresses.[1]

She concludes this interview looking back on a life well-lived, with no regrets, but wishing she had been able to have more education.

[1]The apparel industry classifies garment manufacturing in terms of price points.
- **Budget or mass market garments** are at the low end of the apparel spectrum with clothes that retail at a relatively low cost.
- **Moderate dresses** are medium-priced merchandise, a step above budget. This is the price classification of the majority of clothing.
- **Better dresses** are medium-to-higher-priced merchandise. The fabrics, styling, and craftsmanship are of better quality than lower-priced items.
- **Designer products** cater to the high-priced prestige or luxury market.
- **Haute Couture and Made-to-Measure apparel** is cut and sewn specifically for individual customers and costs tens of thousands of dollars. Source: apparelsearch.com/

Note: This interview has been slightly edited for continuity and readability; in order to preserve the integrity of the conversation, the phraseology remains that of the interviewer and interviewee. Italicized information in square brackets has been added for the purposes of clarification and context.

OA: The only thing I can start off with right now is that I am a Depression baby.

JC: What year were you born?

OA: I was born [*on September 1,*] 1928.... Okay, like I first started at, I was a Depression baby, but I did go to work.

JC: Were you born in Fall River?

OA: Oh, yes. I was born [*at 200*] Choate Street.... See, my grandmother [*Mrs. Antonio Raposo Terceira, Sr., née Maria De Jesus Ferreira Andrade*] had a little grocery store [*at 198 Choate Street, Fall River*] and, of course, during the [*Great*] Depression, she lost everything. But we had a wonderful bringing up, my cousins and I; we had a lot of fun together ... we played games together. Today, children do not play games. That is terrible. They don't know what hide-and-seek is, you know, or jump rope. Forget it. Forget it. I don't know why the children don't play games like we used to play games. And we, um, my grandmother sat on the stoop while we played games, and, of course, when the [*street*] light went on, you know what happened – we had to go home. We didn't stay outside, we had to go home. Once in a while, maybe, if she stayed a little later, or we'd beg her, she would stay a little later.... But we had to go home when that light went on; home everybody went. And a lot of us, our street was about the size, and, ah, I am trying to think, I'm trying to visualize it now because it was so small. It was so small, but we played a lot there.

JC: Can you describe the house you were brought up in?

OA: Sure. It was a six-tenement house. It was my ... aunts, and myself, me, I was brought up there. Well, my, ah, aunt [*Mrs. Manuel Arruda, née Alexandrina Raposo Terceira*] lived on the bottom floor. We lived on the middle floor. And my Aunt Mary [*Mrs. Antonio Raposo Terceira, Jr.*] lived on the top floor. And that is where we were brought up.... My grandmother lived right across the yard in her little apartment....

JC: Were your grandparents immigrants?

OA: My grandfather [*Antonio*] ... he was brought up in [*Feteiras do Sul, São Miguel,*] Azores. My grandmother [*Maria*] grew up in [*Feteiras do Sul, São Miguel,*] Azores, but was brought up in Hawaii. She had quite a travel, you know.... [*Her father, Manuel Ferreira Andrade, and his three children, went to Hawaii following the death of his wife, née Claudina S. Neto; Manuel was employed as a landscaper by a wealthy islander. He eventually immigrated to the United States after the death of his employer.*]

JC: Can you tell us something about that?

OA: Well, I don't know the name of the island of Hawaii that she was brought up in, but when the hurricane came [*on September 21, 1938*], my grandmother told us immediately to go home and put the windows, crack the windows [*in order to equalize the air pressure inside the house with that outside to prevent storm damage*], and stay in the house, and don't go out. Because she [*knew*] ... we are going to have a bad storm. We all laughed because we never had anything like that, but we did get it and we got it good. Yup, and she lived there ... I don't know how many years. [*Mrs. Terceira resided at 198 Choate Street for approximately seventeen years, circa 1923 – 1940.*] But she came from New Bedford, [*Massachusetts*]... and she married my grandfather who set up a little store.

JC: She met your grandfather in Fall River?

OA: No, New Bedford. He heard there was a young girl from Hawaii in New Bedford, so he went up and checked it out and he married her.

JC: What did your grandfather do for a living?

OA: That's what he did, he ran the little store.

JC: A variety store.

OA: A little variety store. Yeah. Yeah. [*Antonio R. Terceira, Sr. is listed as a grocer in the* Fall River City Directory *from 1906 to 1924; the business is listed alternately as 'grocer' and 'grocer, fish market.'*]

JC: And your parents, where were they brought up?

OA: My father [*José 'Joseph' Raposo Terceira, Sr.*] was brought up on Columbia Street [*in Fall River*]; she [*his mother*] didn't have her children yet, but he was born on Columbia Street [*in 1898*]. My mother [*née Rose Souza Farias*] was born in [*1901 in Bretanha, São Miguel,*] Azores. And, uh, that is where she was born, in the Azores. And I went and visited ... and I never saw such a beautiful island in all my life.

JR: You are absolutely right. I went to the Azores also and it is very beautiful. And you wonder why anyone immigrated.

OA: From the [*Azores*], well, they were too poor.

JC: Your parents are interesting pairing. Your father was Lebanese and your mother was Portuguese.

OA: No, no.

JC: Your husband is Lebanese. I'm sorry.

OA: Yes. And my mother-in-law [*Mrs. Nahem 'Nathan' Eid Abdow, née Mary Doumite*] was brought up in the Convent [*of the Good Shepherd*] in [*Cairo*] Egypt. [*She was sent there from Beirut, Lebanon, by her family to live and be educated under the care of her aunt, Sister Marie de la Nativité, who was a nun in the order of Sisters of Our Lady of Charity of the Good Shepard of Angers.*] Her parents [*David and Affie Doumite*] had died, and then she came to this country [*to live with her aunt, Mrs. Morad, in New Bedford, and*] she got married [*in Fall River in 1922*]. And my husband [*Dolor 'Duke' Bernard Abdow*] is Lebanese, and they are a really wonderful family. Really. My in-laws ... they take care of me like I'm a child. They come over here to visit me, make sure I have everything and I have got no complaints.

JC: Was there any difficulty in marrying someone of another nationality?

OA: Well, at the time, at the beginning, you get that in everything and everyone, I think. Because when my husband said he wanted to get married, and my mother- in-law found out I was Portuguese, she didn't like the idea too well. But I am going to tell you, she brought up my two sons [*Steven Dolor Abdow and Keith Bernard Abdow*] while I went to work, because I am a working girl. I worked in the shop, one shop ... was twenty-eight years – that's not counting the others. [*One of the 'others' was the Kerr Thread Mills (American Thread Company), Martine Street, Fall River.*] And my mother-in-law took care of my children while I went to work. So really, they are wonderful people ... and as you meet them and get to know them, you realize what wonderful people they are.

JC: Do you want to talk about your working life?

OA: Well, I used to get up in the morning at seven [*o'clock*], get my baby dressed, put him in the car, and my husband would bring me down to work. We'd leave my baby down with my mother in-law, because at the time, for a while [*after I was married*], I lived [*at 40 North Breault Street*] in Westport [*Massachusetts*] for a few months, so I would leave the baby with her [*at the Abdow residence at 182 Quequechan Street, Fall River*]. But afterwards, my father worked at the Luther Mill [*Luther Manufacturing Company, 240 Hartwell Street, Fall River*]. He was a weaver … so he would get out at three [*o'clock*], so he would pick me up, and the baby, and home we would come. There was always a way that you could have someone help you take care of your child. Really.

JC: Now you worked in the same shop for twenty-eight years?

OA: That's right.

JC: Which shop was that?

OA: Nancy Dress [*Company, 473-475 Pleasant Street, Fall River*].

JC: And which mill was that in?

OA: That's, oh, it was [*the old Durfee Mills*] at the corner, way down the bottom of the Avenue, way down the bottom…. Plymouth [*Avenue*], right down where the statue is. [*'The Hiker,' Spanish-American War Veteran Memorial by Theodora Ruggles Kitson, dedicated in 1938.*] We got the hurricane there one time, too … Hurricane Carol [*August 31, 1954*] blew the windows all right into, into the shop.

JC: What was your job?

OA: My job was making dresses.

JC: So you were on …

OA: The better dress.

JC: So, you were on a sewing machine?

OA: Yes, and it was the better dress. It wasn't the, the cheap quality. We worked on the better dresses and made more money. We got more money by working on the better dress.

JC: Can you describe what the mill was like?

OA: The mill was like? Sometimes, one time my girlfriend said, 'We have a nice carpet down the bottom there.' We go down the bottom, and it was the … it was a cardboard … they didn't take care . . . they should have taken better care of the quality of the …

JC: The work place?

OA: Yes, they should have taken care. We never had hot or cold water. When I went to another shop after years, I went to another shop and it had hot water! I couldn't believe it! I couldn't believe it had hot water.

JC: Did you need permission to go to the bathroom?

OA: No, we had a very good boss. His name was [*Abraham*] Ira Tepper; it was Jewish. He came from New York to begin himself, and he was a very good boss. That, I will say that for him. But, uh, the mill's run down, that's the way it stood.

JC: You didn't feel as though you were being overworked?

OA: Well, we were overworked because we wanted to make money.

JC: The more you did, the more you made.

OA: That's it.

JC: Okay.

OA: That's ... what they called piecework. And we worked hard, and we wanted to make the money, and we made, we made quite a bit of money at the time. [*Mrs. Abdow told her son, Steven, that, when the piecework Standard Rates were being set, the women purposely went slower so that it would be easier to beat the standard allowable time in order to make more money on piecework.*]

JC: You were working forty hours a week?

OA: Ah, no, thirty-seven hours.

JC: Thirty-seven hours?

OA: Yes, it was something like that. I can't even think of it now.

JC: Was there a union then?

OA: Oh, yes, the ILG [*International Ladies Garment Workers Union, Local No. 178 (ILGWU)*] and you had the medical coverage; if you needed anything, you'd stop by there. I know I had trouble with some kind of a – I don't know how to explain it – some kind of a bug, and they gave me shots for it, and I got rid of it. But they would take care of you. They were very good at the ILG[*WU*]. It's too bad that it's closed now. I said that just this week, when we went by it. I says, 'Too bad that place closed down.' [*ILGWU Union Health Center, 304 South Main Street, Room 1, opened in Fall River in 1944. The center moved to Garment Workers Square, 38 Third Street, Fall River, in 1951.*]

JR: Yes, that was down in back of the City Hall.

OA: That's right.

JR: I remember, I think I remember the doctor there was Mrs. Radovsky [*Dr. Anna C. Radovsky, née Anna Pearl Cort, the wife of Dr. Everett Simon Radovsky*].

OA: Yes, yes.

JR: Do you remember her?

OA: Yes, I had her for my examination, and I'd go to her again. They were pleasant, and they were very thoughtful, you know, and if you needed – I was allergic to something – I don't know what it was, they made me go every week. I got sick of it at the end, I stopped going, but ...

JC: They provided a lot of services.

OA: Yes, but the ILG[*WU*] was very good. I mean, I enjoyed working for them, and I ... I even had my tonsils removed from them. And I was a big girl by then.

JR: So did you get a pension from the ILG[*WU*]?

OA: Yes, but what happened was, that I, uh, left the ILG[*WU*]. When I left ... the other shop closed down, so I got less money. So, by the time I went to get my, uh, pension, there was a loss there, there was a loss on my pension.

JR: Quite a bit?

OA: Yes, yes, quite a bit. And I don't think it was a fair deal, but who am I? I am just, just a worker like anyone else. Some people got more, some people got less. Well, I was one of them, I got less.... There was a shop there that opened up for a while [*Rondo Knit Sportswear, 240 Hartwell Street, Fall River*]. I worked there for a while over there, and it brought down my pension right down. Right down, it went right down. [*Mrs. Abdow's pension was $90 - $96 monthly, just enough to initially prevent her from qualifying for MassHealth Insurance; according to her son, Steven, it took her family several years to acquire that benefit for her.*]

JC: Mrs. Abdow, we are talking about your working years. We are talking about 1950s and 1960s. When did you retire?

OA: Well, I retired [*in 1990*] ... and I was glad, because I didn't have to drive to work anymore. Yes, I worked up until that time.

JC: Now, you said that you're a child of the Depression.

OA: Yes, I am.

JC: Would you share with us some of your Depression stories? What it was like for you and your family?

OA: See, like my mother went to work right away [*after she married*]. She got married [*in Fall River on January 25, 1920*], and she went to work. She eloped. She eloped, so she stood here and she went to work.

JC: Where did she work?

OA: She worked at the Har-Lee [*Manufacturing Company, 425 Pleasant Street, Fall River*].

JC: Oh, okay.

OA: She worked at the Har-Lee, pressing all day. So, you know that is no easy one there. And my father worked at the Luther Mill [*Luther Manufacturing Company*] ... he had to get up at five [*o'clock*] to walk to the Luther Mill [*a distance of approximately two miles*] and she had to get up at seven [*o'clock*] to go to the Har-Lee, to get the trolley, because, at that time, we still had trolleys. I think we did at that time. [*The last trolley run of the Eastern Massachusetts Street Railway Company in Fall River was made on September 20, 1936.*]

JC: You sure?

OA: And she would get on the trolley and go to work at the Har-Lee. She would come home at four [*o'clock*]. My father was already peeling the potatoes for supper. And we had, we never went without. We had a good, good upbringing.

JC: How many children now?

OA: Just four – my three brothers [*João 'John' Raposo Terceira; George Raposo Terceira; and José 'Joseph' Raposo Terceira, Jr.*] and myself. And my mother kept on working until my older brother was sixteen [*in 1936*] and then she says, "Well, I, I give up. I'm not working anymore."

JC: So they were working throughout the 1930s, during the Depression. So they were lucky in that way.

OA: Yes.

JC: Because Fall River was really suffering in the 1930s.

OA: That's it, that's why I say in a way, in the long run, I am a Depression baby because, uh, I got away from that. I played outside with my grandmother watching us. And there was my mother, walking to work, sometimes she would walk, sometimes she'd walk to work so she'd have a dime for a cup of coffee. Yup.

JC: Was a different time.

OA: Yup, it was a different time. For a cup of coffee she would walk. I will take a, I will get a coffee today, [*she'd say*]. So she'd get a cup of coffee.

JC: Did you feel in any way deprived, because of …

OA: No, we were all happy, we all played together outside. You know there was nothing. Today's kids don't play games. They don't play like we used to play….

JC: Just one question … you mentioned no hot water at the factory, or mill. Was your home a cold water flat?

OA: A cold water flat? It was a cold water flat. And my mother get the tub out from hanging on the door, and bring it out on the, and it was only once a week. She'd bring out the tub and we would all take a bath. And then my brothers got old enough to go to the [*Fall River*] Boys Club [*at 374 Anawan Street*] – I thanked the Boys Club many times – so they could go swimming, but I had to use the tub. I had to use the tub.

JR: How did you heat the house? I remember my grandmother had coal.

OA: Yes.

JR: Did you have coal?

OA: Yes, my grandmother had coal for … there was coal in the house. There was, uh, let me see, there was a, ah, a closet on the back of the stove and there was a chimney. You had the … you … opened the door and you would get the bale coal and you'd dump it in the stove. And that was what kept the house warm. And then the oil came out. When the oil came out, my father right away changed to oil, because he didn't want that, said he doesn't want that [*coal*] in the house. So, he got the oil.

JR: Did it heat the house better?

OA: The house was always warm. It was warm; it wasn't cold.

JR: I'm kind of curious because you are making me think about my grandmother now. How about washing clothes? Because washing machines …

OA: My mother had the laundry. She went to work, she couldn't be doing laundry, so she got the laundry [*done*]; it was $1 a week to do the laundry.

JR: They picked it up in the house? And they brought?

OA: And she'd hang it out in the clothes line, on the clothes line, that is what she did. [*So-called 'wet wash' laundry was laundered commercially and returned to the customer wet, to be home dried.*] And she would say, 'Don't put the heavier clothes, put the lighter clothes, so we can … get it a little more clothes on the clothes line.' But she always had her clothes line. Everybody in that house has a clothes line. Everybody. Yeah.

JC: Did your parents talk about politics very much?

OA: Ah, my father would say to my mother, 'Rose, you know, maybe we should vote for this guy.' And they'd be talking about it. And she looked at it and she would say, 'No, I don't like that guy. I want the other guy.' My grandmother voted, you know. She went to, she voted with the shawl over her shoulders. And she went to vote. And my aunts [*Maria Raposo Terceira; Mrs. George W. Desmarais, née Regina Raposo Terceira; Mrs. Manuel Arruda née Alexandrina Raposo Terceira; Mrs. Antone Mello, née Adelina Raposo Terceira; and Mrs. Joseph Oliveira Silvia, née Herondina Raposo Terceira*] would tell her to vote for this guy. And she would say 'Ah, no, I heard him over the radio, I don't like him. I want, I'm choosing the one I want.' She was very independent. Yeah.

JC: How about presidents?

OA: President [*Franklin Delano*] Roosevelt was our guiding light – really.

JC: Tell us why.

OA: Why? Do you remember sitting around the radio and listening to that radio when he were saying the war [*World War II*] was broken out? We were all, all of us didn't know what to do or say. He, he was a wonderful president. And, you know, Mrs. Roosevelt [*née Anna Eleanor Roosevelt*] was a wonderful woman, too. She was a very brilliant woman, yeah, she was a very brilliant woman. But Roosevelt … started the March of Dimes. Do you remember the March of Dimes? March of Dimes put a dime in the little thing there. My father got us a card each so that we could put – get a dollar in there. Thank God, for the March of Dimes. I think there would be many more crippled people around. [*The March of Dimes Foundation was founded by President Roosevelt in 1938 as the National Foundation for Infantile Paralysis, to combat polio.*]

JC: Did you know he was crippled? [*Roosevelt was stricken with poliomyelitis while vacationing at his summer home on Campobello Island, Canada, in August, 1921.*]

OA: Yes, we knew that; we knew that right from the beginning.…

JC: Yes.

JR: So I am going to go back a little bit.

OA: Go ahead.

JR: To your house.

OA: It had an aerial, there was no antennas. It was an aerial in the house, right? Because I remember my uncle putting one up for us. The aerial.

JC: For the radio?

OA: Yeah.

JR: When did you get the radio? That was pretty advanced.

OA: Well, that's when we got it. It was a small one, but we got a good reception from it. And, uh, we always, we always put on the radio at night. We heard "the Shadow knows" [*The Shadow, a widely popular radio detective series, aired from 1930 - 1954*], Mr. and Mrs. Brent [*Mr. & Mrs. North, a popular radio mystery series, aired from 1942 - 1954*]. Should I go on?

JR: Yeah, go on.

OA: And of course, Kate Smith, [*Kathryn Elizabeth Smith, a beloved American contralto singer, known as 'The First Lady of Radio'*] she was our angel. That we loved. Kate Smith.

JC: Was your family very religious?

OA: My father wanted us to go to church, hear Mass, and we went to Catholic School.

JC: You did?

OA: The Espirito Santo [*Parochial School, Alden Street, corner of Everett Street, Fall River*]. We went to that school. As a matter of fact there was word that my grandfather helped build that church [*Espirito Santo Portuguese Roman Catholic Church, Alden Street, corner of Everett Street.*] Not that he helped build it, but he got in with other ... how I will say it, other men, together, so they could build the church there [*in 1904*]. Because way down the end of the road. It is way down the end. So, and we also had two islands down there. And they are gone. They took the two islands away.

JC: You mean in the river?

OA: Yes. We had two islands down there. Because we had, we had the last house, and I used to look out the window and we could see the two islands.

JC: I don't know, or remember that.

JR: I don't remember that. That is a surprise.

OA: Yes, two islands where the Bigbury [*Bigberry Stadium, on Front Street at the end of Wordell Street, in Fall River, was*], well if you go further down, and there were two islands there.

JR: They must have filled it in.

OA: They did, they did, because someone told me after a while, they said no, they filled them in. I said, 'That's not right.'

JR: I'd love to hear you tell me about your mother and her cooking.

OA: Oh, her cooking was delicious. My mother was a good cook, she was a good cook. She made sweet rice [*arroz doce, a traditional Azorean dessert*], soup [*caldine*], of course, I didn't like soup, so she would get after me. And my father said, 'Rose, leave that girl alone, because if she don't like it, don't make her eat it.' Because I don't like Portuguese soup [*sopa de couvres*]. I don't like Portuguese soup. But she was a very, very, good cook. But she would get a pan like this and make a big pan of soup. But she wasn't to cook a lot during the week because she had to go to work the next day. But on the Saturday and Sunday she would … sometimes say, "Joe, I think I am going to start some stew." She would make beautiful stew [*ensopedo*]. "So I am going to start it tonight so we can have it tomorrow. So I won't have to make it tomorrow." She would think ahead of time. Try it.

JR: Did she teach you to cook?

OA: Ah, yes, she did. Because when she took a stroke, I took over the house. So I, I did cook a lot, but I don't want to cook anymore. I don't want to cook anymore.

JC: You were the oldest child?

OA: No, my brother Joe.

JR: But, you were the only girl?

OA: Yes. I had to do everything. I had to take over.

JC: You went to Espirito Santo [*Parochial*] School.

OA: Yes, as far as sixth grade. Because my father bought a little house [*at 40 North Breault Street*] in Westport, [*Massachusetts*] so we moved out there [*circa 1941*]. But somehow or other my mother took sick [*She suffered a stroke, then called a 'shock'*]; she didn't like it. We went [*to*] Westport but all I went was as far as the sixth grade [*in Fall River*].

JC: Do you have any memories of the teachers there? What about Espirito Santo School?

OA: Espirito Santo, well … the real memory that I have of Espirito Santo was of Miss [*Mary*] Cabral. I guess you've heard of her? [*Miss Cabral taught kindergarten at Espirito Parochial Santo School for fifty-three years, from 1925 – 1978.*]

JR: I didn't, to tell you the truth.

OA: Well, Miss Cabral taught us how to receive our First Communion. She really, really, was an angel – really an angel; we all loved her. She was a lay teacher, she wasn't um, a … nun. [*First Holy Communion is a Catholic tradition denoting an individual's first reception of the sacrament of the Holy Eucharist.*]

JC: Some of them are nuns.

OA: Some of them were nuns [*Franciscan Missionaries of Mary*], some of them I wish they weren't nuns, but they were nuns.

JC: Tell us why?

OA: Sometimes, let's face it, they have favorites. So sometimes when their child doesn't get the right answer; it doesn't work out too well. So that was it. But I stood there until the sixth grade. And, like I said, [*I was there*] until the sixth grade and then we moved, like I said to, uh, Westport. And my mother took sick….

JR: I can see, I can see that your generation wanted to make sure your children went on to school and graduated.

OA: We really did. We really believed in schooling, as much as we could give … they [*her sons*] did well. They both went to [*Bishop*] Connolly [*High School, 373 Elsbree Street, Fall River*], both of them; I made sure they went to Connolly.

JR: Very good.

OA: As a matter of fact, my oldest boy [*Steven*] was the first one to receive a diploma. [*The Class of 1970 was the first graduating class from Bishop Connolly High School; diplomas were awarded alphabetically, hence Steven Dolor Abdow was the first graduate awarded a diploma.*]

JR: Very good.

OA: He was the first one to receive a diploma. I said, 'Good for you, Steve ….'

JC: You left school…. Did you stay home to take care of your mother?

OA: Yes. I stood home. [*She terminated her formal education during her sophomore year in high school.*] And then after a while, the doctor says to my father, 'Well, you know, Joe, your wife … seems to be doing good. Maybe she can stay alone for a while.' So he says, 'My daughter is not going to work, she has to take care of her mother.' I says 'No, Dad, I'm not taking care of Momma. I am going to show Momma how to do some things that I know she can do, and I will come at night and do it when I come home from work.' I didn't want to be without work.

JC: So what was your first job?

OA: My first job was sewing on the machine. That was my first job.

JR: Now were you already married when you started working?

OA: No, I got married afterward [*on June 18, 1949*]. I got married after.

JR: How did you meet your husband?

OA: If I told you, you won't believe me.

JR: Oh, yes we will.

OA: I met him [*Dolor 'Duke' Bernard Abdow*] on the telephone.

JC: How did that happen?

OA: Well, I was babysitting my godchild [*Dorothy 'Dolly' Ann Terceira*] because her grandmother [*Mrs. José 'Joseph' M. Perreira, née Maria Alfredo*] was sick in the hospital, and my sister-in-law [*Mrs. George Raposo Terceira, née Alice Perreira*] wanted to be with her mother. So I was taking care of her. So the phone rings, I pick up the telephone and I says, 'Hello?' He says, "Hi, Hank, how about us seeing each other tonight?' Hank [*Henry Assad*] was his cousin. I said 'I think you have the wrong number.' And we started, that's it.

JC: How old were you?

OA: I would say about eighteen or nineteen, about that. 'Cause I got married at twenty, and he was twenty himself.

JC: Where did he take you on your first date?

OA: On my first date, my first date, of course, where else? Mark You [*Chinese Restaurant, 1236 Pleasant Street, Fall River*]. Where do you think?

JC: Did he make a good impression?

OA: Well, I thought he was rich.

JR: And did you walk to Mark You?

OA: Yeah, because, first of all we took, we took the bus to, uh, the Durfee [*Theatre, 28 North Main Street, Fall River*]. We saw a nice movie.

JR: Oh, you went to the movies?

OA: That was something. I got all dressed up for that, and I went. I wasn't even dressed up for that – my sister-in-law [*Alice Perreira Terceira*] called me up and she says 'Olive are you keeping that date or not?' I said, 'Are you kidding? I don't even know the guy.' So ... so she says, 'Go out and see if he's there.' So, I looked out the window – and I lived [*at 1433*] Pleasant Street, [*Fall River*] for a while – and I looked out the window, and there he is at the corner. I come back to the phone; I says, 'The poor guy is at the corner waiting for me.' And that is how I met my husband.

JR: Did he come to the house and meet your parents?

OA: No, not in those days you didn't do that. No, he came, I say about a month or so after. I says, 'Hey Ma, I am meeting this guy I went to school with.' I lied. I says, 'I went to school with. So I am going to go to the movie with him.' Well, she says, 'You be careful and be home by ten o'clock.' You imagine? We had to be home by ten o'clock? We still had curfews and yup, especially with girls. Sometimes I hated being a girl. My brothers go swimming to the sandbars. Did you ever hear of the sandbars? I couldn't go, I was a girl. The boys would go. The boys could go swimming to sandbars. I, I couldn't go. [*The sandbar, on the north shore at the outlet of South Watuppa Pond in Fall River, was considered the best place for fresh water bathing on the lake.*]

JR: How about girlfriends, hanging out with girlfriends?

OA: Um, I had my cousins. We were all like friends. Yeah. Yeah.

JR: You went to the movies?

OA: Yes, yes, that's what we spent our... and then the Strand [*Theatre, 1363 Pleasant Street, Fall River*] is close to where I lived. So I would say, 'I am going to a movie today.' So that was alright, she would take it, you know? But to say it about go out with different fellas on dates just wasn't called for. You couldn't go.

JC: Your husband had a good job?

OA: He worked as a repairman for, uh, how can I say it.... He did, he did have a good job ... he did washers and dryers. But commercial ones, not the regular ones, it had to be the commercial ones. And he had a lot of little jobs on the side. They'd call him up and say, 'Duke, my machine is out,' and he would go up.

JC: So he was working for someone else?

OA: He worked at Hoyt [*Dryer Corporation, Westport, Massachusetts*]. That was his regular job. But he worked for himself, really, towards the end. He was working for himself.

JC: So, when you were bringing up your children, things were much better than when you were being brought up.

OA: Of course, [*my son, Keith,*] had to walk to school. [*Bishop*] Connolly [*High School*] was right up the street. We lived [*at 886*] New Boston Road, [*Fall River*] ... so all [*he*] had to do is walk up the street to get to Connolly.

JC: Why did you send them to Connolly?

OA: Because I, I wanted them to have a good education.

JC: Okay.

OA: I wanted them to have, uh, and they did. They were taught at first by the Jesuits [*Society of Jesuits, Brothers of Christian Instruction*]. And you couldn't ask for any better than the Jesuits for a teacher.

JR: I'm going to just jump back a little bit. Because you mentioned [*President*] Franklin Roosevelt and you mentioned listening to the radio when the war broke out. Can you tell us about the war years? And who went into the war in your family?

OA: Well, see, in my family [*two of*] my brothers went; both of them were discharged. My oldest brother [*John, United States Navy, enlisted May 11, 1942*] got discharged honorably [*on September 18, 1942*] because ... he had something let go in his stomach and they had to send him home. And they told him if you sign this paper – that's why when I see this about the veterans getting short-changed, I say my brother got short-changed – if he signed the paper, we will give you a discharge now and you can go home. So he was so sick, he couldn't even walk. I was the one that took care of him; I took care of him and my mother.

JR: That's a lot of responsibility.

OA: You know, but gradually he got on his feet. Then my other brother [*George*] went in [*United States Army, enlisted March 12, 1943*] and my mother is sitting on the porch and sees the Red Cross coming up and says, 'Oh no, something else happened. It has to be George because John is already discharged.' So the woman got out, they knew each other. My brother George was in the Army and she says, 'Don't get nervous, Mrs. Teixeira. There's nothing wrong with your son; he's all right.' You know why he got discharged? He was a sleep walker [*discharged June 10, 1943*].

JR: Oh, jeez.

OA: He was a sleep walker.

JR: Oh, no!

OA: Oh, yes, and he was since he was small, and my father had the lock on the top of the door so he wouldn't leave the house.

JR: Well, that's interesting.

OA: And the lady said, 'Don't get discouraged because there is a lot of them that we had to discharge for being a sleep walker. We can't have them in the army. They can take a gun and shoot someone. Shoot a friend.' So my mother, you know what she told her? 'You know something? You don't want them, I want them, send him home.'

JR: How about your husband? Did he get called up?

OA: Ah, no, he was just too, he just, uh, my mother in-law wouldn't sign the paper for him to go because he used to work [*as a spinner*] in the mills, all kind of hours. He loved it, he loved working in the mills. All kind of hours because she wanted, she'd use his money to live on.

JR: Sure, you had to support your family.

OA: Yeah. So.

JR: They always ask you if you have someone dependent on you before they send you through the service ... I heard you drove a car? You were driving?

OA: Well, I drove, but not for too long. I hated driving a car. I didn't like driving a car. I don't know why, I just didn't like it.

JR: Who taught you?

OA: Uh, I think my husband taught me. Yeah, if anything, it was on the street in Westport up and down the road. And that was it. And I drove for a while. Then of course when he died I got sick and all, so that was it.

JC: How long ago did he die?

OA: My husband, he [*died in 2000*].

JC: How did that change your life?

OA: It didn't change my life, because what I did was, I started to think what is going to happen to me now that Duke is gone. I didn't want to lose him but I lost him like anybody else loses their loved ones. And then I said, I know what I am going to do ... and then I went to live at, um...

JR: In the apartments.

OA: The [*Academy Building*] Apartments, [*102 South Main Street, Fall River*] that's where I went to live, and that's where I have been living until I came here [*Catholic Memorial Home, 2446 Highland Avenue, Fall River*]. I woke up one morning and here I am. I don't know what happened to me ... they said I was very fresh. Can you imagine that? I can't imagine it. Yeah. So life is strange.

JC: Do you have any grandchildren?

OA: I have ... [*Four grandchildren: Nathan Steven Abdow; Tamara (Abdow) Carpenter; Timothy Abdow; Stacia Abdow; and four great-grandchildren: Aisha Abdow; Devon Abdow; Dakota Morgan Abdow, and Riley Abdow.*]

JC: Do they visit you?

OA: Oh yeah. They all come and see Vo [*a diminutive of Vovó, which is the familiar form of Avó, or grandmother in Azorean Portuguese.*] They call me Vo. We always called my grandmother Vo and I stood with Vo.

JR: What do you think of the changes in Fall River from ... your time of growing up and now?

OA: Like my father used to say, 'I don't know why they are building all these banks, who has money to put in all these banks?' But, the trouble, the thing is, it needs to be straightened out a little bit. I don't like to go too much into politics, but we should have a good mayor and a good politician in there. Someone that's good that will teach, not teach – show the people that he is willing and able to run Fall River, because Fall River was a great big city at one time. It was a great big city, because I read the book one time. I couldn't get over it. We had a parade one time, over a hundred people in the parade and it was all from people that worked in mills – that worked in the mills.

JC: The Cotton Centennial? [*The Fall River Cotton Centennial celebration was held from June 19 – 26, 1911 to commemorate the one-hundredth anniversary of the construction of the first cotton mill in Fall River, by Colonel Joseph Durfee, in 1811.*]

OA: Yes, that's it – the [*Fall River*] Cotton Centennial. Yes, now, isn't that enough to be proud of? And then I read a book about this woman that came [*from*] New York ... to live here with her husband. He was a lawyer. She said, 'I never saw such a beautiful city in all my life, because ... there's trees.' It's unbelievable how pretty Fall River is.

GK: President [*William Howard*] Taft came down for that Centennial. [*President Taft visited Fall River on 'President's Day,' June 23, 1911*].

OA: Did he? See? We had a lot to be proud of. I am telling you we have to do something; please, do something, there is so much to be done. You know?

JC: When you look back on your life, do you have any regrets?

OA: I don't have any regrets, marrying my husband, having my children, I just wish ... that I probably could have had a little more education. That is what I think I would have liked, a little education.

JC: You were born too soon.

OA: That's what you get when you're a baby.

JC: Mrs. Abdow, we thank you for sharing your memories with us.

OA: Oh my goodness, I went on, and on, and on, and on. I wish I had more to tell you.

PHOTO GALLERY

2.1 Olivia's grandparents with their children: Standing, left to right: her aunt, Adelina Raposo Terceira; her uncle, Antonio Raposo Terceira, Jr.; her aunt, Maria Raposo Terceira; her father, José 'Joseph' Raposo Terceira, Sr.; her aunt, Regina Raposo Terceira; her aunt, Alexandrina Raposo Terceira; her uncle, Manuel Raposo Terceira. Seated, left to right: Olivia's grandmother, Mrs. Antonio Raposo Terceira, Sr., née Maria De Jesus Ferreira Andrade; her aunt, Herondina Raposo Terceira; her grandfather, Antonio Raposo Terceira, Sr. *"It was a six-tenement house. It was my … aunts, and myself, me, I was brought up there."*

2.2 Olivia's grandmother, Mrs. Antonio Raposo Terceira, Sr., née Maria De Jesus Ferreira Andrade, in later life. *"My grandmother grew up in* [Feteiras do Sul, São Miguel,] *Azores, but she was brought up in Hawaii. She had quite a travel, you know."*

2.3 Olivia's father, José 'Joseph' Raposo Terceira, Sr., and her mother, née Rose Souza Farias, on their wedding day, June 25, 1920. *"She got married, and she went to work. She eloped. She eloped so she could stay here and she went to work."*

2.4 Olivia with her siblings, 1934. Standing, left to right: George Raposo Terceira; João 'John' Raposo Terceira; Olivia. Seated: José 'Joseph' Raposo Terceira, Jr. *"Just four – my three brothers and myself. And my mother kept working until my older brother was sixteen and she says, 'Well, I, I give up. I'm not working anymore."*

2.5 The Fall River Boy's Club, 374 Anawan Street, circa 1930. *"It was a cold water flat. And my mother got the tub out from hanging on the door ... and it was only once a week. And she'd bring out the tub and we would all take a bath. And then my brothers got old enough to go to the Boy's Club – I thanked the Boy's Club many times – so they could go swimming, but I had to use the tub."*

2.6 Olivia strikes a classic 1940s pose. *"Sometimes I hated being a girl. My brothers go swimming to the sandbars ... I couldn't go, I was a girl."*

2.7 A 1950 advertisement for Kerr Thread Mills, a division of American Thread Company, Fall River, Massachusetts. Olivia was employed here until circa 1953 when the company closed.

2.8 The Durfee Mills, Pleasant Street, Fall River, Massachusetts, in an early 20th century postcard; the building at the left later housed Nancy Dress Company, at 473 – 475 Pleasant Street. *"I worked in the shop, one shop* [Nancy Dress Company] *... twenty-eight years – that's not counting the others."*

2.9 *Left:* A Terceira family portrait. Standing, left to right: Olivia's brothers, George Raposo Terceira; José 'Joseph' Raposo Terceira Jr.; João 'John' Raposo Terceira. Seated, left to right: her mother, née Rose Souza Farias; Olivia; her father, José 'Joseph' Raposo Terceira, Sr. *"And we had, we never went without. We had a good, good upbringing."*

2.10 *Right:* Sister Marie de la Nativité, of the order of Sisters of Our Lady of Charity of the Good Shepherd of Angers, at the Convent of the Good Shepherd in Cairo, Egypt, with her niece, Mary Doumite; the girl, would later marry Nahem 'Nathan' Eid Abdow and become Olivia's mother-in-law. Mary was fluent in six languages: Arabic, English, French, Greek, Italian, and Latin. *"And my mother-in-law was brought up in the convent in Egypt. Her parents had died, and then she came to this country* [and] *she got married."*

2.11 Olivia's husband, Dolor 'Duke' Bernard Abdow, circa 1930; the photograph was taken in the yard of his parents residence at 275 Quequechan Street, Fall River, Massachusetts. *"And my husband is Lebanese."*

2.12 Olivia's father-in law, Nahem 'Nathan' Eid Abdow, representing Uncle Sam, July, 4, 1939; the photograph was taken outside the Lebanese American Club on Quequechan Street, Fall River, Massachusetts. Depicted to his left is Gloria Assad, as Martha Washington, and to his right, John Hagg, as George Washington.

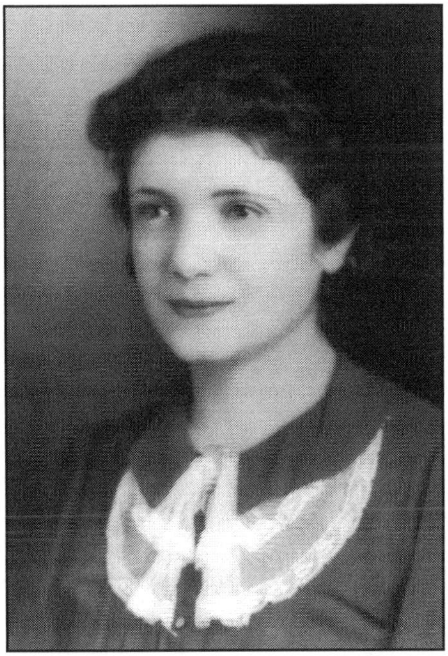

2.13 Olivia's mother-in-law, Mrs. Nahem 'Nathan' Eid Abdow, née Mary Doumite, circa 1940.

2.14 Olivia's husband, Dolor 'Duke' Bernard Abdow, 1948. *"I met him over the telephone."*

2.15 Interior of the Durfee Theatre, 28 North Main Street, Fall River, Massachusetts, late 1940s. *"Yeah, because, first of all, we took the bus to, uh, the Durfee. We saw a nice movie."*

2.16 Mr. & Mrs. Dolor 'Duke' Bernard Abdow on their wedding day, June 18, 1949, posing in the living room of Olivia's parents' residence, 1433 Pleasant Street, Fall River, Massachusetts; her wedding gown has been donated to the Fall River Historical Society. *"Cause I got married at twenty and he was twenty himself."*

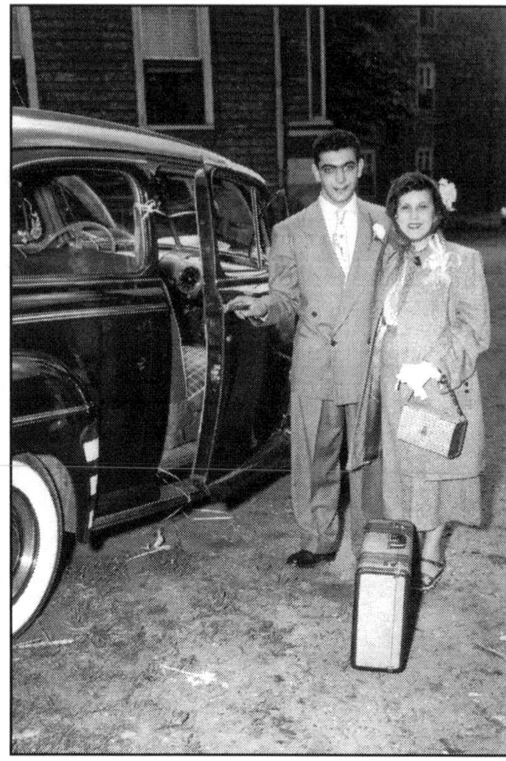

2.17 The newlywed Mr. & Mrs. Abdow leaving for their wedding trip, following their wedding, June 18, 1949.

2.18 The newlywed Mr. & Mrs. Abdow with members of their wedding party returning to her family's residence, 1433 Pleasant Street, Fall River, Massachusetts, following their wedding, June 18, 1949.

2.19 Olivia shortly after her marriage, circa 1950. *"I am a working girl."*

2.20 Olivia and Duke in a 1950s Christmas snapshot.

2.21 Olivia's in-laws, Nahem 'Nathan' Eid Abdow, and Mrs. Abdow, née Mary Doumite, at their grandson Steven's *"5 year old birthday party,"* 1957. A smoker, Mary was a devotee of the *nargile,* the traditional Lebanese water pipe; she holds a *fenjan*, or cup, of *al-qahwa*, strong Arabic coffee. *"Because when my husband said he wanted to get married ... my mother-in-law found out I was Portuguese, she didn't like the idea too well. But I am going to tell you* [she] *took care of my children while I went to work ..."*

2.22 Olivia and Duke with their eldest son, Steven Dolor Abdow at the boy's fifth birthday party, 1957; Olivia would soon give birth to their second child, Keith Bernard Abdow. Olivia captioned the photograph: *"Steven's 5 year old party. Keith was on his way."*

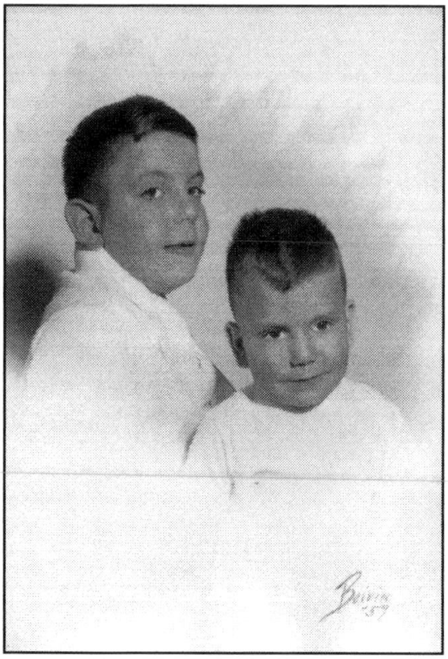

2.23 Olivia's sons, Steven Dolor Abdow and Keith Bernard Abdow, 1959. *"I wanted them to have a good education."*

2.24 Olivia, her husband, Duke, and their son, Steven, dressed for his First Holy Communion, outside the family residence at 85 Massasoit Street, Fall River, Massachusetts, 1959; Olivia's in-laws, Mr. & Mrs. Nahem 'Nathan' Eid Abdow, lived on the third floor of the house in the rear center, 182 Quequechan Street.

2.25 Olivia's mother-in-law, Mrs. Nahem 'Nathan' Eid Abdow, née Mary Doumite, striking a pose with one of her beloved *nargile*, the traditional Lebanese water pipe, early 1960s. *"They are wonderful people ... and as you meet them and get to know them, you realize what wonderful people they are."*

2.26 Olivia and Duke, 1965. *"I don't have any regrets, marrying my husband, having my children, I just wish … that I probably could have had a little more education. That is what I think I would have liked, a little education."*

2.27 The Robeson Mills, 240 Hartwell Street, Fall River, Massachusetts, 1870s; reincorporated as the Luther Manufacturing Company in 1903, the structure later housed Rondo Knit Sportswear. *"There was a shop* [Rondo Knit Sportswear] *that opened up for a while. I worked there for a while over there, and it brought my pension right down. Right down, it went right down."*

2.28 The Fall River Cotton Centennial celebration was held from June 19 – 26, 1911, to commemorate the one-hundredth anniversary of the construction of the first cotton mill in Fall River, Massachusetts, by Colonel Joseph Durfee in 1811; this image depicts a parade held on June 21st. *"It was a great big city. We had a parade one time, over a hundred people in the parade and it was all from people that worked in the mills – that worked in the mills."*

2.29 President William Howard Taft addressing the crowd at the Fall River Cotton Centennial celebration on "Presidents' Day," June 23, 1911. *"See? We had a lot to be proud of."*

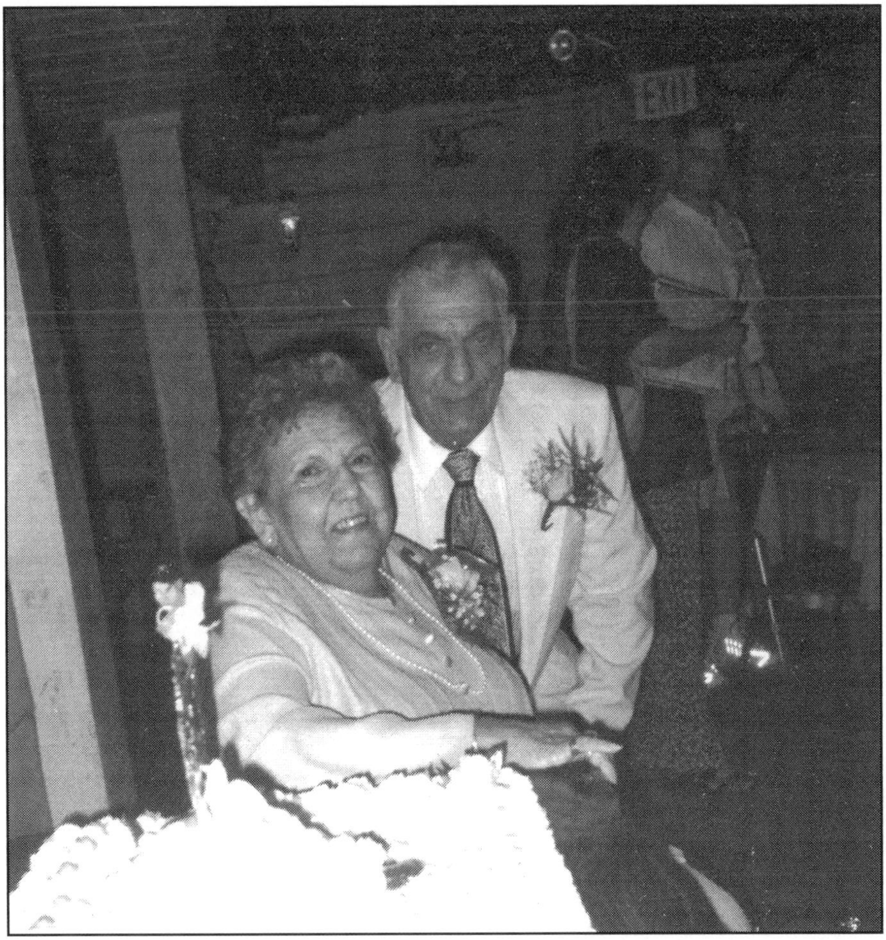

2.30 Olivia and Duke at their Golden Wedding Anniversary celebration in 1999. *"I didn't want to lose him but I lost him like anybody else loses their loved ones."*

THREE:

DOLORES ALMEIDA, NÉE SILVIA

Personal Statistics

Name: Delores Silvia
(Mrs. James "Jimmy" Francis Almeida, Jr.)

Date of Birth: October 18, 1937

Place of Birth: Fall River, Massachusetts

Father: Seraphine Peter Silvia (1896-1972)

Mother: Virginia Rapozo Salgado (1909-1999)

Siblings:
Alphonse "Al" Peter Silvia (1921-1983)
Lawrence "Sonny" Peter Silvia (1931-1997)
"Female Baby" (1935)
Margaret Silvia (1939-2008)
---(Mrs. Frank Owsney)
"Stillborn Male" (1942)
Note: Delores' father's first wife, Elisa Martin (1901-1935) was the mother of Alphonse and Lawrence Silva; she died on December 4, 1935, due to the effects of childbearing; the child also died at birth. Thus the two eldest boys were Delores' half-siblings

Spouse: James "Jimmy" Francis Almeida, Jr.

Date of Marriage: May 30, 1956

Children:
Louis William Almeida (1958-1993)
Lori Ann Almeida
---(Mrs. Antonio Pereira)
Kevin James Almeida

Employment history:
Pleasant Curtain Company, Fall River
Atlas Manufacturing Company, Fall River
K & G Manufacturing Company, Inc., Fall River
Novelty Boys Wash Suit Company, Fall River
Servall Manufacturing Company, Inc., Fall River

EDITED TRANSCRIPT

Interview with Mrs. James "Jimmy" Francis Almeida, Jr., née Delores Silvia

Interviewer: (JR) Joyce B. Rodrigues, Fall River Historical Society

Interviewee: (DA) Delores (Silvia) Almeida

Date of Interview: June 10, 2015

Location: Somerset Ridge Center, Somerset, Massachusetts

Summary by Joyce B. Rodrigues:

Delores (Silvia) Almeida was born in Fall River, Massachusetts, on October 18, 1937. She came of age at the height of her native city's garment manufacturing period. She graduated in 1953 from eighth grade at the Susan B. Wixon Elementary School, and like her sister and brothers before her, immediately went to work to contribute to the household.

Work Experience:

Fall River factory work was plentiful and jobs were readily available in the 1950s and 1960s. As an example, there were 101 factories listed in the 1951 edition of the *Directory of Massachusetts Manufacturers,* which lists companies employing fifty or more production workers. These jobs were diverse and included the manufacturing of curtains, ladies dresses, men's shirts, children's wear, luggage, loose-leaf binders, and lighting fixtures.

Delores' career took her to:

- Pleasant Curtain Company, 237 Pleasant Street
- Atlas Manufacturing Company (curtains), 288 Plymouth Avenue
- K & G Manufacturing Company, Inc. (ladies dresses), 187 Pleasant Street.

By the late 1960s and throughout the 1970s, American factory and garment workers were facing growing overseas competition. Commenting on this period, Delores notes the impact of this development on the local economy: "There [were] so many factories in Fall River. … They are all gone. All [*the*] shops are gone."

Like the textile decline in the 1920s, Fall River in the last quarter of the twentieth century would once again face economic instability and the prospect of an uncertain future.

Family Life:

Delores is a second-generation Portuguese-American. Her grandparents immigrated to the United States from the island of St. Michael in the Azores; her father and mother were born in the United States in 1896 and 1909 respectively.

Delores was brought up on a farm. Her father worked as a farm manager for a family in Swansea, Massachusetts, and for the George Magan family in Tiverton, Rhode Island. She was brought up "old-fashioned." Her father's job on the Magan farm came with a rent-free house and fresh milk every day.

The family eventually moved to Fall River. "My father always worked on the farm, and then, when the farms started fading away, he went to work at the Truesdale Hospital [Inc., 1820 Highland Avenue] helping out in the kitchen."

Delores started working at the age of sixteen, and retired at age sixty-two with a pension from Social Security and with no pension from the ILGWU union because she did not have enough years.

Delores met and married James Francis Almeida, Jr., "the boy across the street"; Their wedding was at the Santo Christo Church on Columbia Street, on May 30, 1956. The couple had three children.

After retirement, Delores took care of her grandchildren and, at the time of this interview, was active as the president of a senior residents' council.

Note: This interview has been slightly edited for continuity and readability; in order to preserve the integrity of the conversation, the phraseology remains that of the interviewer and interviewee. Italicized information in square brackets has been added for the purposes of clarification and context.

JR: This is June 10, 2015. We're at Somerset Ridge and this is Delores Almeida who we are interviewing today, and the interviewer is Joyce Rodrigues. So we are going to get started. Let's get started. Okay, Delores, I heard a lot about you. Tell me about your family; tell me about your parents and grandparents.

DA: My … grandparents were born in the Old Country in [*Saõ Miguel, Azores*] Portugal. [*The interviewee's paternal grandparents, José "Joseph" Peter Silvia, and his wife, née Rita de Jesus, immigrated from Capelas, São Miguel, Azores; her maternal grandparents, Louiz 'Luis' Rapoza Salgado and his wife, née Margarida 'Margaret' Soares, immigrated from Relva, a civic parish in the municipality of Ponta Delgada, São Miguel, Azores*].

JR: You mean the Azores?

DA: The Azores – and my mother [*née Virginia Rapoza Salgado*] and father [*Seraphine Peter Silvia*] were born here in the United States. [*The interviewee's mother was born in Fall River in 1909; her father, was born in Somerset, Massachusetts, in 1896*]. And I learned Portuguese through my grandparents, who couldn't speak a word of English, so that's how come I can now speak both languages. My mother and father spoke English; they spoke the two languages.

JR: And when did the grandparents come to the United States?

DA: I don't know, it was way before I was born – way before that. [*The interviewee's paternal grandparents, the Silvias, immigrated to the United States before 1896; her maternal grandparents, the Salgados, before 1909.*]

JR: Did they work in Fall River when they came here?

DA: My grandfather [*Louiz 'Luis' Rapoza Salgado*] did. He worked at the – at the cotton mill in Fall River, the mill that was ... on Rodman Street [*Richard Borden Manufacturing Company, 440 Rodman Street*]. He worked in that cotton mill. I remember taking the cotton off of his whiskers in the morning. My grandmother [*Mrs. Louiz 'Luis' Rapoza Salgado, née Margarida 'Margaret' Soares*] was a stay-at-home wife; she stood home taking care of us.

JR: And how many children did they have?

DA: My grandmother only had my mother and my aunt [*Sarah Rapoza Salgado, who later married her first cousin, Manuel Rapoza Salgado*]. And they – my aunt [*Sarah*] came to this country [*when*] she was twelve years old. But, my grandparents had to leave her behind [*when they immigrated*] so they could come to this country and try to make a life. So, once they got their lives situated, they sent for her, and then, in the meantime my mother was born here [*in Fall River*].

JR: Okay, and tell me about your mother and your father.

DA: I had a wonderful mother [*née Virginia Rapoza Salgado*] and father [*Seraphine Peter Silvia*]. They were very good, and I was brought up old-fashioned, you know, they took good care of us. My father worked, my mother tried working, but then we were always sick so she stood home to take care of us, you know, always with a cold or something like that. But, uh, other than that, my father was the breadwinner of the house. [*The interviewee's mother was the second wife of Seraphine Peter Silvia; the couple married in 1936. His first wife, née Eliza Martin, whom he married circa 1919, was a native of the Azores, having immigrated to the United States in 1918; she died on December 4, 1935, giving birth to the couple's third child, a 'female baby,' who also died. The cause of death Eliza's death was 'pre-partum hemorrhage (acute separation of placenta); shock following Caesarian section.' The couple's two surviving children, Alphonse 'Al' Peter Silvia, born in 1921, and Lawrence 'Sonny' Peter Silvia, born in 1931, were the interviewee's half-brothers.*]

JR: And where did your father work?

DA: My father worked on the farm. He did farm work – milking cows, cultivating the land, and all of that. Back then, when we got a job, the house came with the job.

You didn't pay any rent because that came with the job, and the milk came with the job. So, we had fresh milk every morning, right from the cow to the house. My father would bring the pail and my mother had another kind of a pail to put it in to keep it in the refrigerator.

JR: Now, where was this farm?

DA: The farm was in Tiverton, [*Rhode Island, at 405*] Nanaquaket Road; George [*Sousa*] Magan [*owned it*]. We lived there – it was a nice house, very nice.

JR: This is the first time I'm hearing about that.

DA: Oh yeah, my father worked for him for a long time – for years. In fact, I used to go with Mr. Magan's cousin [*Elizabeth Magan*]; we would go collecting the money for the milk every Saturday morning, because people would, they'd have their customers, and at the end of the week ... we would go collect the money from the milk they delivered all week.

JR: Now, did you get involved in the farm? Did you work on the farm?

DA: No, no, we didn't work on the farm. My father did the work.

JR: And the house was there.

DA: The house was there – I don't know if it's still there now.... We had like a two-tenement house and we lived on the second floor....

JR: How many children were there at the time?

DA: There was only myself and my sister [*Margaret Silvia, later Mrs. Frank Owsney*]. My two brothers [*Alphonse 'Al' Peter Silvia, and Lawrence 'Sonny' Peter Silvia*] were married, so they were on their own, doing their own lives. But we would see them on weekends, and we go have a nice get-together on a weekend. My mother would do the cooking and we would all have our lunch together.

JR: Now, were you born in Tiverton, [*Rhode Island*]?

DA: No, I was born in Fall River.

JR: So, at the time, where were you living in Fall River when you were born?

DA: Well, my father and my mother were living in Swansea, [*Massachusetts, on Warren Road*]. Before Mr. Magan, there was another farmer that he worked for, and then he took them to be my god-parents; they became good friends. His name was Michael [*Miguel S.*] Massa – that's who he worked for.

JR: Ok, I am going to write that down.

DA: The one that I, [*it*] was Michael [*Miguel S.*] Massa [*and his wife, Mary C. Massa*] who became my godparents.

JR: And Mr. Magan.

DA: And … Mr. George [*Sousa*] Magan was on Nanaquaket Road in Tiverton, Rhode Island.

JR: So, those were the two farms?

DA: Those are the two farms that I can remember. My father always worked on the farm, and then, when the – when the farms started fading away, then he went to work at the Truesdale Hospital [*Inc., 1820 Highland Avenue, Fall River*], helping out in the kitchen.

JR: So, he was always working.

DA: My father was a good worker; he was a good breadwinner. He never wanted my mother to work.

JR: Did he ever tell you stories about the [*Great*] Depression?

DA: No, they never did. We never did.

JR: I know times were tough.

DA: Yeah, those times were tough, but they never told us anything about that.

JR: So, you grew up with a sister and two brothers.

DA: Yes.

JR: And, did you have your own room?

DA: No, I shared a bed with my sister. We shared our room, we both slept in the same bed – no separate beds back then. It was a little house, it was only a little apartment [*at 308 Ferry Street*], you know, when we came to the city [*circa 1939*]. But even on the farm … we both slept in the same bed.

JR: So, how did you get along?

DA: We got along good. She was cranky sometimes but, you know, just like siblings do, but we loved one another.

JR: Now did you go to school in Tiverton, [*Rhode Island*] or was it in Swansea, [*Massachusetts*]?

DA: I went to school in Tiverton … I went to school in, umm, oh, Fort Barton [*Elementary*] School [*99 Lawton Avenue*] in Tiverton, when we lived on Mr. Magan's house….

JR: You were born in nineteen …

DA: I was born in 1937, October 18, 1937. Yeah.

JR: Now, were there any duties, any particular duties that you had to do in the house?

DA: Oh, yes, we had to clean, you know, I'd help clean the house on the weekend. And, you know, girls weren't – in my house was like that – the outside is for the boys, the girls stay indoors, doing your homework when you get out of school, and whatever she [*the interviewee's mother*] had planned for us to do, we did it. And on the weekends, I remember beating the carpets with the wire thing with a handle … put it out on the line, and beat the carpets. And we cleaned the house, and my mother did the cooking.

JR: Did you also learn how to cook?

DA: Yes, I did.

JR: What were the favorite recipes?

DA: Well, no recipes. We – back then, they don't have recipes. Even myself, I never had a recipe, I did it the way I saw them do it. We'd marinate the meat when it was roast meat, roast chicken, turkey, we'd marinate it. Make beans, we made the baked beans. In fact, I handed down the recipe, well, I made up the recipe, because it wasn't – my mother made the baked beans, and I did it like her. So, then, when I came into this nursing home [*Somerset Ridge Center, 455 Brayton Avenue, Somerset, Massachusetts*], I handed down to my daughter [*Mrs. Antonio Pereira, née Lori Ann Almeida*] and my son [*Kevin James Almeida*], how to make the baked beans, and they make it. Very simple, so.

JR: I remember growing up with my grandmother, and we used to do a lot of house cleaning, and we used to put curtains on a stretcher.

DA: On the stretcher with the pins that stuck up, and we'd stretch that good, and those curtains were beautiful after they got dried up and put them on the window. I remember having the organdy curtains; those were tough, but put them on the stretcher – you didn't have to press them. They take two people … we took it out, and I remember my sister on one end and I'm on the other end folding in half, make the crease, fold again, make another crease, so by the time they hung on the window, they were nice. The creases were beautiful, yes.

JR: Did you have a washing machine?

DA: Well, my mother, we didn't get a washing machine until later on, and the first washing machine we had was a Maytag [*Washing Machine Company, later Maytag, Inc. Newton, Iowa*] with the rolling pin [*Maytag Wringer Washer*]. We put the [*wet*] clothes through the roller – how many times they got stuck going around the roller – release it. But those were good days.

JR: So, before that, you probably had to wash [*laundry*] by hand.

DA: We would boil the clothes before that, we would boil the clothes. I remember my mother and my grandmother [*Mrs. Louiz 'Luis' Rapoza Salgado, née Margarida 'Margaret' Soares*] putting the clothes – they save a special pan just to put the clothes, dirty clothes in there – and then they boil the clothes, and then wash it on the scrubbing board. The clothes come out nice and white, and [*they used*] Octagon [*Laundry*] soap, [*manufactured by Colgate-Palmolive-Peet, New York, New York*] and bluing during laundering for the white clothes. [*Bluing was a product habitually used to improve the appearance of white textiles; added to the water during rinsing, it added a hint of blue dye to the fabric, enhancing its brilliance*].

JR: You are bringing back a lot of memories for me, also, because my grandmother had a washing machine with a ringer, and then she would turn the ringer around, so that the clothes could go into the rinse.

DA: Right, the water would go back into the – yes, that's how we did it.

JR: And the bluing was in that water.

DA: Right, to make the clothes white-white. And the clothes did come out nice and white.

JR: The dryers. We hung things outside.

DA: No dryers. We hung things outside on the line, yes, and then, when the laundry came, then we would send the jeans and the clothes to the laundry, but never to wash and dry. We always dried it on the line … always on the line. [*So-called 'wet wash' laundry was returned to the customer wet to be home-dried.*]

JR: So, how did you heat the house in those days?

DA: In those days, we helped warm the house with kerosene heaters, kerosene stoves, and also came along the combination stoves, half gas, and the other half kerosene.

JR: I haven't heard about that.

DA: Oh, yeah, my [*maternal*] grandmother had one, and we had one. It was half kerosene and the other half was the gas stove. A big long stove, and then the top we polished it on the Saturday, we polished that with a black polish [*called 'stove black'*], and boy, that would shine beautiful.

JR: I think before that, too, my [*maternal*] grandparents had wood; they had wood and they also had coal.

DA: I don't remember the coal and the wood. When I was growing up, it was kerosene. And the heaters and the stoves would have two, uh, tanks. You'd fill one and then you would have to fill the other one, so during the night you wouldn't – the house wouldn't get cold – in the morning, we would get up, the house was cold. Run down the cellar, go fill it up with kerosene, and then get the stove going again and warm it up.

JR: So, you went to ... Fort Barton Elementary School. Did you go to another school after elementary school?

DA: No, then we came – my father, by then, the farm gave up – and then we went to Fall River [*circa 1948*], and then I went to the Susan H. Wixon Elementary School [*263 Hamlet Street*] and I graduated from there [*in 1953*]. [*The interviewee resided with her parents in Fall River at: 308 Ferry Street, circa 1939-40; 76 Hunter Street, circa 1942-44; 22 Danforth Street, circa 1948-49; and 616 Third Street, circa 1950 – until her marriage in 1956. During the years for which there are gaps, her father was employed as a laborer on farms outside the city.*]

JR: From the Susan H. Wixon Elementary School.

DA: From the eighth grade, and then from there I went to work.

JR: That was very typical. That happened to my mother as well, from grade eight, and she would have been older than you, but it was in the '30s and you know it was the [*Great*] Depression and times were tough.

DA: I remember during the war, World War II, we all had [*coupon*] books – we had the ration then, and we'd get them once a month – we'd wait in line to go get sugar and flour and meat, and it was very scarce. And back then I remember that there wasn't even nylons for the women to wear. That's when they would start coloring their legs [*so-called 'paint-on-hosiery'*] with a spray to make it look as though they had stockings on – nylons on. That was during World War II ....

JR: Tell me about holidays and birthdays.

DA: Holidays was very nice; we'd all be together. Birthdays, we didn't make too much of birthdays – my mother never made too much of birthdays. But, holidays we were always together. And every night, all family oriented, always. So, we had, I had good memories.

JR: And were you brought up with the Catholic Church or...?

DA: Yes, the [*Roman*] Catholic Church. I went to Santo Cristo Church [*240 Columbia Street, Fall River*], and ... when I got married [*in 1956*], I also went to Sts. Peter and Paul Church [*Snell Street, corner Dover Street, Fall River*]. But, I took [*First Holy*]

Communion in Santo Cristo Church, [*the sacrament of*] confirmation, [*and*] I got married in Santo Cristo Church.

JR: I think it's the oldest Portuguese church [*in Fall River.*]

DA: Yes, it is, I think so … they are all gone now, most of them. [*The parish history can be traced back to the founding of the first mission in Fall River established to serve the Portuguese community in 1876.*]

JR: Okay, I am going to ask you a little bit more about the community of, well, actually, Swansea, [M*assachusetts,*] and Tiverton, [*Rhode Island,*] and Fall River. Tell me about the community that you grew up in. What was that like? Your neighbors?

DA: Neighbors were very – well, in Tiverton and Swansea neighbors were far apart. I don't know too much about Swansea, like I said, when I was born, we were living there, but I remember mostly Tiverton, and Fall River – where we lived, you know, everybody was very, uh, looking after one another. They would not – if you were sick, and [*they*] knew you were sick, they'd make you some chicken soup, and take it over to the neighbor because that neighbor was sick, and sit with that neighbor for a little while to see how they, you know, if they needed any help, they would help them. There were more, it was more get-togethers with neighbors. Not all the time, but most of the time.

JR: What neighborhood was that in Fall River? Where was that?

DA: That was around, uh, Hunter Street and Columbia [*Street*]. Hunter, Hope [*Street*], that was where we lived ….

JR: So, you must have seen a lot of the Portuguese [*religious*] feasts and processions.

DA: Oh, yes, we went to those processions. I remember taking some sweetbread [*massa sovada*] when they have the Holy Ghost Feast [*Festas do Espirito Santo*] at Santo Cristo Church, and my grandmother [*Mrs. Louiz 'Luis' Rapoza Salgado, née Margarida 'Margaret' Soares*] would make the home-made sweetbread, and wrap it up … and tie it with red ribbon, the red ribbon, so I could take it to the church, and I would take it, my sister and I would take it. [*The Festas do Espírito Santo, or Holy Ghost Festival, plays an integral role in the lives of devout Azoreans, and Azorean-Americans, and usually begins on Pentecost Sunday, running through the spring. The festival was founded by the 13th century Queen Saint Elizabeth (Isabel), formerly a princess of Aragon, who was Queen Regent of Portugal, the consort of King Denis; a devout model of Christian charity, she was noted for her religious piety, charity, and devotion to her work for the poor.*]

JR: Did you march in the processions?

DA: Yes, yes, and also I handed that down to my daughter, too; she went in the processions a lot.

JR: I am going to jump ahead a little bit and you mentioned World War II, and you said you had two older brothers. Were they drafted?

DA: My oldest brother [*Alphonse 'Al' Peter Silvia*], he volunteered because they were going to be drafted, but he volunteered to go into the service [*United States Army, enlisted January 5, 1944*].

JR: Did [*he*] come home?

DA: [*He*] came home.

JR: That's wonderful. Your mother must have been very worried.

DA: Oh, yeah, she was worried. We wouldn't have Christmas. My mother would say, 'No Christmas, your brother is in a war. We're not having a Christmas. We will have a Christmas when he comes home.' And we waited and waited, and I remember they would have the lights go off, the, oh, what was that? You know, like, air raids. I remember the air raids we had, and have to shut your curtains, and the shades – back then were [*black out*] shades – and no lights on because you'd have the police [*Air Raid Wardens*] knocking at your door; they patrolled to see who had lights on. For [*when*] the air raid came you had to have everything in darkness, 'til they put out another ... a different kind of a sound that it was over, and then you can put the lights on again. It was always at night that would happen; I remember that.

JR: Do you remember where your brother served in the war?

DA: My brother was [*a Private First Class*] in the infantry.

JR: Was he overseas ... ?

DA: Yes, he was over there, and it was a very nice – a very happy day when [*he*] came home.

JR: That's wonderful; many families lost brothers.

DA: I know. I had a friend of mine [*Teresa L. Pacheco*], she lost her brother [*Fernando Pacheco*], missing in action, and her mother [*Mrs. João "John" Pacheco née Hortencia Domingos*], from that day on, her mother never walked, never talked, stayed bedridden until she died. Yeah, a lot of things back then. [*Fernando Pacheco, United States Army, Private First Class, was killed in action on September 17, 1944; he had enlisted on March 11, 1943. His remains were interred in Notre Dame Cemetery, Fall River, on August 20, 1948.*]

JR: Let's go back to the Wixon School. After you graduated and you said you went to work, how did that transition take place?

DA: I went to work, we used to walk to work.

JR: Where did you work?

DA: I worked, I started working at the Pleasant Curtain [*Company, 237 Pleasant Street, Fall River*] first. Folding curtains, upstairs from, uh, it used to be Rogers Restaurant [*Rogers Cafeteria, 261 Pleasant Street, Fall River*], you know, [*Francis*] Rogers [*and his wife Theresa C. Rogers*] from Somerset, [*Massachusetts*]? They used to have a little restaurant.

JR: I know where that is, and over that restaurant was Pleasant Curtain?

DA: Pleasant Curtain, and I worked there for a long time. Then I went …

JR: What did you do there?

DA: I folded curtains.

JR: Folded?

DA: I folded curtains.

JR: After they've already been sewn?

DA: After they were sewed, and they would go through a press, where the man – the fellow – would feed it through this machine, and we would be on the other end, and it will come out all pressed, and you fold it in half, and then put it on a box. Then we go to the table and fold it, and then put it in packages for the different sizes.

JR: Was that piecework?

DA: No, it wasn't piecework. We had to put out a certain amount – a quota – we had a quota to put out, but it was not piecework.

JR: But they, probably – the sewers?

DA: The sewing machines, the sewers were all on piecework. The rod and hemmers, and the people who did the drapes – because they also did drapes – and they were all on piecework, but we weren't, we were on time work.

JR: How did you get that job?

DA: A friend of mine [*Teresa Sousa, the wife of the interviewee's cousin, David Sousa*] knew my mother, and … 'My daughter is looking for a job, she needs to get a job,' so she spoke to me and I got the job. Making seventy-five-cents an hour back then [*and*] that was working forty hours a week. Coming home, don't touch your pay, they put it in the envelope, they staple it, and I give it to my mother.

JR: They gave you cash?

DA: It was cash, back then they gave you cash; no checks, it was all cash.

JR: Then, you brought that home.

DA: Brought it home to my mother the way they gave it to us, then my mother would give me two dollars a week.

JR: I saw my family do something with the – the cash – that was brought home; they used to call it in Portuguese, 'countar' [*pronounced coon.tar*].

DA: 'Countar,' yeah. Well, that means they would figure out the money, count the money. They make the countar about this for rent, this for food, this for this, this for that. Pay this bill, got your furniture bill, or a store. Back then a lot of people would buy groceries and pay it at the end of the week. Some grocery store who knew you, the grocery man, yeah.

JR: And then you put some money into the envelope for insurance.

DA: Insurance, yes, like $2 a week, $2.50 in for the insurance man; by the time he came, we had our money. And money for church, we had to put money for church – you'd better put seventy-five cents – we put it in the envelope for church, and we'd have to go to church every Sunday. You don't go to church, you don't go out; we couldn't go to a movie because you didn't go to church. And when you get home, the clothes you used for church, we take them, put them away, and use other clothes. That Sunday clothes, they were special.

JR: Just for Sunday.

DA: Just for Sunday. Shoes, dress, no matter what it was, it was just for Sundays.

JR: I think on Sunday, too, you had a family dinner.

DA: We had the family dinner and then we would sit around and talk. Yup, very nice.

JR: Now, your brothers, I guess …

DA: They're both passed. [*Alphonse "Al" Peter Silvia, died in 1983, and Lawrence "Sonny" Peter Silvia, who chose to cease contact with his family for decades, may have died in 1997.*]

JR: They contributed to the house, too, and your sister?

DA: Yes, they did. My sister [*Margaret Silvia, later Mrs. Frank Owsney*] did, but already the times were different, because I was two years older than her … things were different. My brothers and all, they come in, they give the money to my mother.

JR: Did she work after school? Did she go right to work right after school or did your sister go on to high school?

DA: No, my sister didn't go to high school, she went to work.

JR: How about your brothers, did they go to high school?

DA: No, they didn't. They all went to work. Back then you had to go to work because you had to help contribute money to the house because, when my father worked on the farm, they were only getting $35 a week, and was working from sun up to sun down. But we didn't have to pay rent, we only had to buy food, and pay no electric because everything came together.

JR: But that was a total of six people to support, and that is quite a responsibility.

DA: But we managed. A lot of soup and different things, you know?

JR: How could you save any money on your allowance?

DA: Well, I tried putting it away. We would save a little bit just at Christmas so we could buy something for one another, for our parents and our brothers. A little bit of something, like an ashtray or something – just a little memento, that we would do, so.

JR: What did you do for, I should say, recreation? Movies? Or going out?

DA: I remember going to the Plaza [*Theatre, 381 South Main Street, Fall River*] for fifteen cents.

JR: Oh, my.

DA: And we would get a chapter, we'd get the world news [*newsreels*], we'd get two movies [*double-feature*]; I could spend a whole day in the show, in the movies at the Plaza Theatre. Fifteen cents we paid, and then the other movies were like fifty-five cents, and then they went up to seventy-five cents. We'd get two movies, two coming attractions – and two movies, at other theatres.

JR: This would be when you were a teenager?

DA: When I was working. When I was a teenager I couldn't go to the movies, my mother wouldn't allow us to go to the movies. But when we worked, you know, it was different, they let us go. But we had to be home by a certain time. 'Movies should be done by four o'clock; you should be in this house by five o'clock,' and we would have to be.

JR: How did you get home? Were you walking?

DA: We walked. We walked home. We were in walking distance, so we'd walk home. [*The Silvia family residence at 616 Third Street, Fall River, was approximately three city blocks from the Plaza Theatre.*]

JR: Very good. Now how did, you started with Pleasant Curtain and what was the next job?

DA: The next job – I worked there a long time – then after I went and worked at the Atlas Curtain [*Atlas Manufacturing Company 288 Plymouth Avenue, Fall River*] ... I worked there. I worked until I got married [*in 1956*], and I worked there a good five, six years.

JR: And when did you get married?

DA: Then when I got married? I got married [*on May 30,*] 1956, and I had my oldest boy [*Louis William Almeida*] in '58.

JR: How did you meet your husband?

DA: He [*James Francis Almeida, Jr.*] was the boy across the street. He lived across the street from me [*at 621 Third Street, Fall River*]. Yeah, so we got to talking, him on the outside of the fence, me on the inside of the fence; we weren't allowed to go out with any boys.

JR: And how many in his family?

DA: My husband had two sisters [*Patricia Ann Almeida, later Mrs. Joseph George Andre Cormier, and Natalie Almeida*]; that was it.

JR: This was on Hope Street?

DA: No, no, this was on, by then we were living [*at 616*] Third Street [*in Fall River*]. We, my mother had moved. My father was then working at the Truesdale Hospital [*Inc., as a 'kitchen helper'*] and ... my aunt [*Mrs. Manuel Rapoza Salgado née Catherine R. Medeiros*] bought a house on Third Street, and that's where we lived – and my husband lived across the street from me.

JR: How did you get to know your husband? I mean, he lived across the street but did you go out on dates?

DA: No dates. Not until I was about a good seventeen years old, almost eighteen. No, we didn't date too much back then. It was at the fence, our dating was at the fence. I said to my mother, 'He wants to go get a chow mein sandwich.' 'You better take your sister with you' – we always had to have a sister with us, couldn't go alone.

JR: Always had a chaperone.

DA: All the time.

JR: So, someone would squeal on you if something went wrong.

DA: Yeah.

JR: How long did you court? I have to use the word courting.

DA: Two years, two years; then we got married.

JR: At the Santo Cristo Church.

DA: At the Santo Cristo Church, yes.

JR: Tell me about your children.

DA: My children, I had three. My oldest one's [*Louis William Almeida*] passed already [*in 1993*]. Now I have my daughter [*Mrs. Antonio Pereira, née Lori Ann Almeida*], and my son [*Kevin James Almeida*] who come to visit me almost every day.

JR: And how were they brought up? I know it was …

DA: They were brought up the same way I was brought up.

JR: Is that right?

DA: Yes, I did. Although, when my daughter was going with her husband I was a little more lenient, I let her go. But I would tell them, 'You better not do anything, nothing better happen, or else.' I'd say that, and honest to God, I said that for two years. He [*the interviewee's son-in-law, Antonio Pereira*] says to me, 'I am sick of hearing it.' 'You are going to hear it until you walk her down the aisle.' I did.

JR: What were your activities together as a family, with your children?

DA: We would go on, like, every year we would go on vacation. No more than maybe three [*days*]; that was enough for me, living out of a suitcase. Yes, we go to New Hampshire – they loved to go to New Hampshire – we would go up towards the White Mountains.

JR: Very nice.

DA: Then, we go out together, go for rides together, and you know, we'd do a lot of things.

JR: Different, you do different things.

DA: We did it, yes.

JR: You had those vacations. But your husband ...

DA: My husband worked, I worked, and...

JR: What kind of work did your husband do?

DA: My husband worked at [*Esterline]* Haskon [*Aerospace*] in, uh, Taunton, [*Massachusetts*].

JR: Haskon, I don't know that place.

DA: They made a little thing, little parts of airplanes, and then when they come in to do going up, with space, about space, he also did some things for the space thing. Whatever. I don't know if they are still there, but that is where he worked for twenty-three-and-a-half years.

JR: Well, I ask those questions because so many of the companies have gone out of business.

DA: I'm sure they've gone. They've gone. [*Esterline Haskon Aerospace, closed its Taunton, Massachusetts facility in 2010*].

JR: For example, curtain manufacturing. There are so many, so many factories in Fall River that were curtain factories. I know I had a cousin that was, uh, I can't think of the name of the shop now, it's on Pleasant Street, further up.

DA: Louis Hand [*Inc., Division of Aberdeen Manufacturing Corporation, 847 Pleasant Street, Fall River*].

JR: Louis Hand – that was one. That is out of business.

DA: Louis hand – that was a big one.

JR: That was very big.

DA: That was big, there was another one down north [*Paroma Draperies, Inc., 2 Weaver Street, Fall River*], and that's all gone. They are all gone. All shops are gone.

JR: I think a lot of it was competition from overseas.

DA: It was competition; the union, they didn't care that the boss didn't want to go with them, do what they wanted to do. That's what happened when I worked. I also went back to work after my daughter was born [*in 1963*], a year-and-a-half later, and I worked at the K & G dress shop [*K. & G. Manufacturing Company, Inc., dress manufacturers, 187 Pleasant Street, Fall River*] and, uh, the union shut him down. He was a wonderful person to work for.

JR: How did that happen? Why would they shut that place down?

DA: Because they wanted him to do – to join in on the union with certain things, and he didn't want to. So, the union just come in and they shut him down. You know, they would pay people to come during the night and destroy the material, and he couldn't work the next day.

JR: Who owned that shop?

DA: Al [*Abraham Albert*] Leshinsky.

JR: Okay.

DA: That was at the [*former*] Union Mills [*Union Cotton Manufacturing Company, Pleasant Street, Fall River*].

JR: Yeah, I know where that is. Now, when did you join the union? Were you a union member early on, maybe back at Pleasant Curtain?

DA: Yes, we were in the union. Then, that was Amalgamated Union [*Amalgamated Clothing Workers of America, Locals Nos. 177 and 376, 142 Second Street, Fall River*]. The dress shops was the ILG [*ILGWU, International Ladies Garments Workers Union, Local No 178, Garment Workers Square, 38 Third Street, Fall River*].

JR: So, how did that work out for you, I mean, in terms of getting a pension?

DA: Well, I didn't …

JR: Two different unions.

DA: Yes, but no, I didn't, we didn't bother to claim that other one at the Amalgamated [*Clothing Workers of America*]; it wasn't worth it. And then when it came to work to get the money from, when I retired, from Ladies International [*ILGWU, International Ladies Garments Workers Union*], my husband said, 'It's not worth it.' I had, like twelve years in that union, so my husband said it wasn't worth it, he said, 'Let it go, what are you going to get for twelve years?' So, I just let it go.

JR: So you never got a union pension?

DA: No, I lived on my husband's pension, my husband's pension.

JR: That's disappointing, to put in all those years and not get a union pension.

DA: I know, I know, but – we wouldn't make much, we didn't pay that much into the union, so you wouldn't get much, unless I had my thirty – even having, uh, what, thirty years in the union, it was no more than one hundred something dollars.

JR: And that was in ILG[*WU*]?

DA: Yes, they didn't pay much.

JR: I am going to go back a little bit and just ask you things like when you got your first telephone.

DA: Oh, we were living on Nanaquaket Road [*in Tiverton, Rhode Island,*] when we got our first telephone. I was single. And it was – you hold up with one hand and you put the other piece in your ear. 'Hello?' Four party line and then they'd take too long. They'd say, 'Get off the phone! We need to use the phone!'

JR: But that was pretty exciting.

DA: It was exciting back then, yes. Oh, we had our telephone, yes.

JR: Who could you call? You had to have family [*members*] that had a phone.

DA: I called my brother [*Alphonse 'Al' Peter Silvia*] in Fall River, we would call my brothers. I don't remember [*about*] my aunt – my aunt had a phone, but I don't know when she got her phone. But we would, you know, call people.

JR: Did you always have electric light or gas light?

DA: I remember, we always had electric. When I was growing up it was electric. The electric had come in to…

JR: Now, how about a car? How about a first time your family had a car?

DA: My father bought a car. He had bought a Hudson [*Hudson Motor Car Company, Detroit, Michigan*] and we'd go out on the Sunday for a drive. During the week, that was for him to go to work.

JR: Any other thoughts about your family and the changes that you went through from the '30s to the present?

DA: No, it was okay, we had a good, you know, we had a good relationship all the way through. We were always a very close family all the, all the way – we were always very close.

JR: What do you think of some of the events today? Like the women's movement in the 1960s and '70s and the way, um, we are interacting today. It's very different from when you were growing up.

DA: Oh yes. But still – I'm so old-fashioned. To me, a woman's job is a woman's job, and a man's job is a man's job. I can't see, I don't like, or don't care to see, I wouldn't care to have anyone in my family doing a man's job. But, if that was what they wanted, you know? It's different today, but I'm still from the old school. A man's job is a man's job, a woman's job is a woman's job.

JR: And what do you think of computers and the way with that?

DA: That to me, a computer is the worst thing they come out with – computers. There is Facebook, and everything – the whole world knows your business. I don't like it. I never did, I never did like computers.

JR: Good point.

DA: The way of the world; it's become a lazy world.

JR: That was what I was going to ask you. How do you see the world changing since when you were young?

DA: Yeah, it's, it's terrible what the way it goes, you know, everything [*is*] going, so, people killing people. We wouldn't hear that – never around here, never. But, it's horrible today. No one can talk to one without using something that they shouldn't be using.

JR: The world has changed …

DA: Very much so, yes, it has. It's sad because you are not safe nowhere; today, no one is safe anymore.

JR: So, when you retired, what was some of the interests that you had after retirement. Your grandchildren?

DA: After retirement, I put myself taking care of my grandchildren.

JR: Well, I think … if you want to conclude it at that point. [*But*] I can ask you a few more things. I asked you about women's liberation, civil rights, 'ya know, you've seen all of that change.

DA: Yes.

JR: You've seen all of that change.

DA: It's too bad that – it's good that people can get out there and vote, but, the way it is today I don't know – it's the world is upside-down, the world is upside-down today. It's not a world like when I was being brought up. Yes, I just, I get that I had a wonderful life, and now I am here [*Somerset Ridge Center, 455 Brayton Avenue, Somerset, Massachusetts*]. I have another life here, and I am happy here.

JR: And I heard that you're, um …

DA: I am President of the Residents' Council.

JR: So, you're a leader. What is that all about?

DA: Well, it's those who cannot speak for themselves now. When I say, 'Those who cannot say, those who cannot speak for themselves,' are the people with Alzheimer's; they can't speak for themselves, so I'm here to speak for them. I feel like if I had a parent who had a sickness like that, I would want someone to speak up for them if something wasn't going right.

JR: So, you kind of check on them and make sure things are going right?

DA: Well, we talk together and I'm friendly with everyone and I keep my eyes open, and we see everything, and it's a wonderful place. I fell into a beautiful place here.

JR: Excellent. Very good. So, you are involved in the leadership here.

DA: I never thought in my life I would ever become President of [*a*] Resident's Council, but here I am.

JR: Okay, well I am going to stop at this point.... I really enjoyed talking with you.

DA: I enjoyed talking with you.

JR: Thank you.

DA: No ... thank *you*.

PHOTO GALLERY

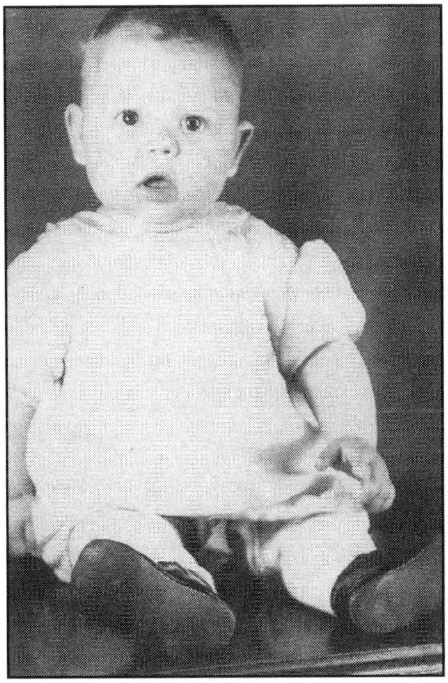

3.1 Delores Silvia, 1938. *"I was born in Fall River."*

3.2 *Above:* Delores' mother, Mrs. Seraphine Peter Silvia, née Virginia Rapoza Salgado, with her youngest child, Margaret Silvia, circa 1941. *"I shared a bed with my sister."*

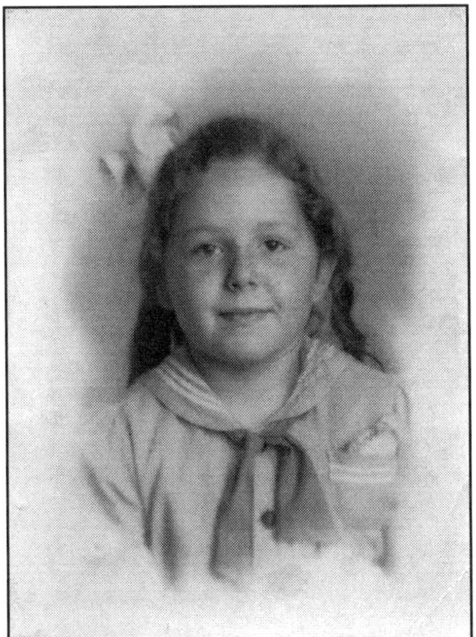

3.3 *Left:* Delores Silvia, circa 1945; her mother made her banana curls using rags. *"I was brought up old-fashioned, you know."*

3.4 Delores' father, Seraphine Peter Silvia, at work on the farm owned by George Sousa Magan, 405 Nanaquaket Road, Tiverton, Rhode Island, early 1940s; the Silvia family resided on the property. *"My father worked on the farm. He did farm work – milking cows, cultivating the land, and all of that ... the milk came with the job."*

3.5 Delores' parents and two of her siblings in a snapshot taken on the farm owned by George Sousa Magan, 405 Nanaquaket Road, Tiverton, Rhode Island, early 1940s; the Silvia family resided on the property. Standing, left to right: Delores' father, Seraphine Peter Silvia; her eldest brother, Alphonse "Al" Peter Silvia; her mother, née Virginia Rapoza Salgado. Front row, left to right: her sister, Margaret Silvia; Delores. *"Back then, when we got a job, the house came with the job. You didn't pay any rent because that came with the job."*

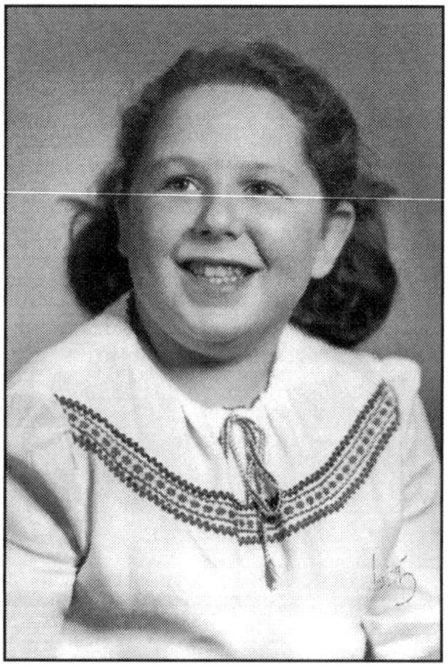

3.6 Delores Silvia, circa 1947.

3.7 *Above:* Santo Christo Church, 240 Columbia Street, Fall River, Massachusetts, 1930s; the oldest church in the city established to serve the Portuguese community, its origins can be traced to 1876. *"I went to Santo Christo Church. I took* [First Holy] *Communion in Santo Christo Church,* [the sacrament of] *confirmation,* [and] *I got married in Santo Christo Church."*

3.8 *Above:* The Susan H. Wixon Elementary School, 263 Hamlet Street, Fall River, Massachusetts. *"And then I went to the … Wixon … School."*

3.9 Delores' family residence, 616 Third Street, Fall River, Massachusetts, as it appeared in 1980; the building was constructed with four tenements for housing mill workers, circa 1868. The Silvias moved to an apartment on the second floor in 1950. *"My aunt* [Mrs. Manuel Rapozo Salgado, née Catherine R. Medeiros] *bought a house on Third Street, and that's where we lived."*

3.10 Delores' posing with her parents on the day of her graduation from the Susan B. Wixon Grammar School, Fall River, Massachusetts, 1953. Left to right: Her father, Seraphine Peter Silvia; Delores; and her mother, née Virginia Rapoza Salgado. *"I graduated from there in* [1953] *... I went to work."*

3.11 *Right:* The former Union Mill, Pleasant Street, Fall River, Massachusetts, as it appeared in 1934. Delores was first employed in 1953 at Pleasant Curtain Company, 237 Pleasant Street, on the second floor of the building depicted in the far right of the photograph. Several years later she worked at K & G Manufacturing Company, Inc., dress manufacturers, 273 Pleasant Street, which was located in the approximate center of the photograph. *"I worked, I started working at the Pleasant Curtain first ... and I worked there a long time."*

3.12 Delores casually posing on a Packard automobile, early 1950s.

3.13 A Holy Ghost Procession, Fall River, Massachusetts, 1950s; the Festas do Espirito Santo plays an important role in the lives of devout Azoreans and Azorean-Americans. *"Oh, yes, we went to those processions. I remember … my grandmother would make the home-made sweet bread, and wrap it up … and tie it with red ribbon … so I could take it to church."*

3.14 Delores' mother and maternal grandmother. Left to right: Mrs. Louiz "Luis" Rapoza Salgado née Margarida "Margaret" Soares; her daughter, Mrs. Seraphine Peter Silvia; née Virginia Rapoza Salgado. *"My grandmother was a stay-at-home wife, she stood home taking care of us."*

3.15 621 Third Street, Fall River, Massachusetts, where Delores' future husband, James "Jimmy" Francis Almeida, Jr. resided with his parents and two sisters; the mansard roof structure was constructed in 1889 with accommodations for five families. The Almeida family occupied an apartment on the first floor. *"My husband lived across the street from me."*

3.16 Delores and Jimmy in a snapshot taken on Third Street, Fall River, Massachusetts, 1950s. *"No, we didn't date too much back then. It was at the fence, our dating was at the fence."*

3.17 Delores and Jimmy dancing at the Ponta Delgada Club, 31 Shove Street, Tiverton, Rhode Island, 1950s. *"I said to my mother, 'He wants to get a chow mein sandwich.' 'You'd better take your sister with you' – we always had to have a sister with us, couldn't go alone."*

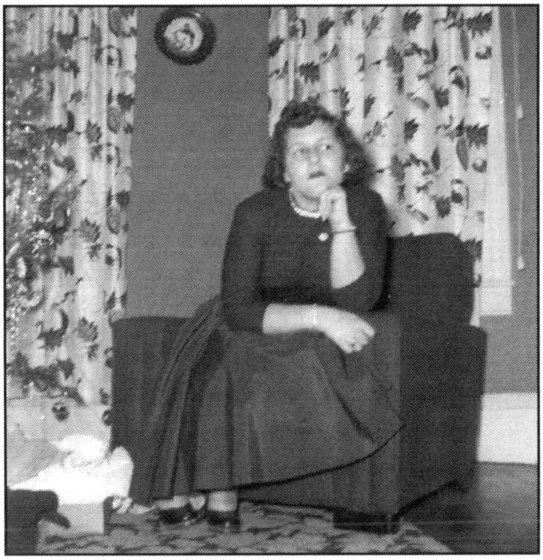

3.18 Delores in a 1950s Christmas snapshot, decades later, she still remembered her outfit: *"Navy dress with a taffeta skirt, rhinestone necklace."*

3.19 Mr. & Mrs. James Francis Almeida, Jr. on their wedding day, May 30, 1956. Standing left to right: the groom's brother-in-law, Joseph George Andre Cormier; the groom's sister, Mrs. Joseph George Andre Cormier, née Patricia Ann Almeida; the groom; the groom's sister, Natalie Almeida. Seated, left to right: the groom's father, James Francis Almeida, aka "Jimmy the Barber"; Delores; the groom's mother, née Harriet Pacheco. *"We* [courted] *two years, two years; then we got married."*

3.20 The former Richard Borden Manufacturing Company, Fall River, Massachusetts, as it appeared in the 1970s; Atlas Manufacturing Company, curtain manufacturers, 288 Plymouth Avenue, was located in the building in the upper left corner of the complex. *"I went and worked at the Atlas Curtain."*

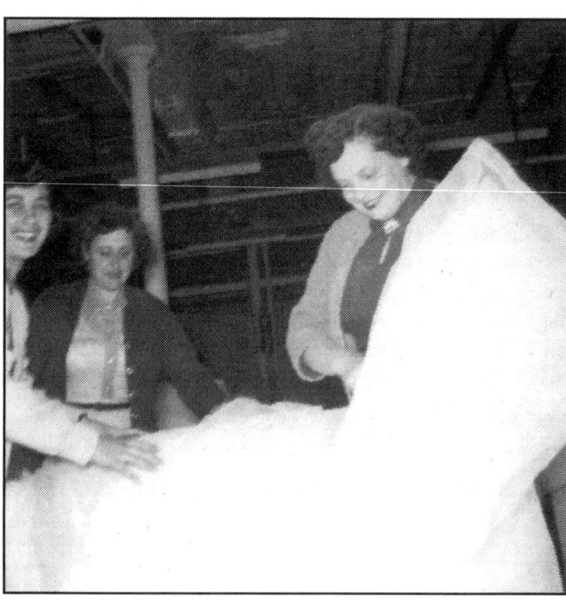

3.21 Delores, at far right, folding curtains with two unidentified co-workers at Atlas Manufacturing Company, 288 Plymouth Avenue, Fall River, Massachusetts, late 1950s. *"I folded curtains ... we go to the table and fold it, and then put it in packages for the different sizes."*

3.22 Sts. Peter and Paul Church, Snell Street, corned Dover Street, Fall River, Massachusetts. *"When I got married, I also went to Sts. Peter and Paul."*

3.23 Delores as Santa Claus, hamming it up at a Christmas party at Novelty Boys Wash Suit Company, 164 Pleasant Street, Fall River, Massachusetts, circa 1960. Delores' friend and co-worker, Teresa Sousa, who was the wife of her cousin, David Sousa, is standing, second from the right. *"A friend of mine* [Teresa Sousa] *... spoke ... and I got the job."*

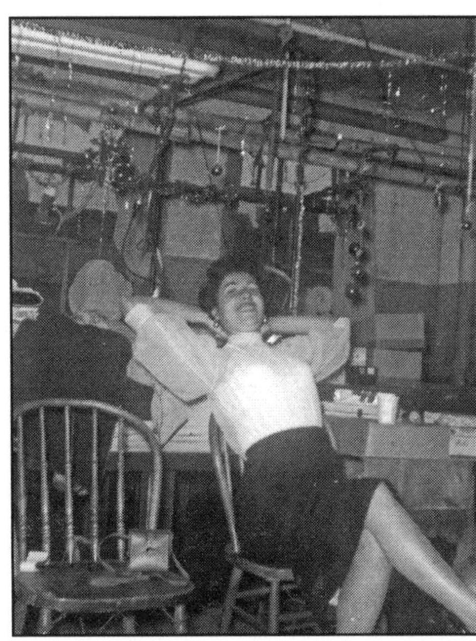

3.24 Delores' friend and co-worker, Teresa Sousa, who was the wife of her cousin, David Sousa, at a Christmas party at Novelty Boys Wash Suit Company, 164 Pleasant Street, Fall River, Massachusetts, circa 1960. *"Yes, we were in the union."*

FOUR:

HORTENCIA PACHECO AMARAL, NÉE RIBEIRO

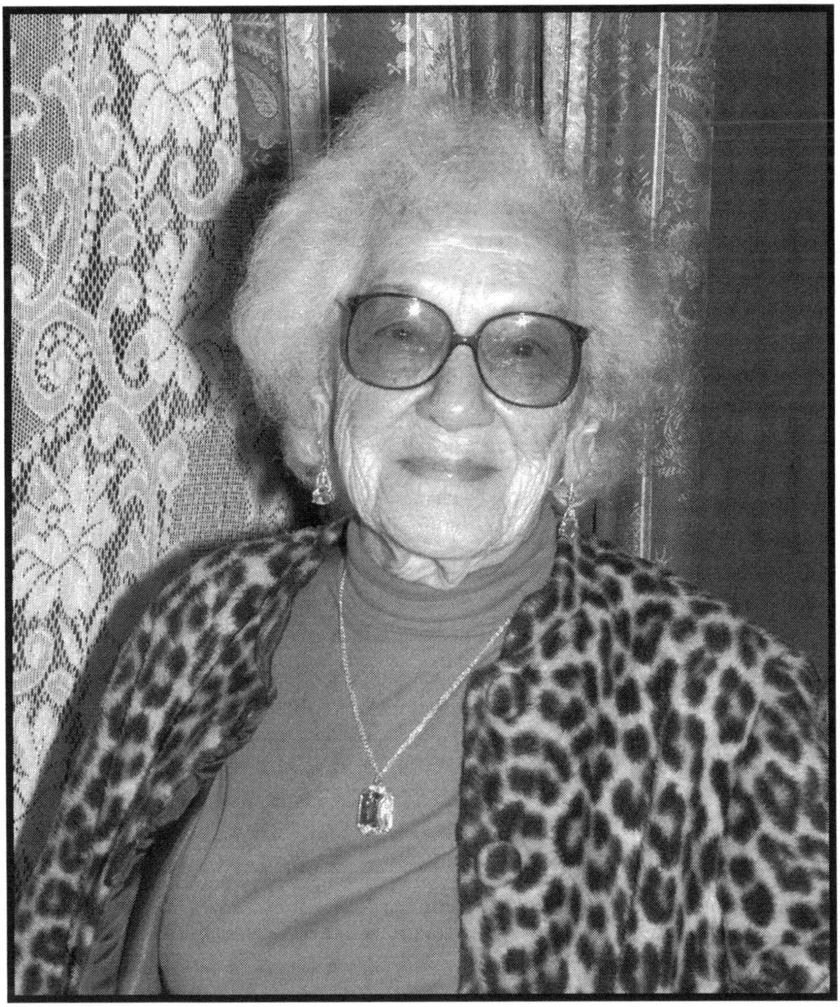

Personal Statistics

Name: Hortencia "Ester" Pacheco Ribeiro
(Mrs. Manuel Amaral)

Date of Birth: September 25, 1916

Place of Birth: Fall River, Massachusetts

Father: José Pacheco Ribeiro (1886-1976)

Mother: Maria Amelia de Paiva Mello (1891-1962)

Siblings: John Pacheco Ribeiro (1909-1979)
Mary Pacheco Ribeiro (1910-1962)
---(Mrs. Manuel Alves Faria)
Joseph Pacheco Ribeiro, Jr. (1918-1999)
Antone Pacheco Ribeiro (1920-2001)

Spouse: Manuel Amaral (1917-1998)

Date of Marriage: March 7, 1942

Children: Paul Joseph Amaral

Employment history:

Bourne Mills, Fall River
United Rayon Mills, Fall River
Massasoit Manufacturing Company, Fall River
Maplewood Products Company, Fall River
Lyn Sportswear Company, Inc., Fall River
Firestone Rubber & Latex Products Company, Fall River
Gamma Leather, Inc., Fall River
Frito-Lay, Inc., Fall River
Raytheon Company, North Dighton, Massachusetts
Center Garment Company, Inc., Fall River

EDITED TRANSCRIPT

Interview with Mrs. Manuel Amaral, née Hortencia "Ester" Pacheco Ribeiro

Interviewer: (JR) Joyce B. Rodrigues, Fall River Historical Society

Interviewee: (HA) Hortencia "Ester" Pacheco Ribeiro Amaral

Additional Commentary: (PA) Paul J. Amaral, Hortencia's son

Date of Interview: November 12, 2014

Location: Fall River Historical Society

Summary by Joyce B. Rodrigues:

Hortencia "Ester" (Ribeiro) Amaral was born in Fall River on September 21, 1916.

Her parents immigrated to the United States from the island of St. Michael in the Azores. They met in Fall River and were married at the Santo Christo Church, Columbia Street, in 1907.

There were five children in the family. Hortensia had an older brother and sister and two younger brothers. The family lived in the south end of the city, close to the Tiverton, Rhode Island, line in mill housing: the Bourne Mills Block, owned by the Bourne Mills.

The Ribeiro family – grandfather, father, mother, brothers and sisters – all worked in the Bourne Mills. Hortencia started working at the Bourne in 1931 at the age of fifteen. She left in 1932 to seek other employment after a strike that lasted nine months.

Hortencia married in 1942 and had one son. Her brothers and husband all served in World War II. She was also the family caregiver to her parents and a bachelor brother.

Her career took her to factories in Fall River: Bourne Mills, United Rayon Mills, Massasoit Manufacturing Company, Maplewood Products Company, Lyn Sportswear, Firestone Rubber & Latex Products Company, Raytheon Company (Dighton, Massachusetts), Gamma Leather, Inc., and Center Garment Company, Inc.

Hortencia retired in 1978 at the age of sixty-two after forty-seven years of employment. At the time of this interview, she was active in senior centers.

Hortencia's century-long work and family life parallels Fall River's economic history from the decline of the textile industry through the transition to the garment and wartime industries, and finally postwar manufacturing.

Note: This interview has been slightly edited for continuity and readability; in order to preserve the integrity of the conversation, the phraseology remains that of the interviewer and interviewee. Italicized information in square brackets has been added for the purposes of clarification and context.

JR: When were you born?

HA: I was born September [*25*], 1916.

JR: And where were you born?

HA: The Bourne Mills Block, the lower block that belonged to the Bourne Mills. They owned them blocks. [*Bourne Mills Block was located north of State Avenue in Fall River; the Ribeiro family resided in a building at 45 Clement Street from circa 1908 to 1924.*]

JR: So you were born in the United States.

HA: Yes, Fall River.

JR: How about your parents?

HA: My mother [*née Maria Amelia de Paiva Mello*] was born in Portugal and my father [*José Pacheco Ribeiro*] was born in Portugal.

JR: And do you know where they were born, in what village or town?

HA: My mother was born in the city, somewhere in [*Ponta Delgada, São Miguel, Azores*].... My father was [*born in*] Lagoa, [*São Miguel, Azores*].

JR: And why do you think they immigrated? Did they ever tell you why they immigrated?

HA: All I know is they got married [*in Fall River on September 28, 1907*] ... my father was twenty-one when he came here. My mother was already here with my grandfather [*João de Paiva Mello*].

JR: Do you remember your grandfather?

HA: Oh yeah, he lived with us.

JR: And your grandmother?

HA: No, I never knew my grandmother [*née Francisca Augusta Cunha*]. She, uh, they separated. That was strange for them days, you know?

JR: Now, were there other children in your family?

HA: Yeah, five, three brothers and my sister and I. I was the middle one ... my brother [*John*], my sister [*Mary*], were born first, then it was me, then my two brothers [*Joseph, Jr. and Antone*].

JR: Now, did your parents work in the mills?

HA: Yes, my father worked in the [*Bourne*] Mills. My mother worked in [*the*] small Shove mill. Not sure if you ever heard of that. A mill right before you get to the Bourne Mills, right there on Shove Street. Until she got her children. And then she never worked again. Then my father worked in the Bourne Mills. As a weaver.

JR: What about your mother, what kind of work did she do?

HA: She worked in the spinning room [*as a spinner*].

JR: And your grandparents?

HA: My grandfather used to work upstairs, used to put some kind of a cotton in round cans, tall cans. [*He was possibly a rover in the carding department of the mill.*] I don't know what kind it was.

JR: In the Bourne Mills?

HA: Yeah, he worked upstairs.

JR: And then you also worked in the Bourne Mills?

HA: We all did. My [*older*] brother was a weaver. My sister and I and my two brothers were fillin' carriers. [*A filling carrier kept the filling boxes at the looms supplied with full bobbins of filling.*] They used to put the bobbins in the can where we used to put it.... I worked there until I was about fifteen. And then they went on strike [*circa 1931*]. The union was always butting in, you know? So we went on strike.... We were on strike for nine months. Nothing coming in. Nothing. We had nothing for nine months. So, finally, I decided to go and look for a job. And I went and worked in United Rayon [*Mills at 460*] Globe Street. I worked there for $6 a week. I used to run forty-eight machines.

JR: Forty-eight machines? What kind of work was it?

HA: Cotton, cotton. Rayon. United Rayon [*Mills*]. I worked there for quite a while.

JR: So what kind of work was that on these machines?

HA: It was like spinning.

JR: And you had to run forty-eight machines?

HA: Yeah, I used to run them. I was a son-of-a-gun for working. That's why. All my bosses admired me for my job. They used to hate to lay me off … even today I am still at it. I still like to, but I can't like I used to, you know?

JR: You like to keep busy.

HA: Yeah, when I see someone doing something it bothers me because I can't go over and do [*it*] with them…. I worked hard all my life.

JR: So you decided to go to work to help your family?

HA: Yeah, because there was nothing coming in, no one was thinking of going to look for a job. Everyone was sitting around. So I said I am going to go, I was a go-getter. So I went and … [*Manuel Alves Faria, who later married her sister, Mary*] was the boss … in the United Rayon [*Mills*], so through him I got the job. I was lucky, for $6 something. And then, when I was working for $6 a week, when [*President Franklin Delano*] Roosevelt came in [*in 1933*]. Anyway, when he came in, the pay went all the way up to $12 and something. I felt like a rich woman. I ran the first time I got my pay, I ran all the way home. I couldn't afford to take the bus. I had no money. So I ran from Globe Street all the way to [*our home on the state line near*] Tiverton [*Rhode Island*]. Run to show my mother all that money I was making.

JR: So … that would have been around the 1930s.

HA: In the Depression. So, but Roosevelt came as a boost. What a difference from $6. And I used to work forty hours a week. You know? [*Pay increases were due to the National Industrial Recovery Act instituted in 1933.*]

JR: Do you remember what Fall River was like in those days?

HA: Oh, yeah.

JR: What was it like?

HA: I don't know, it was just you used to go down to the city with all the beautiful stores: [*R.A.*] McWhirr's [*Company, department store, 165-193 South Main Street*], Cherry & Webb [*Company, ladies' and misses' fashions, 139-149 South Main Street*], Newbury's [*J.J. Newberry Company, five-and-ten-cent store, 107 South Main Street*], and then the market in the corner [*Arruda's Market, 2629 South Main Street, corner*

Last Street]. That is where all the poor people used to go and buy all their food. Hardly anything. The men used to buy a dozen eggs for twenty-five cents them days. You bought a pound of steak for twenty-five cents. And my mother couldn't afford to buy all that because we weren't working. But it just happened that the man who had the grocery store [*Antonio Medeiros Arruda, Jr.*], he used to say 'Mary, you buy it for the children ... and you pay a little bit by the week.' So every week my mother would give them whatever she had to give him. We went without. And we ate more, a lot, because my father used to go down to the water and get clams, quahogs, that's why I love seafood. My father used to bring home lobsters and walk up the hill at Hooper Street [*in Tiverton, Rhode Island*]. The steep hill with two buckets of clams and what not. That was how we ate because we had no money. We had nothing. I never had anything for Christmas. I never owned a doll because we never had nothing. When we put our stockings up for Santa Claus, we used to, all we got was walnuts and Christmas candy. That was good, that was wonderful. But no gifts. That's it.

JR: Well, I am going to ask you to describe your home then. Did you live in your own home, or did you rent?

HA: We couldn't afford nothing. We couldn't afford a car, couldn't afford anything. Couldn't afford to eat, never mind.

JR: Did you pay rent? Or did you have your own home?

HA: We worked in the Bourne Mills, [*we rented*] in the Bourne Mills block for $4.

JR: $4 a week?

HA: Yeah. That was a lot of money then. We didn't have it. Somehow my mother must've managed. My mother was like me, a go-getter. She hold on to her money. She know what to do.

JR: Did you have your own room in your house or did you have to share a room with your sister?

HA: I had to do with my sister, and [*for*] my brothers, it was three in a bed. And ... my mother happened to have a big room with a little alcove or something and she had like a couch. Then one of my brothers [*would*] sleep there. And the other ... would sleep with my oldest brother. When they used to raise all kinds of cane.

JR: Tell me about going to school.

HA: What do you want to know?

JR: When did you start and what school did you go to?

HA: I started, went to first grade. I must have been seven years old then. I went to Mount Hope Avenue School [*655 Mount Hope Avenue, Fall River*]. And they used to call me Ester. I don't know if I should tell you this. They [*family and friends*] used to call me Ester; the moment I went to school, the teachers were calling everyone's names, you know. So they were calling my name, which is Hortense. And I never said anything. You know? And then she said again, 'Hortense Ribeiro.' I didn't answer. And then they said, 'That's you.' I said, 'No, that's not my name. My name is Ester.' [*She said,*] 'No, your name is, Hortense.' No one ever told me my name was Hortense. They used to say it in Portuguese [*Hortência*] but never told me in English that my name was Hortense. I always figured it was Ester. I was crying, I was, 'No, it's not, my name is Ester.' I don't know where my mother got that name. I told my mother, 'I will never forgive you for giving me that name.' I still haven't forgiven her. I hate that name.

JR: Did you speak Portuguese at home?

HA: Oh, yeah, my father didn't understand English. So we always had to talk Portuguese. When we used to talk English, my father would say, 'Hey, speak Portuguese so I know what you are talking about.' But after, he learned. And then he got to be an American citizen. My mother. My mother was smart, she went to school here. She come here at age nine. And she went to school. She had two brothers. I had two uncles, Manuel and Joe [*Manuel Paiva Mello and Joseph Paiva Mello*].

JR: Did they also work in the mills?

HA: Yeah, we all worked, everybody worked in the Bourne Mills. And did you know that people used to walk, I don't know if you know where Columbia Street is? And you know where the Bourne Mills is? You know those people used to walk from there, five o'clock in the morning all the way to the Bourne Mills [*a distance of approximately 2.5 miles*] because they couldn't afford to take the bus.

JR: The bus or a trolley? Was it a trolley?

HA: Yes, there was a trolley.... And with us too. All kinds of storm[s] and mud, we all used to go to school the same way, they didn't cancel.... You had to walk. Because we had no money to take the bus or trolley at the time.

JR: Let's get back to the Mount Hope Avenue School. How many grades were in that school?

HA: Four. [*The Mount Hope Avenue School housed grades one through three.*] And then I went to Hicks School [*Harriet T. Healy School at 726 Hicks Street, Fall River*]. And Hicks School I think it was until sixth [*grade*].

JR: Did you quit from the Hicks School?

HA: No, I quit school from Slade [*School, South Main, corner Slade Street, Fall River*] when I was fifteen.

JR: So this is the ... school on Hicks Street?

HA: Yeah, I worked, I went right through there, then I went to Slade Street [*School*]. But I never got around to ... graduate. I never graduated from the eighth grade. Because as soon as my father, when we were old enough, my father would pull us out ... to work. [*Ester left school to go to work at the age of fifteen.*] So I never had the chance to graduate. They wouldn't. My father said, 'You know you weren't born to go to school. Just to have children.' And then they had old fashioned ideas.

JR: So he was thinking that you were going to get married and have children.

HA: Yeah, I didn't get married until I was twenty-five years old.

JR: Did you have a lot of friends in school? A lot of girl friends?

HA: Oh yeah, the boys used to pick on me all the time. You know, I used to get up, the teacher used to tell me to come to the desk. And this guy, I could kill him, even today. Every time I go by, he would put his foot out and I would go flying.

JR: He tripped [*you*]?

HA: All the time. He always did that to me.

JR: Maybe he liked you.

HA: Yeah, he was trying. But I didn't like him. And when I saw my husband [*Manuel Amaral*], I met my husband when I was thirteen years old.

JR: Where did you meet him?

HA: Down at South Park. And I said to myself, 'That is the guy I am going to marry.'

JR: How did you know that?

HA: I don't know, I just liked him.... I used to be with him and his friends. And he never said anything to me. He would just wave. And I'd think that guy is not going to ask me for a date. I will have to go ask him.

JR: That is kind of shocking, isn't it? I mean to ask a guy?

HA: I told you, when I make up my mind I want something, I used to go and get it. So finally I went looking for him.

JR: Did you know his family? Did you know who he was?

HA: No, I didn't know. I just knew him, I liked him. That was it. And I told him, 'Hey why don't you ask me for a date? Why don't you go out with me?' He says, 'I can't afford you.' The Depression. Nobody worked. He didn't. When he went out with me, he didn't even have a nickel to put me in the bus. But he was a poor thing. He had no mother or father. [*His mother, née Evangelina Mendonca, died in 1926 at the age of thirty-three, having given birth to eleven children, four of whom survived her; his father, Manuel Amaral, aka Manuel Amaral Malaco, died in 1929 at the age of forty-six.*] I said, 'Look. You go out for me, your luck is going to change.'

JR: How was he living?

HA: He lived with his grandmother [*the widowed Mrs. Antonio Mendonca, née Antonia de Jesus; his uncle, Joseph Mendonca, and his family; and his sister, Josephine*]. He used to go for handouts. Welfare. That is how everybody lived. But in my time, they didn't have that. So my father used to go hunting down the water for clams, quahogs, peeniewinkles [*periwinkles*]. My mother used to make me sit down and do the peeniewinkles to keep me out of trouble. I was always in trouble.

JR: I am going to ask you about dating your husband. Where did you go if he had no money?

HA: We would go for walks. We would go down to South Park. All the girlfriends and boyfriends went down the South Park. Where else could we go? And walk. We used to walk from my house all the way down [*a distance of approximately 1.8 miles*], and he lived [*at 954*] Langley Street [*a distance of approximately 3.7 miles from the park*].

JR: That is a long way.

HA: He used to walk.

JR: Did he meet your father and mother?

HA: Finally, I brought him home one time. He had never had much to eat at home so my mother used to feed him. My mother was … nice, she would feed anybody that came to her house.

JR: What are your memories of going out with him? Was he able to take you to the movies or anything like that?

HA: Well, yeah, no, I used to pay my own. You know, you go to Park Show [*Park Theatre, 1425 South Main Street, Fall River*], you pay ten cents to go in…. That was a lot of money. So I let him pay sometimes, other times I pay for him. And I felt sorry for him. Then … he went in the service…. He was a National Guard. [*National Guard, Coast Artillery Corps, Private First Class, enlisted September 16, 1940.*] He was one of the first ones to go in. I was just going out with him then. Oh, then, before him … I got a few boyfriends, you know? I was going to get married. I had all my bridesmaids all picked out and I decided I didn't want to get married.

JR: Now could you save your money for the wedding?

HA: What money?

JR: Well, from your job at the mill.

HA: No one used to give me money. My mother, never.... We never got spending money in those days. We couldn't afford it. Then if I needed something, she would buy it for me, you know?

JR: So your income went to the house? Your salary, the income you made went [*to*] your father and mother.

HA: My mother, I used to adore my mother. I used to tell my mother, she used to work so hard.... She always had cotton dresses that were smocks. [*I used to say*], 'If I ever make money working, my first pay [*is*] going to be for you to go out and buy yourself a nice dress.' I always said that since I was a kid.... So finally, when I went to work at Bourne Mills, I got my first pay. See, in them days when my sister and my brother get their pay, they had to go and bring it to my father. The pays had to go to the father, you couldn't hold it. So, when I got my pay, I didn't give it to him, I held onto it. But he never said anything. So, on his way home, we walked. My father says, 'Don't you have any intention of giving me your money?' I said, 'No.' [*He said,*] 'What do you mean, no?' I says, 'I promised Mom I was going to give her that for a dress and that is what she is going to get.' But he didn't say anything. She bought a beautiful navy blue dress with chiffon sleeves, I was so proud of her. But I kept my promise.

JR: Now, after that, did you have to turn your money in?

HA: Yeah, that I had to do, but that first one was for my mother. I was always buying her things.

JR: Your mother sewed her own clothes? And she made clothes?

HA: And that's one thing about the teachers, they used to love my Mom ... in them days, there were flares and pleated. I used to tell my mother how to make my dress. I used to tell her, 'I want it this way.' So one day a teacher said, 'Hortense, you always look so nice in your clothes.' She says, 'How do you do it? Who does your dresses?' I said, 'My mother.' She said, 'Oh, very nice....' I says, 'I tell her how to make it. That's the way I want it.' They couldn't believe it. I was only fifth grade [*at Harriet T. Healy School*]. Miss [*Lillian Louise Kearney*] O'Hearn. Fifth grade [*teacher*] ... she was tough. Used to whack us around like nothing. Yup, used to whack us. Can't do that today.

JR: So you did you learn to sew from your mother? Did she teach you how to sew?

HA: As much as I wanted to learn to sew, I could never learn. But ... I learned to crochet ... yet I couldn't learn to sew.

JR: Did you have to do your chores around the house?

HA: Of course. My mother didn't have to tell me what to do.

JR: What did you do?

HA: I did housework. Sometimes I come home from work, my mother would be ironing, I would say, 'Mom, give me that iron,' and I would do all the ironing. I used to do it. You know, washed floors. We used to have stairs. I used to clean all those stairs. I used to do the beds, everything.

JR: Did you have a washing machine?

HA: No. Scrubbed.

JR: How did you heat the house … was there a stove, a wood stove?

HA: It was a wood stove when my mother lived in the Bourne Mills Block. That was a wood stove. When we were kids. But when I was about fifteen, we moved [*to 582*] State Avenue to this cottage [*in Fall River, on the Tiverton, Rhode Island, line, circa 1932*]; we had a heater. [*From circa 1925 to 1931, the Ribeiro family resided at 132 Last Street in Fall River.*]

JR: So, they had to chop the wood?

HA: Oh, yeah, [*and*] buy coal. My mother used to save all year for coal. They used to buy a ton of coal, and a ton was $45 them days. My mother had to save all, put aside every week some money … to buy coal.

JR: And did a ton of coal last the whole winter?

HA: We tried. We used a lot of wood. And that is how mom used to cook on that and all. Although she had a gas stove … she seldom used it when the stove was [*burning*] during the winter. And she used to cook the roasts…. And my mother was a good cook.

JR: Did you have to learn to cook with her?

HA: Oh, yeah, but we didn't fit in the kitchen with her because the kitchen was small and she was a little chubby…. Remember? She looked nice though, I was proud of her. I loved her so much. She weighed about two hundred pounds. But she was tall. But she looked good. And she had nice arms. One time she tore her arm and I cried because her arms were so nice, and I couldn't see it. I was a softy when it was for my mother.

JR: What were some of her favorite recipes?

HA: Chourico [*a highly seasoned Portuguese pork sausage*]. We loved chourico. And no matter what we cooked, there was chourico in it. I don't know. But chourico had to be in it. I used to love chourico. That is what used to give it the taste.

JR: And did she make her own bread?

HA: Yes, her own ... bread. She used to knead it in a big pan and cover it and put it back on the stove and it used to rise up from the heat.... She made biscuits. She used to make a sweet bread [*massa sovada*]. She would make five [*small ones*]. We each had a sweet bread. The five of us. And she would make the big ones. She had the big ones with the egg. They used to put [*whole*] eggs [*in them*].

JR: You made those sweetbreads for Easter?

HA: Yeah. [*Folar de Páscoa is an Azorean Easter tradition. Whole raw eggs, symbolizing Christ's resurrection, are set into the surface of the dough before baking.*]

JR: Did you cook like that for your family?

HA: Yeah, not like my mother but I cooked. I did pretty good. My husband didn't starve. He'd eat anything because he never had anything so, no matter what I gave him, he ate.

JR: I am going to ask you if you had a radio in those days.

HA: When we were in the Bourne Mills Block, we didn't even have electricity. There was no electricity. It was ... kerosene. And my mother used to have a mirror in back of it [*a lamp*] and it gave a big light. You know.... So one time, I was in the Bourne Mills Block, I was about six years old or seven. I tell my mother, 'I'm hungry. I'm going to have bread and butter.' That was all we could eat, bread and butter. We had nothing else. My mother said she was busy in the kitchen. So Momma says, 'Wait a minute, when I get through with this I will give it to you.' ... at the time there was an old fashion ice box ... and my mother had a big ... bowl with fish in it. A big one, not a small one, a big one, on top of the ice box. So I opened the door of the ice box and I put myself over it and [*was*] swinging ... back and forth. My mother said, 'Get away from there. Don't do that.' [*I said,*] 'No, I want bread, give me bread, Ma.' And I'm swinging back and forth. All of a sudden, the ice box tips over, I escaped in time, or I would have been killed. There goes the fish slapping down on the floor. There we go all over the place. And I ran out. Oh, when I saw that, I ran out. My poor mother, she had to clean that up. So after she got rid of it, she says, 'Hey Ester, come on, I will give you the bread now.' I said, 'No, never mind, Ma, I'm not hungry.' And I didn't go 'cause she would have killed me.

JR: Now, when you were growing up with your family, did you have any illnesses, any sicknesses or health care problems?

HA: No.

JR: Everyone was healthy?

HA: The normal, um, the only thing we got was the measles. My mother had the three of us with the measles. My two younger brothers, [*Joseph, Jr. and Antone,*] and I at the same time. My mother worked so hard. That's why I would have done anything for her. She had to take care of the three of us. That's the only sickness we had. Even now I haven't, thank God at my age I have no cuts in my stomach, nothing. Thank God, no operations. Maybe I will get it after, but my body is like it always was.

JR: There was a lot of [*sickness*] during the Depression, it was hard to pay for doctors. And your brothers and sisters, were they born at home?

HA: They were all born at home. A lot of them, well, we had Dr. [*Joseph Jacome Travassos*] Lima.... He was our doctor; he never charged. My father used to work for him in his garden [*at his home at 107 State Avenue in North Tiverton, Rhode Island*]. But ... we were lucky and we were never charged, you know?

JR: So ... now to the mills. You started working at the Bourne?

HA: When I was fifteen.

JR: And then how long did that last?

HA: That didn't last too long, because right after that the union butt in, wanted more money, and ... the place wouldn't give it to them. So they closed down the place, it was nine months. I'll never forget that. That was when I went to get the job, I worked in about seven or six different places.

JR: Can you remember all of those places for us?

HA: I got the names here ... Bourne Mills [*844 State Avenue*], United Rayon [*Mills, 460 Globe Street*], The Rag Mill [*Massasoit Manufacturing Company, 136 Pocasset Street*], Maplewood Yarn Mill, [*Maplewood Products Company, 1290 Stafford Road*], Firestone [*Rubber & Latex Products Company, 172 Ferry Street*], Pocket Book Place [*Gamma Leather Company, Inc., 288 Plymouth Avenue*], Lyn Sportswear [*Company, Inc., 129 Martine Street*], [*Frito-Lay, Inc., 638 Quequechan Street*], Raytheon [*Company, 600 Spring Street, North Dighton, Massachusetts*], and Center Garment [*Company, Inc., 62 County Street*]. [*I retired from*] Center Garment. That's a Jewish [*owned company*]. That was the better place....

JR: Tell me more about that.

HA: I used to be an examiner [*in the finishing department*], I used to examine the garments ... I know his name was Abe. He was so good.... Trieff, Abe [*Abraham*] Trieff.... And his son, what was his name?

JR: Harvey, I think his son is Harvey.

HA: Harvey is one of them. Yeah, Harvey was the older one, the two brothers, Harvey and Nate.... [*The 'two brothers' she is referring to are Harvey Ian Trieff and Richard Paul Trieff. "Nate" was Nathan Trieff, who founded Center Garment Company, Inc. in 1946. He was Abraham's father, and Harvey and Richard's grandfather.*] And ... I used to examine the material. They were very good to me. They were very, very good to me.

JR: Now, how about Firestone. That was a huge plant.

HA: Yeah, I worked all over Firestone. I did pillows [*in Department 5*], I did everything. Well, there is a picture of me over there doing pillows.

JR: I didn't know they did pillows.

HA: They had pillows, mattresses, my husband used to work there, too. Mattresses, everything. I started working upstairs in the spinning, I was spinning the threads for Firestone.

JR: I thought they were always involved in the war, doing gas masks.

HA: During the war they did gas masks. They had a department upstairs for gas masks. I wasn't working there then. This was after the war, I didn't have a job so I used to get my check, they used to give us money then, you know? And they got me that job. That was the best thing they did.

JR: When you got there, to Firestone, did you have to get training to do this work? Did someone show you?

HA: Yeah, they had to show you what to do, naturally. All my jobs were trained, even at the shops, the old shops. That is how I worked in all these places. Every time Firestone laid me off, through the union – the union again – I had to go to get another job. That was how I found all these jobs.

JR: You paid into the union? Did you have to pay into the union?

HA: I think I had to pay twenty-five [*cents*] a week.

JR: What union was that? What was the name of that union?

HA: Oh, I don't know. [*United Rubberworkers of America, Local No. 261*] Oh, that was Firestone.

JR: The dress shops had a different union.

HA: Yeah. [*International Ladies Garment Workers Union, Local 178*]

JR: Were you able to get a pension from those unions?

HA: Yes, I get very little. I only get thirty-some dollars from the union. Because worked only ten years. You have to work there ten years. But see, I never worked there long enough, because as soon as Firestone called me, I used to go back. And they used to tell me I was crazy to go back. The boss didn't want to let me go. They said, 'No, don't go.' I would say, 'Hey, that's money in the bank. I am going to go back there.'

JR: How long did you work at Firestone?

HA: Oh, over ten years. [*She was employed at Firestone on and off over a span of seventeen years.*]

JR: So, was there any pension from the Rubberworkers?

HA: I got not much.... But uh, I got the insurance. It would have been through my husband, too.

JR: Now ... about President Roosevelt. He brought in the Social Security [*in 1935*].

HA: He brought in a lot of things, God bless him. But that raise, that was beautiful, I still can't get over it. I had hardly any money.... I would make three or four dollars a week. And the shop, Lyn Sportswear, that's one of the first shops I worked in. Lyn Sportswear. But they were all nice, they were all good bosses. But Firestone ... I had to clock and I had a certain amount. I always went in.

JR: Was that piecework?

HA: Yeah, I would always go over. And my boss would come and take it away. And [*at*] the end he would say, 'God bless you.' 'Cause I always used to make more than I was supposed to. I was always a good worker. One time the big boss was watching me.

JR: I was going to ask you ... about all these jobs. Some of them were dangerous. Some of them may have been dangerous. Like at Firestone.

HA: That was a men's job. The [*dangerous*] jobs was mostly for men. Not for women.... I know I did the pillows. I did the pillows, that's all I can remember. And ... upstairs, I did the thread. And then I worked for Mr. [*Clarence J.*] Boyer [*a foreman at Firestone*], on something else.... I worked almost every department.

JR: Do you remember the salary there? What you were earning? And your husband?

HA: Thirty-two dollars.

JR: Thirty-two dollars a week. That was pretty good, wasn't it?

HA: We were rich. Um, what you call it, I can't think of it now. We had better times then, the Depression was over. So Roosevelt was there, it [*wages*] kept going up. That was the best paying place in the city.

JR: Now, was your husband drafted? Did he go into World War II?

HA: Oh, yeah, I wasn't married to him then. He was in the National Guard and he joined the National Guard so he could have a little bit of money for himself. He had no money.... His grandparents didn't have any money either. So he joined the National Guard so he could get some money. He would only get enough to buy things.... I think it was thirty a month. He didn't make much. It was enough to keep him, you know, so naturally when the war started in '42 ... is when I got married.

PA: He was due to be discharged from the National Guard in January, 1942. Of course, [*the Japanese attack on*] Pearl Harbor was a month before that. So he was interned for the duration.

JR: He had to stay in the National Guard because war broke out?

HA: Yeah, he had to go. He was one of the first ones to go. He went to New York, he stood there for a while. Some place in New York, then from there they went overseas.

JR: Do you remember where he went overseas?

HA: Germany, England, and France.

JR: That must have been very difficult for you.

HA: Well yeah, I missed him. There was nothing I could do. Then my two brothers went, and my three brothers went. [*John, Private, U.S. Army, enlisted February 23, 1942; Antone, Private, U.S. Army, enlisted August 15, 1942; Joseph, Private, U.S. Army, enlisted June 14, 1943.*]

JR: Were they single at the time? [*John and Antone were unmarried when they enlisted; Joseph was married.*]

HA: My oldest brother never married.

JR: So you had three brothers in the war and your boyfriend at the time.

HA: Until 1945, the war was over.

JR: And did they all come back? They all made it back to Fall River?

HA: My husband wasn't the same when he came back [*discharged November 8, 1945*]. He was a sick man. They got the best of him. But he got over it. He was alright. My brother John was never the same [*discharged November 8, 1945*]. They never were the same when they came back [*her brother, Antone, was discharged December 10, 1945; and Joseph was also discharged sometime late in 1945*].

JR: So during that time, you were always working at Firestone, or did you try the dress shops?

HA: I was working at the dress shops. Firestone was after the war.

JR: Okay. Now you went to Lyn Sportswear.

HA: That's the first one.

JR: What kind of work did you do there?

HA: Dresses.

JR: On the sewing machine?

HA: No, I didn't sew. I was an inspector.... I tried, I tried to sew ... and I couldn't learn it. I learned everything. No matter where I went. Even one time I was at Firestone. I was doing something and this big boss come and was standing behind me, watching me. And after a while I never paid attention to him, I did my work. He says, 'You seem like you like your job.' I said, 'No, I don't.' He said, 'You seem like you are enjoying it.' I said, 'Well, I have to do it. So I am doing it. It isn't because I like it.'

JR: What did you really want to do? Did you ever have an idea on what you wanted to do?

HA: No, just happened some jobs I didn't care for. But I would do it the best I could. Some people used to mess everything up, not me. That is why they always liked me.

JR: How about Gamma Leather. What kind of work was done in Gamma Leather, a factory with pocketbooks?

HA: Well, they made pocketbooks.

JR: But you have to sew those too.

HA: I put them together, they used to sew them, I put them together from what I can think of now. It's been so long.

PA: I think you did the framing ... once it was together you put the frame on, the metal frame.

JR: Let's move ahead to your family because you got married after the war.

HA: I can tell you this about getting married. My husband was in the service ... so the war come out with something that every month our family would get a check. Every month, you used to get a check. So it would be sent to wherever they [*the enlisted men*] wanted it to. So he told his grandmother, 'Grandma, I am going to send a check to you, but you have to help me and save some of that money so I can get married.' She is like, 'Oh no, I can't do that.' So he said, 'Then I can't send you that check. 'Cause I am going to need it to get married when I come out.' So anyway, so he started to get on my back, you know, we should get married. I said, 'My mother doesn't want me to get married. My mother says I shouldn't get married while you're in the service because you might die.' Anyway, I got married without anyone knowing [*on March 7, 1942; Manuel was on a twenty-four hour leave*].

JR: Oh? In Fall River?

HA: Yeah, at [*Our*] Lady of the Angels church, my church. So I got married. Nobody knew. Just his sister [*Josephine Amaral*]. She stood up for my wedding and one of his friends from the service. So, finally, my mother ... says, 'Alright, you can get married.... My husband says, 'We are already married.' Do you know that she went to church and tried to have it annulled?

JR: No.

HA: The priest said, 'Hey, go home, they are married. Go home, forget about it.'

JR: But you were already of age.

HA: I was twenty-five. My father never said a thing. But my mother never forgave my husband. But after, my husband was very good to her. You know? But it was a shock to her when she found out. So I said, 'You didn't want me to get married. So that was for the check to come to me.' And I used to get it, I used to put it in the bank.

JR: So then he went off to the war?

HA: Then he went to [*Fort Hood in Killeen,*] Texas. He come back. Before he went to the war, overseas, he went to Texas. So I went and stayed there with him. What can I say about Texas? It was beautiful. I loved it. What did they say, a two-horse town? It used to have the sheriffs on horseback with their guns. Just like in the movies. Just like it. It was beautiful. They had mostly Protestant churches. But they finally made one [*Catholic*] church for us. So that was very good. I wanted to go to the regular church.

JR: That's quite an adventure. Not a lot of girls went to Texas.

HA: Oh my husband wanted to be with me, although I couldn't be with him. 'Cause he was in the camp and I was living [*in Gatesville, Texas,*] with a couple [*Herschel C. Britain and his wife, née Alta O'Neal*]. I still write to them. The couple I lived with.

JR: Now, when did he come back from the war?

HA: 1945. I lived with my mother for a while.

JR: You lived in Fall River when he came back?

HA: Yeah. And did you know, when we got married, you know my [*mother*] wouldn't let him sleep with me? 'Home. You're not staying here. Get out, go home,' [*she said*]. The poor guy used to have to leave.

JR: I guess he was trying to get along. He was trying to get along with your mother.

HA: He was soft. He was soft. I had a wonderful life.

JR: When he came back from the war, you set up your home in Fall River.

HA: I lived with my mother.

JR: And then when your husband came back, you had your home in Fall River?

HA: I lived with my mother in Fall River in a cottage. We lived right on the state line. Here is Fall River right on this side, and the other sidewalk was Tiverton [*Rhode Island*]. I lived there until I was put in an apartment up in the Common Fence Point [*Rhode Island, circa 1946 - 1947*]. And then after I lived [*at 594*] Bradford Avenue [*in Fall River, from circa 1947- 1952*]. We moved. My mother cried so much because I was always with her, I took care of them, my mother and father. I took care of them.

JR: So tell me about your family ... when did you start your family? Do you have children?

HA: God, yeah. Got him.

JR: That's it?

HA: Little rascal. He is one. I have a wonderful son, a beautiful son [*Paul Joseph Amaral*]. He was born in '48. My husband come back in '45, and he was born in '48 because I didn't want kids. But my husband loved kids. Loved children, so I said, 'Okay.' So he says, 'I would love to have five,' and my husband, I loved him, I said I'd do anything for him. So I said, 'Okay. We will have five, we will have this one first.' After we got this one, my husband said, 'Never mind, we don't want five. He's a rascal. Drives us nuts.' Well, all kids are. He would say, 'Ma, I wanna do this.' 'Ma, I wanna.' 'Mom, wait, I only go two hands.' 'Okay, do that with one hand do that with the other hand,' I said. 'I will fix you, you talk to me like that.'

JR: So you were a disciplinarian? You were tough?

HA: I had to be tough. But he's good.

JR: I am thinking about after the war, and then some of the years you spent before the war. Some of the big events that happened in Fall River ... the Hurricane of [*September 21,*] 1938.

HA: Oh, what a year, about that hurricane. Let me tell you?

JR: Yeah, I want to hear about that hurricane.

HA: Well, I used to work in United Rayon then, on Globe Street. And I used to work with my girlfriend [*Mary Arruda*], so we come out of work, and I don't know if you ever heard of Shove Street. So we were walking and then it started to get windy, you know? So, in them days, our dresses were flared. So I told my girlfriend, 'Gee, it's kind of windy.' My flare started to go up over my head and started rolling it in, and then it go up from the back, you know? So I started holding the front and the back, and the damn thing would still float, so I said, 'The hell with this,' and let it go. So the flare is going over my head. I had no slip on. I never wore slips them days. So up it goes. My girlfriend and I.

JR: That was during the storm? The hurricane was on its way?

HA: I didn't know it was a hurricane then, I just thought it was windy until I got home.

JR: There were no weathermen to tell you about the storm coming – there was a big fire in [*Fall River on February 2,*] 1928.

HA: Oh, yeah, it burned the whole down[*town*].

JR: Down in the Granite Block area [*on South Main Street*]. Do you remember that? Describe that.

HA: You could see it from my house. All that smoke and all that.

JR: So you retired from the Center Garment. What year did you retire?

HA: I retired from Firestone.

PA: No, Center Garment. That was the last job you had, Center Garment. You were a floor lady.

HA: Oh, yeah.

PA: You were a floor lady at Center Garment. 1978.

HA: Good thing you came. I thought it was Firestone.

JR: And that was a supervisory position if you were a floor lady. You were like a supervisor.

HA: Yeah, I was smart.

JR: What kind of work did you do as a floor lady?

HA: I used to help with examining. I used to tell some of them what to do and not to do, you know?

JR: You had to distribute the work?

HA: Yeah. And I used to, it was nice. That [*Abraham*] … Trieff. When I retired … from there … he gave me a check of $100. Let me see. [*He said,*] 'I hate to see you go, Ester.' I said, 'It's time for me to go.' 'Cause I used to work hard. You know, I used to take care of my father. And my brother, my oldest brother never married. He lived with my father. And he had arthritis in his hands. And his fingers were all twisted…. Someone would have to come wash him and take care of him. He used to love me…. I used to take care of them. So my father used to say, 'You know I took care of you, now you take care of me.' I said, 'That's right, Dad.' And I used to take care of them. My mother. I worked hard.

JR: So you retired in 1978, and what have you been doing ever since?

HA: Raising hell.

JR: I hear you are pretty active. I heard you have a schedule. You have a lot of things that you do?

HA: I worked at [*a*] Senior Center.

JR: Which one? Which center is that?

HA: In Tiverton [*Rhode Island*].

JR: When did you learn to drive?

HA: Oh, [*in 1961*] I was living [*in Tiverton*]. So I never had a car. I never drove. My husband drove. He never had car in his life, either. The first time when we got married, we bought a car, [*a used Dodge described by their son as 'tired'*]. One time I was looking for him and I didn't see him. I said, 'Where in the heck is he?' I go in the garage, he is in the car. Just he had never had anything in his life. He was sitting there admiring the car. Never had anything. That's why I gave him anything he wanted. I used to let him have it.

JR: What kind of work did he do after the war?

HA: He went to Firestone. No, he worked in the King Phillip Mills for a while [*as a bobbin filler*]. And then after … Firestone was hiring all the veterans, so I said, 'Why you don't go try working there?' because he wasn't happy in that other job. And that's how he got a job there. Me, I got a job by accident.... I got laid off, and so they found me this job, at Firestone.

JR: So did your husband teach you to drive?

HA: Yeah. I was ready to divorce him. But I went. It took a while, but I did it. It's a good thing, I needed it. Because I was asking other people, I would depend on other people to take me. Sometimes they would forget to pick me up. I would be waiting at the bottom of the hill and they would forget me. So he says, 'Honey,' he used to call me 'Honey' all the time, 'I'll get you a car.'

JR: So I am thinking about all the other things that came in after the war. Like television. Do you remember getting your first television?

HA: Ah, yeah, my mother ... got one, too. [*And the telephone*] ... oh, when we get the telephone, we didn't know what to do. We never had a telephone in our lives. And finally we had a telephone. We were living with my mother and was still single. We didn't know what to do with the telephone, then we got a radio. We had a radio when we were young.... Because my brother and I used to get out of bed without my mother knowing, we would go in the parlor and listen to the radio without her knowing.

JR: And when did you get your television?

HA: It was on Bradford Avenue [*1947-1952*].

JR: What do you think about computers today?

HA: I think it's wonderful. And not only that, computers, kids six years old doing that. I can't get over it. I don't even know one button from another. And they know it. I feel like a jerk. The way they are so smart.

JR: So what do you think is different today than years ago? If you were going to tell me about Fall River then and life today, what's different from those two periods of time?

HA: Oh, I don't know. It's much nicer now than it was before.

JR: That's right. I really appreciate your time today.

HA: I hope I was a help.

JR: I think it was very insightful.

HA: Was it helpful?

JR: I know how important it was for you to help your family. And then you had a very interesting life.

HA: I had a beautiful life. I was a rascal. I used to drive my mother crazy. I was always climbing in trees.... She would be looking up, calling, 'Ester! Ester! Hortência!'

JR: We are going to end this now....

HA: Yeah, okay.

JR: Thank you so much. Ester, I am going to call you Ester.

HA: Yes, I rather you did!

JR: Okay.

HA: I'm tired, I never talk so much in my life.

PHOTO GALLERY

4.1 Hortencia's father, José Pacheco Ribeiro, as a young man.

4.2 Bourne Mills, Hortencia's first place of employment, circa 1931, at the age of fifteen. *"When we were old enough, my father would pull us out* [of school] *to work."*

4.3 Working girls at the Bourne Mills, circa 1928. Hortencia's sister, Mary Pacheco Ribeiro, is at the far right. *"We all worked, everybody worked in the Bourne Mill."*

4.4 Hortencia's brother, John Pacheco Ribeiro, strikes a comic pose for the camera, 1940s; behind him is the Bourne Mills Block, where the family resided from circa 1908 to 1924. *"When we were in the Bourne Mills Block, we didn't even have electricity. It was ... kerosene."*

4.5 Downtown Fall River following the devastating conflagration of February 2, 1928 (Great Fire of 1928); a view looking north from City Hall tower. *"You could see it from my house. All the smoke and that."*

4.6 The Ribeiro family cottage at 582 State Avenue, Fall River; the family purchased this property circa 1932. *"We lived right on the state line. Here is Fall River right on this side, and the other sidewalk was Tiverton, Rhode Island."*

4.7 Manuel Amaral (second from right) and his buddies during World War II. *"...he joined the National Guard* [in 1940] *so he could have a little bit of money for himself."*

4.8 Hortencia's mother, Mrs. José Pacheco Ribeiro, née Maria Amelia de Paiva, circa 1938. *"My mother, I used to adore my mother."*

4.9 Hortencia's father, José Pacheco Ribeiro, circa 1938. *"...my father didn't understand English. So we always had to talk Portuguese. When we used to talk English, my father would say, 'Hey, speak Portuguese so I know what you are talking about.' But after, he learned."*

4.10 *Left:* Hortencia's mother in the yard of the family residence at 582 State Avenue, 1940s. *"My mother was like me ... a go-getter.... She knew what to do."*

4.11 Hortencia in the 1940s.

4.12 Mr. and Mrs. Manuel Amaral on their wedding day, March 7, 1942. *"My mother* [said] *I shouldn't get married while* [he was] *in the service because* [he] *might die."*

4.13 Hortencia and Manuel as young newlyweds. *"'Honey,' he used to call me 'Honey' all the time."*

4.14 Firestone Rubber & Latex Products Company, Inc., Fall River, Massachusetts, circa 1956. *"I worked all over Firestone."*

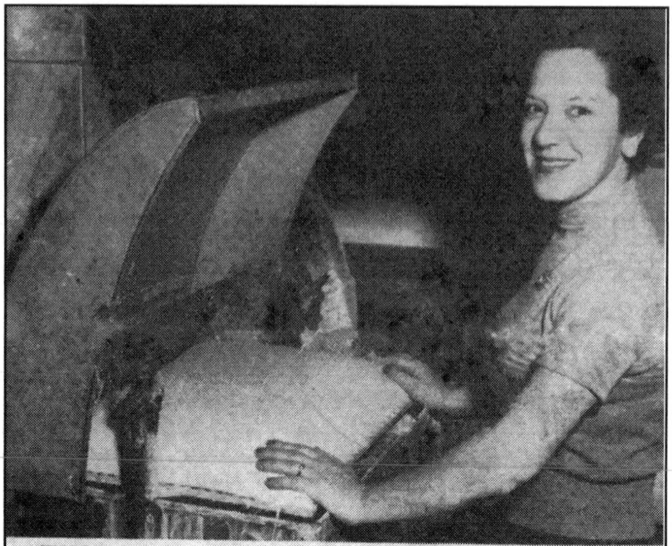

THIS IS EASY: Hortensia Amaral operates a new machine designed to coat the underside of pillow sections with cement preparatory to their being pressed together. The machine is new to Department 5.

4.15 Hortencia at work at Firestone Rubber & Latex Products Company, Fall River, Massachusetts, late 1940s or early 1950s. A Firestone "big boss" in conversation with Hortencia: *"You seem like you like your job." "No, I don't.... I have to do it, so I am doing it. It isn't because I like it."*

4.16 The former Kerr Thread Mills, Fall River, Massachusetts. Lyn Sportswear Company, Inc. operated from this location from circa 1962 to 1971. *"Lyn Sportswear, that's one of the first shops I worked in."*

4.17 Workers at Gamma Leather Company, Inc., 288 Plymouth Avenue, Fall River, Massachusetts, 1966; Hortencia referred to this company as the "Pocket Book Place." *"I put them together - they used to sew them - I put them together. ..."*

4.18 Hortencia posing with a negligee set in salmon rayon satin trimmed in beige machine-made lace that she wore in the 1940s; the garment was donated to the Fall River Historical Society in 2013.

FIVE:

MARY VINCENT CORREIRA, NÉE ARRUDA

Personal Statistics

Name: Mary Vincent Arruda
(Mrs. Joseph Tavares Correira)

Date of Birth: November 5, 1928

Place of Birth: Fall River, Massachusetts

Father: Manoel "Manuel" Vincente d'Arruda, Sr. (1901-1968)

Mother: Maria Souza (1901-1992)

Siblings:
Manuel Vincent Arruda, Jr. (1925-2010)
John Vincent Arruda (born 1931)
Irene Vincent Arruda (born 1939)
---(Mrs. Robert James Rigby)
Daniel Vincent Arruda (1941-1964)
David Vincent Arruda (1942-1963)
Rita Vincent Arruda (born 1943)
---(Mrs. Luis Silva)
Leo Vincent Arruda (born 1944)

Spouse: Joseph Tavares Correira (1925-1993)

Date of Marriage: November 24, 1949

Children:
Joanne Correira
Joseph Anthony Correira
Lorianne Correira

Employment history:
Berkshire Fine Spinning Associates, Inc., Fall River
Shelburne Shirt Company, Inc., Fall River
Farinha's Restaurant, Fall River
Bomark Corporation, Fall River
Klear-Vu Corporation, Fall River

EDITED TRANSCRIPT

Interview with Mrs. Joseph Tavares Correira, née Mary Vincent Arruda

Interviewer: (JR) Joyce B. Rodrigues, Fall River Historical Society

Interviewee: (MC) Mary Vincent (Arruda) Correira

Additional Commentary: (JC) Joanne (Correira) Cadieux, Mary's daughter

Date of Interview: October 17, 2015

Location: Correira residence, Westport, Massachusetts

Summary by Joyce B. Rodrigues:

Mary Vincent (Arruda) Correira was born in Fall River, Massachusetts, on November 5, 1928. Her narrative tells the story of the Arruda/Correira family and provides unique insights into Portuguese-American religious practices and cultural traditions.

Work Experience:

The Arruda family worked as weavers, carders, and spinners in the Davis and Parker Mills. These mills and several others, located in the Quequechan (River) Valley Mills Historic District, represent the last major area of textile development in Fall River from the late 1890s into the early 1900s.

The Davis Mills, 749 Quequechan Street, manufacturers of fine and fancy cotton goods, employed 800 operatives; it was liquidated circa 1930. The Parker Mills, 20 Jefferson Street, produced fine yarns. It was sold in 1931 to Berkshire Fine Spinning Associates, Inc., a company that managed to survive the Great Depression and prosper during and after World War II.

Mary started working at the age of fifteen, and retired at the age of sixty-eight with a pension from both Social Security and the ILGWU union. Her career took her to the following manufacturers that were all located within walking distance of her home in the so-called Flint section of the city:

- Berkshire Fine Spinning Associates, Inc.
- Shelburne Shirt Company. Inc. Located at 135 Alden Street in the Flint Mills, Shelburne was founded in 1933 as a family-owned enterprise and was one of Fall

River's largest employers and a leading American manufacturer of men's shirts. At its peak, the company employed 800 workers and produced three-million shirts annually. Shelburne closed in 1988. The factory reopened as Fall River Shirts soon after and reorganized in 2009 as New England Shirt. Today, it is a niche industry as a high-end shirtmaker, and employs sixty workers.

- Klear-Vu Corporation. Klear-Vu, located at 420 Quequechan Street, was established in New York in 1924 and relocated to Fall River in 1965. The company manufactures chair pads, rocking chair cushions, bench pads, decorative pillows, and other products. Today, it is located on Airport Road and employs over 100 workers. In 2015, the company earned the Made in USA CERTIFIED® Seal.

Family and Church:

Mary's parents both immigrated to the United States from the island of St. Michael in the Azores in 1920. They became acquainted in Fall River and were married in 1925 at the Espirito Santo Church located on Alden Street.

Espirito Santo Church was founded in 1904 to minister to the Portuguese-speaking Catholics who lived in the Flint Village. The Espirito Santo Parochial School, established in 1910, was the first Portuguese-Catholic grammar school in the United States. The church and school continue to serve the Portuguese-speaking community today.

There were eight children in the Arruda family, five boys and three girls; Mary was the second oldest. All the Arruda children were born at home, and attended the parish grammar school. Mary graduated in 1943 and went directly to work to help support the household.

Mary met and married Joseph Tavares Correira, who grew up in the same neighborhood. The wedding was at the Espirito Santo Church on November 25, 1948; the couple had three children.

During the interview, Mary's daughter Joanne noted the importance of religion to their family: "... in my growing up years and listening to family stories ... religion was a major, major part of your life."

Mary and her daughter describe in detail the Portuguese religious tradition of the Festas do Espírito Santo (Holy Ghost Festival). The feast plays an integral role in the lives of devout Azoreans and Azorean-Americans, and usually begins on Pentecost Sunday and continues through the spring. The festival was founded in the 13th century by Queen St. Elizabeth (Isabel), Queen Regent of Portugal, who was noted for her religious piety, charity, and devotion to the poor.

The Holy Ghost Feast is celebrated not only in Fall River but also in Portuguese Roman Catholic churches and Holy Ghost clubs throughout the state of Massachusetts, New England, and anywhere you find a large Portuguese or Portuguese-American community.

Note: This interview has been slightly edited for continuity and readability; in order to preserve the integrity of the conversation, the phraseology remains that of the interviewer and interviewee. Italicized information in square brackets has been added for the purposes of clarification and context.

MARY CORREIRA

JR: Where were you born, Mary – when were you born, and where were you born?

MC: 11-5-28 and I was born in Fall River … I forgot the name of the street.

JC: It was [*310 Alden Street*]. [*The Arruda family resided at 310 Alden Street, circa 1925 – 1929; at 293 Jenckes Street, circa 1930; and at 249 Jenckes Street, circa 1931 – 32.*]

JR: How about your parents? Were they also born in Fall River?

MC: Portugal.

JR: And, do you have any idea where about?

MC: My mother [*née Maria Souza*] was in Nordeste, [*Saõ Miguel, Azores*], and my father [*Manoel 'Manuel' Vicente d'Arruda*] was [*from Bretanha*], St. Michael's.

JC: Saint Michael's.

MC: They met here [*in Fall River*].

JR: Oh, they met here. Were they married here then, and do you know the church, by chance?

MC: Espirito Santo [*Church, 275 Alden Street, Fall River, in 1925*].

JR: Very good.

MC: On Alden Street. Yup.

JR: What did they do for a living?

MC: My mother was a spinner in the mill, and my father was a [*weaver*] … in the mill.

JR: And, did your mother tell you what mill she worked in?

MC: As a matter of fact, I started, I started in that mill, too. I used to, we used to walk every morning, then I got a problem with my legs, so I had to quit the job, and that is when I got into the shops. [*According to the interviewee, her parents had been employed at the Davis Mills, 749 Quequechan Street, Fall River; the mill was liquidated circa 1931. In the 1940 edition of the* Fall River City Directory, *the interviewee's father is listed as 'weaver, Parker,' likely a reference to the former Parker Mills, 20 Jefferson Street, Fall River, which were sold to Berkshire Fine Spinning Associates, Inc., in 1931. The interviewee's father was employed by the latter company for many years.*]

JR: When you were working in the mill, what kind of work did you do?

MC: I was, uh, I used to clean like the spinners; I used to clean it. I was, I was a helper … we all worked there; then I had to quit because I couldn't walk that far. That's when I started in the shops.

JR: So, before we get to that, let me just work on growing up …

JC: They moved to [85] Cash Street, [*Fall River, circa 1939. The Arruda family resided at 72 Everett Street, Fall River, circa 1933 – 1936*].

MC: We lived [*at 71*] Pitman Street, not too long [*circa 1937 – 1938*]; then we went to Cash Street.

JR: And what was that neighborhood like?

MC: It was nice; everyone knew everyone.

JR: Was that a single family home, or a three-family?

MC: No, it was, well, by the time my mother had me, and it was two of us [*the interviewee and her elder brother, Manuel Vincent Arruda, Jr.*], it was like two or three children in each family. [*85 Cash Street was a three-family tenement*].

JR: And how many children were in your family?

MC: Eight. I was the second oldest. [*Manuel Vincent Arruda, Jr.; Mary Vincent Arruda; John Vincent Arruda; Irene Vincent Arruda, later Mrs. Robert James Rigby; Daniel Vincent Arruda; David Vincent Arruda; Rita Vincent Arruda, later Mrs. Luis Silva; and Leo Vincent Arruda.*]

JR: And, can you tell us a little bit about all those children?

MC: It was Manny, it was me, and then it was Irene. Then it was David, he died [*in 1964 at the age of twenty-two; the cause of death was cancer*].

JC: She has a sister, Rita, she has a brother, Leo, a brother John, and her brother Manny, who died two years ago.

JR: Very interesting, very interesting. Now, how did you manage all these children? How did your mother manage all these children?

MC: We all lived in one house. I will never forget it. Every time a baby was born, my grandmother would come and say, 'You watch him.' She would bring him in the room, close the door, then all of us would be, 'Oh, no, another one.' They would come and bring them to me because they had them at home.

JR: That was what I was going to ask you. All these children were born at home?

MC: They were all at home, and then she'd come and bring them to me, and I would say, 'Another one? Another one for me to take care of?' Hey, I was the oldest girl. But it was – my [*maternal*] grandmother [*Mrs. Manuel Carreiro de Souza, née Senhorinha Moniz Borges*] lived with us, so she was a great help, she was. Then she, we moved, [*to 72*] Everett Street, [*Fall River*]. Then we moved, she moved to [85] Cash Street, *[Fall River*]. That was where I got married from [*in 1948*], Cash Street.

JC: It's funny how they stayed in the same neighborhood. They moved from one street just to the next street over. And I think a big part of that, in my growing up years and listening to family stories, is it was very important to stay in the parish because religion was a major, major part of your life.

JR: So, tell me about the religious background in your family.

MC: Oh, we all went to Espirito Santo Church. Sunday, we, everybody had to go to church.

JR: And how about your brothers, were they altar boys?

MC: No.

JC: No, but my grandfather [*Manuel Vicente Arruda, Sr.*] was very involved in [*the*] Espirito Santo [*Church*] procession [*Festas do Espírito Santo*]; he'd carry the bust of Christ. [*The Festas do Espírito Santo, or Holy Ghost Festival, plays an integral role in the lives of devout Azoreans, and Azorean-Americans, and usually begins on Pentecost Sunday, running through the spring. The festival was founded by the 13th century Queen St. Elizabeth (Isabel), formerly a princess of Aragon, who was Queen Regent of Portugal, the consort of King Denis. A devout model of Christian charity, she was noted for her religious piety, charity, and devotion to her work for the poor.*]

MC: He used to collect at the churches; he collected the money at the churches. If there was anything to be done, he would be right there.

JR: I know that the churches had a lot of [*religious*] processions.

MC: We were in that every year.

JR: And Mary, you marched those processions, did you carry anything?

JC: We have the crown. We actually own a sterling silver crown. It's at her apartment ... so we carry our own crown. [*The crown is a replica of the crown of Queen St. Elizabeth (Isabel); it is accompanied by a scepter surmounted with a dove, symbolizing the Holy Spirit*].

JR: Did that come from Portugal?

JC: Yes.

MC: My sister-in-law [*Mrs. Henri Charette, née Emily Correira*] gave me that one because someone gave her one. So she gave me hers.

JC: But it is from Portugal.

JR: So, there are a lot of Portuguese traditions in your family.

JC: We have the last, what they call them, the Dominga, and the church picks seven families. Probably four years ago was the last time we had put our name in because it's … a lot of work…. We had the Dominga here; I set up an altar in my living room with the candles and we had prayers, and we had open house for seven days. [*Considered a great honor, the crown remains on display with each family for a one-week period, during which a continuous open house is held; traditionally, the crown is never left unattended.*]

JR: That's right, open house for seven days. That was a lot of entertaining.

MC: Oh, yeah.

JC: A lot of food.

MC: I enjoyed everything.

JR: A lot of food, and the days you are talking about, it was a lot of people in the neighborhood, the same people in the neighborhood.

MC: And people that had the Dominga would come, too. They would come – like, let's say they had the second, and third Dominga – they would come to mine, and I'd go to theirs. But it was, it was all right.

JR: It was kind of like a fundraiser for the church? Was that how it was?

JC: It's not really a fundraiser, because when they come to your house, the concept is they light a candle … you collect a dollar for the candle, and that does get donated to the church. And then, in the end, there is a procession to the church. In honor of the story of the Holy Ghost, which is an interesting story. It's the story of Queen Isabella, who sold her crown to feed the poor. And that is why, when we have the feast, it's the Portuguese soup [*soupa de couvres*]; you don't pay, everybody who goes to the feast eats for free.

MC: I looked forward to that. Oh …

JR: That is a lot of … dinners. My mother went to a lot of those events in Espirito Santo [*Church*]….

MC: I was already, I was already married.

JR: Okay. I don't know if your parents let you go to these things unchaperoned.

MC: When I was little, I had to march in all of them.

JC: But what about when you were dating? How did that happen? What was that like, if you wanted to go out? Did you have to take your sisters with you, or your brothers?

MC: No, that was when I was working at the shop. That is where I met [*my husband*]. I was, what, seventeen? I started going out with my husband [*Joseph Tavares Correira*].

JR: You started going out at seventeen? Not before that?

MC: No. If I went out on a date, I had to be home by ten [*o'clock*] because my father got home from work at ten, and I had to be home before him. That went on for a long time. And after, I went out with my husband, what, five or six years, 'cause I told my father, I says, 'You know, Joe is going to give me a ring, and, you know, want to talk about getting married.' He said, 'Oh, no, we have to go to Portugal first.' I says, 'I don't want to go to Portugal. You are not going to marry me off out there.'

JR: Oh, was that the idea?

MC: Oh, yeah. So finally, we started going out. I had to be home by ten. Then, when he finally gave me the ring, the only one I could talk to was my mother, so I told her, 'You know, Ma, Joe is going to give me a ring.' I says, 'I am not going to keep going out with him. We are going to get married.' 'Oh yeah?' 'Okay.' My [*future*] mother-in-law [*Mrs. Manuel Tavares Correira, née Evangelina Soares-Farias*] had it all planned.

JR: Oh?

MC: Oh, yeah, I had to move in with her.

JR: Oh? So did she have daughters?

MC: Oh, yeah. [*Mrs. Manuel Estrella, née Mary Correira; Mrs. Henri Charette, née Emily Correira; Mrs. George Vallee, née Francelina Correira; Mrs. Emilio Dispirito, née Emma Correira; and Mrs. Joseph Costa, née Evangelina Correira.*]

JR: But you had to move into her house?

MC: I had to move in there.

JC: She didn't want to let go of my father [*her only son, Joseph Tavares Correira*].

MC: So we went, got married [*at Espirito Santo Church, Fall River, on November 25, 1948*]; I was there for what, nine years.

JR: Nine years in your mother-in-law's house?

MC: And let me tell you, I went through hell.

JR: Was that in the same neighborhood? Was it in the east end as well?

MC: [262] Pitman Street, [*Fall River.*]

JR: And you went through hell? I am not making light of that – I can imagine. How did you, how did you work through all those problems?

MC: I put one kid to bed, and then it was about maybe nine [*o'clock*]. And I would say, 'I got to work tomorrow, you know?' Here comes Emily [*her sister-in-law, Mrs. Henri Charette*] with her two kids [*Robert Charette and Barbara Charette*]. She was right in my bedroom, and she takes a kid out of the crib. I says, 'Emily, I got to work tomorrow.' 'Oh, you will be fine.' Oh, I didn't go for that.

JR: So, you had your children in your mother-in-law's house?

JC: She had just me [*Joanne Correira, born 1953*]; I was an infant. But the problem with my grandmother was that her house was Grand Central Station. All of her daughters, nieces, nephews …

MC: They lived downstairs, so it was like open house.

MC: I didn't have, the first five years I didn't have any kids. I had a problem, I didn't have any. After that … I told him, 'I got to get out of there.' Yeah, then, after, I told my husband, 'I can't keep up with this.' I says, 'We have to get a place.' Because he was so tied up with his mother, you know?

JR: Now, did he have brothers?

MC: Only sisters.

JR: So, just sisters, so she was kind of, didn't want him to leave. Didn't want her son to leave. Is that it?

JC: The only son and the youngest.

JR: Well, you had to pay into the house, didn't you? I mean, you had to pay for the food; you had to pay board.

MC: Oh, yeah.

JR: How did you work this out? How about the cooking and the buying groceries?

MC: Well, we used to take me and her shopping, you know? And, uh, she did the cooking. There was only supper time 'cause they had to work, and he worked. But like I said, I paid for my sins, let me tell you.

JR: How about chores around the house? Did you have to do a lot of housekeeping?

MC: My room.

JR: Just your room?

MC: And her [*her daughter, Joanne's*] room, and after I got fed up with that, I said, 'Joe, I can't keep up with this.' So, finally, I says, 'Look, either you go with me or you stay here.' Then I talked to my insurance man. He says, 'I got this here apartment for you.' I says, 'Where?' He says, [*'At 132*] Harrison Street, [*Fall River'*]. I says, 'Oh.'

JR: Not too far away.

MC: Oh, yeah, so I says, 'Yeah? Where is this?' He told me, he says, 'Come and see me tomorrow.' He was nice, he was real nice.

JR: So your insurance man owned the property.

JC: Mr. [*Frederick H.*] Sahady, wasn't it?

MC: Huh?

JC: Fred Sahady, Sahady Insurance? [*He was an agent for Prudential Insurance.*]

MC: I'm telling you, he was a nice guy; he saw what I went through. I have to set out my laundry; the laundry would come in, I would have to hang it all out, then take it all in. It was a bugger. Finally, when ... I talked to him [*her husband*], I says, 'Joe, we have to get a place, this is ridiculous.' So I told him, we came for a ride, we saw Tilly [*Mrs. Jesse Costa, née Clotilde 'Tilly' Camara, a co-worker and friend of the interviewee, who resided at 185 Gifford Road, Westport, Massachusetts,*] and she says, 'All that land is all free. All by one owner.' I says, 'Really?' So we bought it.... But my husband built the house; he did it himself.

JR: He was very talented ... you told me he was a mechanic in the shops.

MC: He fixed machines, he fixed everything.

JR: Sewing machines.

MC: Yeah.

JR: And he was a carpenter, too?

JC: He would work on the house 'til dark, and I can remember laying in the car.

MC: My father would come and help, too … and my mother would come, and she would sit downstairs, and watch my father spread the …

JC: Cement, for the bricks.

MC: Like I said, everything turned out okay.

JR: He knew that he wanted to provide for his family. I am going to go back to Pitman Street. Because we didn't cover the school, Espirito Santo [*Parochial*] School, [*Alden Street, corner Everett Street, Fall River*], this was a Catholic School. Tell me a little bit about Espirito Santo; how many grades were in that school, and how were the teachers?

MC: Eight grades.

JR: Eight grades. What about you? How about when you were going?

MC: Oh, I was doing fine. Oh yeah, I loved it. 'Cause there, when I got to sixth, no, eighth grade, I will never forget her, Mother Anjou [*of the order of Franciscan Missionaries of Mary, later known as Sister Lia Oliveira; a Fall River native, she taught sixth grade and religious instruction at Espirito Santo Parochial School for over forty years. Following retirement, she taught the Portuguese language in all grades in the school, and in several local parishes.*] She talked to me, says, 'Mary, would you like to come and see' – I don't know where the hell this place was, where the nuns were. [*The Franciscan Missionaries of Mary, Holy Family Convent, 385 Fruit Hill Avenue, North Providence, Rhode Island, was the novitiate of that religious order; the Mother House was in Rome. In Fall River, the Sisters resided at 621 Second Street.*]

JC: The convent.

JR: Oh, she was thinking you were going to be a nun?

MC: So, I says, 'Sure.' My mother almost flipped out. I went, I saw what they went through and all, and I says, 'Not for me.' Now, I graduated from there [*circa 1943*]. I went to [*B.M.C. Durfee*] High School, [*on Rock Street, Fall River,*] for two months.

JR: Very good. What happened there, two months?

MC: I went to work. My mother, my father, they needed the money.

JR: That was a very common thing.

MC: I was the second oldest one, so I had to go to work.

JC: And Uncle Manny [*the interviewee's brother, Manuel Vincent Arruda, Jr.*] was already working, right?

JR: Where was Manny working? Was it a mill, or a factory?

MC: I forget where he was working; then, he had to go in the service [*United States Navy, enlisted October 20, 1944, discharged April 24, 1946*].

JR: Okay, when you left [*B.M.C.*] Durfee High School, when you went to work to help.

MC: I went to work in the mills.

JR: Where did you work – what was that job?

MC: It was spinning.

JC: At the [*Berkshire*] Mill [*Berkshire Fine Spinning Associates, Inc.*].

JR: And that was where you met your husband?

MC: No, I met him [*Joseph Tavares Correira*], it was out of the shop, right near the mill. [*He was employed as a shipper at Compton Manufacturing Corporation, bathrobe manufacturers, 420 Quequechan Street, Fall River.*]

JR: It was after the Davis Mill – yeah.

MC: Yeah, they were making jackets [*Joseph Chromow & Co., women's and children's clothing, 420 Quequechan Street, Fall River; located in the same building as Compton Manufacturing Corporation, where Joseph Correira was employed.*] And I liked these jackets, they were nice; I wanted a black one. So, he was like, a … mechanic or whatever, he come up and says, 'What are you looking for?' I says, 'I like these jackets, I want to get a jacket.' He goes and gets me a red one. I says, 'I don't want a red one.' 'Oh, this is a nice color.' I says, 'I want a black one,' and he's looking, 'But the red one is better.' I says, 'Look, either I get a black one or I don't get one at all.' So, he got me a black one, and he started giving me a ride home, and that is how I met him.

JR: And this was a factory that made jackets?

MC: Yeah.

JR: Ladies jackets?

MC: Right upstairs, women's jackets.

JC: Do you remember what street that one was on?

MC: Quequechan Street.

JR: Quequechan Street, okay.

JC: Was it upstairs from Stella Anne [*Frocks, Inc.*]? Because we had Stella-Anne [*Frocks, Inc., 420 Quequechan Street, Fall River*], and we had Shelburne Shirt [*Company, Inc., 111 Alden Street, Fall River*], then we had Klear-Vu [*Corporation, plastic accessories, 420 Quequechan Street*].

MC: I forgot. But, anyway that was where I worked. Not for too long, 'cause, hey, I had to walk it, you know? Then, that's when I went into ... Shelburne making cuffs ...

JR: Okay.

MC: Shirt cuffs.

JR: And maybe that was what year?

JC: I was in kindergarten. So, that would have been approximately ... 1957.

JR: 1957 ... okay. I've heard Shelburne was a pretty tough place to work in, it was very demanding. Is that true?

MC: The head floor lady – she was tough. The hell was her name?

JR: You were on cuffs. How does, how do you do cuffs on a shirt? If you want to describe that?

MC: We didn't put it on the shirt, I made the cuff.

JR: Oh, you did.

MC: You take the one that had the button [*hole*], and I put it on the other one, and stitched it right around. Every time she would get tired she would come and sit, and say, 'Mary, let me see something.' She would sit at my machine and sew. I would say, 'This is pretty good.'

JR: So, you made the cuff that would go to another person, and then that ...

MC: She would attach it to the shirt. It was nice, I liked working there.

JR: Was that piecework?

MC: Oh, yeah. Then after that I went downstairs.

JR: We talk about all the years working [*and*] there is a lot of technology that pertains to our life, and I will go back a little bit, and I will ask you, in your family, on Pitman Street, did you have a radio? Do you remember when you had a radio?

MC: Oh, yeah.

JR: When was that?

MC: We had a radio in the house.

JR: When you were growing up, or was it later?

MC: No, when I was brought up.

JR: Just one radio, I imagine. And what about the – heating the house? Were there wood stoves or coal stoves? I'm going back to my own grandmother at this time, because she had coal stoves.

MC: I don't remember.

JR: Or, gas heaters?

MC: I don't know.

JC: I am going to jump in and say it was gas heaters.

JR: Do you remember your refrigerator?

MC: Oh, yeah, we had to put ice in it.

JR: And I bet it was a small one.

MC: A lot of times, my father would say, 'Come on,' and he would go get the wagon and go down and get ice. Oh …

JC: Thinking back now, on the Cash Street apartment, as a child, the toilet was a pull chain and the tank was above your head, and I can remember … you always worried the water was going to tip over on you, on top of you.

JR: Of course, I don't think any of those apartments at the time had hot water. You had to …

MC: No, we had to warm the water.

JR: You had to heat your water.

MC: No [*bath*] tubs. We had this big thing like this, and I would say, Saturday was, it was Saturday nights, I would say, 'Okay.' The baby was first, the little one was first, wash them, and the second one, and the third. Then, empty that [*water*] out and get some more warm water for the others. By the time it was my turn, I just laid in there. My mother would say, 'Hey, you going to sleep there or what?' I says, 'Right now I am tired, too tired to sleep.'

JR: You are spunky, Mary, you are pretty spunky.

MC: So, I had to take my bath; it was rough. But it was, the people were nice on Cash Street.

JR: Shopping in that area, where did you go for your groceries?

MC: My father did the shopping. Where the hell did he go?

JR: I know there weren't any supermarkets like today.

MC: No, there wasn't. There was this big place where they sold like fruit and vegetables; [*I*] forgot the name of the bloody place. And I used to laugh, at the end of the summer, my father would say, I says, 'Oh boy here we go.' We should go to the places where they just sold fruit so we could make the wine.

JR: Okay, so, he made that from purchased fruit, because I know a lot of people in that area of Fall River had grape vines.

MC: We used to buy the pigs; kill them, and then bring them home.

JR: That also was very popular. I think it was done during certain times of the year, especially maybe, tied into [*the church*] feasts, where a family would butcher a pig and make their chourico [*a spicy Azorean pork sausage*], and morcela [*Azorean black pudding, a highly-seasoned blood sausage*].

MC: My father used to do that, and I was right in the middle of it.

JR: And also, peppers, too, I think; very popular at the end of the summer.

MC: We used to go to all these stores on Pleasant Street [*in Fall River*].

JC: I still remember their hands being swollen – she [*the interviewee*] and my [*maternal*] grandmother, as a child I used to watch – they had the grinders, and they would grind the pepper and onion, and they would make these sauces and can them, and I can remember their hands being like blistered from that.

JR: So, canning, you did canning in the house at the end of the summer? I know that was a popular thing to do as well.

MC: Yeah, well, a lot of the [*hand-cranked*] grinder, pepper [*pimenta moida, an Azorean relish-like condiment, often used in cooking*], cut up onions, and stuff like that. We used to put it in the big jars, oh, yeah.

JR: Now, you were born in 1928. So you were kind of coming in just before the Great Depression … you were growing up during the Depression. What was that like?

MC: A lot of people knew my father.

JR: Was he working during those years?

MC: He worked at the mill.

JR: He was working?

MC: He used to go in – what – twelve o'clock, and come home at ten.

JR: That was unusual, because a lot of people weren't working, you know?

MC: He was, he was, and my mother, too.

JR: So, the Depression, you would have been a small girl at the time, growing up … and you had older brothers, and older family members.

MC: I only had one older brother [*Manuel Vincent Arruda, Jr.*]; the others were all younger.

JR: And they were working?

MC: No, only my….

JR: They weren't working during that time?

MC: Nope.

JR: What did they end up doing? What kind of work did they end up doing? I know this was a time when a lot of people were on welfare, too.

MC: No, not us.

JC: My grandparents were too proud to ask for any help, and they all went to school. I mean you [*the interviewee*] were working, Uncle Manny [*the interviewee's eldest brother*] was working, but all the others were in school.

JR: In school at the Espirito Santo [*Parochial School*] … you had to pay tuition, I think. Did you have to pay tuition in the Catholic school? I know they do today, but I am not sure in those days.

JC: I don't think they paid tuition, because my grandfather worked at the church on Sunday – he would pass the collection boxes. But he also did a lot of the work on the Church grounds, so if there were some kind of a barter program – he worked at the church and volunteered so much – then the children were probably allowed to go at a greatly reduced rate, is what I am guessing. Because there was no money; it was almost a bartering system.

JR: Yeah, interesting, very interesting. You mention one favorite teacher at the Espirito Santo [*Parochial School*], and I didn't catch her name.

MC: Mother Anjou [*Franciscan Missionaries of Mary, later known as Sister Lia Oliveira*].

JR: Anjou. That's angel, isn't it? I am trying to …

MC: She was great; she was the one that was trying to talk me into being a nun.

JR: I think that was probably what a lot of the nuns did, you know, try to do a little recruiting.

MC: They even took me to some place in [*North*] Providence. [*The Franciscan Missionaries of Mary, Holy Family Convent, 385 Fruit Hill Avenue, North Providence, Rhode Island*].

JC: That was the convent.

MC: To go look at the place. [*The Holy Family Convent was the novitiate of the order of the Franciscan Missionaries of Mary.*]

JC: They only had one lay teacher at the Espirito Santo [*Parochial*] School, and that was their kindergarten teacher, who was Miss [*Mary Espirito Santo*] Cabral, and what is amazing is that my mom [*the interviewee*] had her for kindergarten, and so did I, so, she was there for a very long time. [*Miss Cabral taught kindergarten at Espirito Santo Parochial School for fifty-three years, from 1925 – 1978.*]

JR: I think you went on a little bit already about your marriage. You know, when living with your mother-in-law. When you set up your own home, you had your landlord, you were with your mother-in-law, then set up your own home. Then, you had another child?

JC: My brother Joey [*Joseph Anthony Correira*]; he was born in 1957, I was born in '53. [*The couple's third child, Lorianne Correira, was born in 1963.*]

JR: And you were working at the Shelburne then, and that was in the '50s?

JC: Late '50s.

JR: That would have been a big change for you to leave the city to come to the country.

MC: I couldn't wait.

JR: I can imagine, and Gifford Road [*in Westport, Massachusetts,*] probably was very, very rural.

JC: As a child, we could walk and not see a house, and we could be free to roam.

JR: So, what were some of your traditions? How did you celebrate holidays?

MC: We did them like everyone else.

JR: And all the relatives come here? This is the central point?

JC: This is the …

MC: The downstairs was all finished…. But it was always open house, and especially when it was the Holy Ghost. It was open house. Oh, God, it was really something.

JR: I remember the Flint [*section of Fall River*] a little bit too, and I remember the movies you could go to in the Flint, and the restaurants.

MC: Yes, that was on Pleasant Street, the Strand [*Theatre, 1363 Pleasant Street, Fall River*].

JR: And a lot of good restaurants.

MC: Oh, yeah, Farinha's [*Manuel Farinha, restaurant, 160 Alden Street, Fall River*] was right at the corner there.

JC: Farinha's was at the corner of Alden [*Street*] – it's just at the bend … almost diagonally across from Shelburne Shirt, and as a kindergartner, I would walk from Espirito Santo [*Parochial School*] to this Farinha's Restaurant to meet my mother for lunch. And then she would leave Shelburne, have lunch with me, [*and*] I would walk back unescorted, unattended, at four-and-a-half years old.

MC: She didn't have to cross no street.

JC: She would cross me and then I would walk three blocks to Espirito Santo [*Parochial School*] … and you didn't have to worry.

JR: That's amazing.

MC: Mrs. [*Maria J.*] Farinha, [*the wife of Manuel Farinha*] hired me.

JC: The lady in the restaurant?

MC: 'Maria,' she says, 'Go to work for me.' I said, 'I have got to work,' she says, 'No, just at noontime…. You work for me, you get free meal.'

JR: So, you were working at noontime when you were supposed to be having your lunch.

MC: So after, everybody's all fed, she would say, 'Okay, sit down, what do you want to eat?' Then she would go get my plate.

JR: Was this while you were still working in the Shelburne? You didn't miss a minute.

JC: A working lunch hour.

MC: She was good.

JR: That is something in a good Portuguese.

MC: It was, it was.

JR: There was another restaurant up on Pleasant Street which was very popular, and it really speaks to the fact that that was a neighborhood of Portuguese and Lebanese, certainly the French [*Canadians*].

MC: Oh, yeah, there was a mixture there.

JR: It was very diverse, and people talk about diversity, but it was a good mix of various immigrant groups.

MC: It was good.

JR: So, looking back at all of this work in Fall River, if you want to pick up on some of these factories, think of any of the factories that you were working in.

MC: Yeah, I went from Shelburne, I went to …

JC: You made pillows; Klear-Vu.

MC: Then I went to the other one. I forgot.

JC: Bomark Manufacturing [*Bomark Corporation, pillow manufacturer, 135 Alden Street, Fall River*] is where she went after Shelburne, and that was right next door.

JR: And that was what kind of work in Bomark?

JC: You were making pillows; they made pillows and cushions. Actually, that was her last place of employment.

MC: Yeah.

JR: So, you retired from Bomark.

MC: That was the one when I told the boss, 'This is my last week here.'

JC: He is the one who gave you the $100 to stay?

MC: No, he sent me upstairs to the head boss, because when there was a Portuguese people coming in, I would be the one to go teach them, you know? This lady, I says to her, you know, 'Fars â sin,' ['*Do it this way,*'] then he'd come and talk to me, and she says, 'How come he comes to talk to you in English?' I says, 'Would you understand him?' She says 'No.' I says, 'Well'.

JR: So you were kind of interpreting and kind of training at the same time.

MC: After, when I told them the week was [*over*] on a Friday. I says, 'I got to talk to you.' He says, 'Come by my office.' I go in his office, he says, 'What is the matter?' I says … 'This is my last week.' 'What do you mean, this is your last week?' I says, 'My husband is home, I am working,' I says, 'I don't think that's fair.' So, he looked at me, says, 'Alright,' [a*nd*] he sent me back to my chair. I continued finishing the work that day, all of a sudden I see him come up to me. I says, 'Oh no,' he says, 'Mr. Mintz would like to see you.' I says, 'Oh, shoot.'

JR: Let's hear that name again?

MC: Mr. Mintz; he was the head one. [*Jacob 'Jack' Mintz, president, Klear-Vu Corporation, and Bomark Corporation*]. I went upstairs, I was there for a long time, and he gets up, he comes and locks the door…. Then he goes, and goes and locks the other door. I just sat there. So, he said, 'I can't talk you out of it?' I says, 'No.' I says, 'I got to retire. It's about time I did.' So, he says, 'Well, are you going to finish the week, the day, or what?' I says, 'This is my last day.' He says, 'Oh,' then he gets up, so I got up, and he come up to me, and says, 'Well … if you ever change your mind, just call me.' I says, 'Okay.'

JR: You were a good worker, so he didn't want to lose good workers.

MC: So, he comes, shook my hand, he said, 'I wish you a lot of luck'. I says, 'Thank you' … he just shook hands, and I said to myself, 'what the hell did he put in my hand?' I walk out the door; he put $100 in my hand. I said, 'I'm not going to change my mind.'

JR: How old were you then, and how many years had you been working?

MC: Let me see, I retired …

JC: You were about sixty-eight.

MC: I was almost, it was almost time for me to retire in my sixties.

JR: You were in your sixties.

MC: Yeah, so my husband was home, so, what the hell? What was he doing home? I should be home.

JR: He was already retired.

MC: Oh, yeah. So, I retired, and that was it.

JC: He was a good boss, Mr. Mintz, though.

MC: Oh, yeah, he was.

JC: You used to talk about how he would deliver ice cream to all the workers on Fridays in the summer.

MC: When he came downstairs, I wouldn't even look at him.

JC: Why?

MC: Hey, I didn't want to get too chummy with him, he would talk me out of it.

JR: You were one of the favorites. They had favorites in the shops, and there were favorites everywhere – wherever you work, there is always a little bit of favoritism.

MC: When he used to come downstairs, and we see him walking up that hallway, he come straight to my machine.

JR: Now, Mary, when you retired, what were you going to be getting as a retirement? Where you worked, did they have unions, did they have union dues?

MC: Oh, yeah.

JR: So, what was the union then? You were retired from?

MC: I don't know.

JC: The check that I get for you every month is from the International Ladies Garment Workers Union [*ILGWU, Local 178, Fall River*].

JR: International Ladies Garment Workers Union. Okay, because Shelburne was Amalgamated [*Clothing Workers of America, Local No. 177 and 376, 413 South Main Street, Fall River*].

MC: That's right.

JR: Shelburne was Amalgamated [*Clothing Workers of America*], so, you kind of had two different unions there. How did that work out, did you get money from both?

MC: I don't remember.

JR: It's okay, I'm just going to go back a minute and try to figure out, when you retired, where your benefits were coming from; if they come from the union? You are probably going to get Social Security, too.

JC: She gets a monthly Social Security check, and ... she gets a monthly union check. Right, Mom, you get two checks every month? You get the one from Social Security, which is your big check, and then you get the small check.

JR: Which is, you said, is from ILGW [*International Ladies Garment Workers Union*], and I guess somewhere in there, I'm trying to think ... you might have not had enough years in the Amalgamated [*Clothing Workers of America*]. You probably lost those years ... I know my mother did. She was right there from the beginning of Amalgamated, and then left ... and she was short a few years, even though she was already vested in it. So there was a big disappointment ... when you worked that long and you pay in, and you don't get anything back. I think we have done about an hour of this .... I am going to leave it at this point ... I want to thank you so much for helping us.

PHOTO GALLERY

5.2 Mary's father, Manuel Vincent Arruda, Sr., 1920s. *"A lot of people knew my father."*

5.1 Mary's father, Manoel Vincente d' Arruda, Sr., as a young man; upon settling in the United States, he anglicized his name to Manuel Vincent Arruda, Sr. *'My father was* [from Bretanha] *... St. Michael's"*

5.3 Mary's parents, as attendants at the wedding of an unidentified couple, late 1920s. Standing: Mary's father, Manuel Vincent Arruda, Sr.; and her mother, née Maria Souza. *"They met here."*

5.4 Mary's mother and maternal grandmother looking out the window of the family's second-floor tenement at 293 Jenckes Street, Fall River, Massachusetts, 1929. Left: Mrs. Manuel Vincent Arruda, née Maria Souza; right, Mrs. Manuel Carreiro de Souza, née Senhorinha Moniz Borges. *"We all lived in one house."*

5.5 Mary with her father, Manuel Vincent Arruda, Sr., and her eldest brother, Manuel, Jr., circa 1930; the photograph was possibly taken in the yard of the family residence at 293 Jenckes Street, Fall River, Massachusetts. *"I was the second oldest."*

5.6 Espirito Santo Church, 295 Alden Street, Fall River, Massachusetts, 1962. *"Oh, we all went to Espirito Santo Church. Sunday, we, everybody had to go to church."*

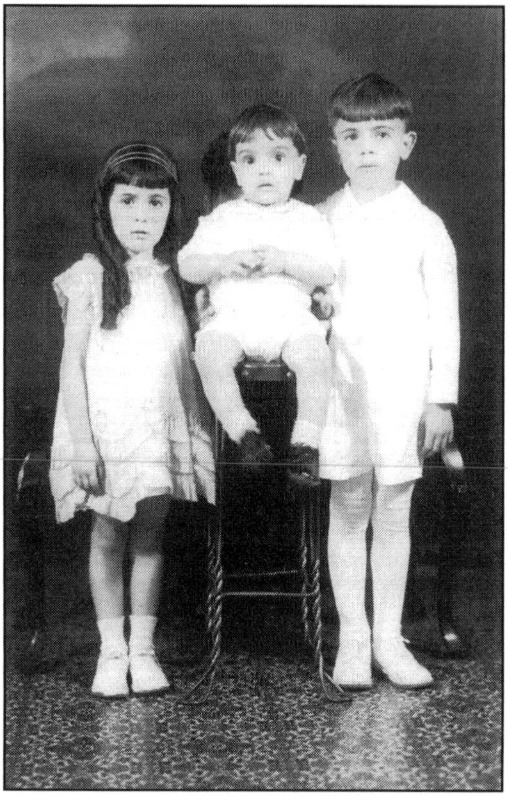

5.7 The three eldest Arruda children, circa 1932. Left to right: Mary Vincent Arruda; John Vincent Arruda; and Manuel Vincent Arruda, Jr. *"It was Manny, it was me, and then it was* [John]*."*

5.8 Mary's maternal grandmother, Mrs. Manuel Carreiro de Souza, née Senhorinha Moniz Borges, in a photograph taken on her eightieth birthday, 1960; she lived with Mary's parents, and was "a great help." *"I will never forget it. Every time a baby was born, my grandmother would come and say, 'You watch him.' They would come and bring them to me because* [my mother] *had them at home."*

5.9 Mother Anjou, Franciscan Missionaries of Mary, later known as Sister Lia Oliveira. *"She was great; she was the one that was trying to talk me into being a nun."*

5.10 Mary's graduating class from Espirito Santo Parochial School, Fall River, Massachusetts, June 21, 1944; Mary is in the middle row, second student from the left. *"I graduated from there. I went to high school for two months. I* [left and] *went to work. My mother, my father, they needed the money."*

5.11 An unidentified woman inspecting cloth at Berkshire Fine Spinning Associates, Inc., Fall River, Massachusetts, 1940; Mary was employed here in 1944. *"We all worked there."*

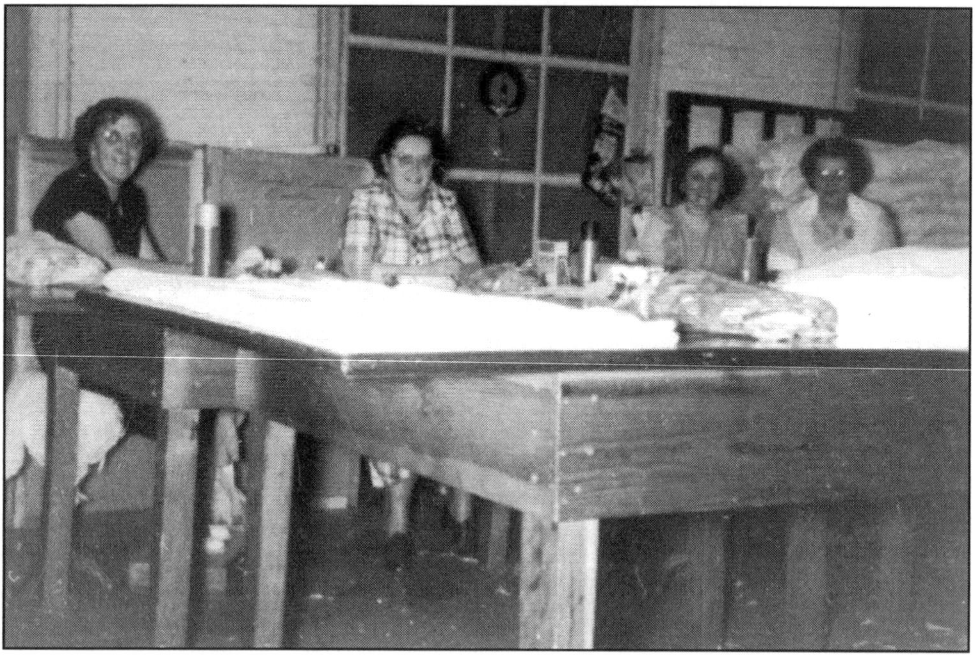

5.12 A group of unidentified women enjoying their lunch break, Berkshire Fine Spinning Associates, Inc., Fall River, Massachusetts, 1950s; Mary was employed here in 1944. *"I was, I was a helper."*

5.13 Mary in a 1940s snapshot; she never learned how to ride a bicycle.

5.14 Mary's mother, Mrs. Manuel Vincent Arruda, Sr., née Maria Souza. *"Hey, you going to sleep there or what?"*

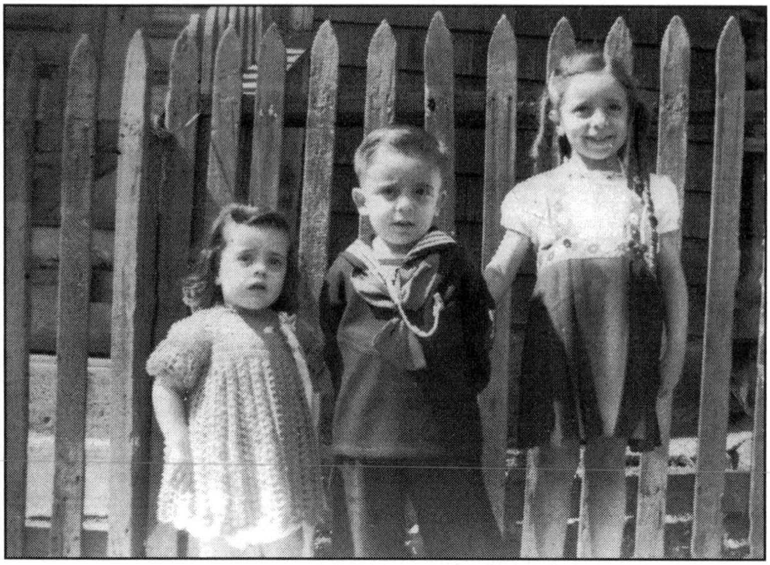

5.15 Three of Mary's siblings, circa 1946. Left to right: Rita Vincent Arruda; David Vincent Arruda; and Irene Vincent Arruda. *"I would say, 'Another one? Another one for me to take care of?' Hey. I was the oldest girl."*

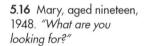

5.16 Mary, aged nineteen, 1948. *"What are you looking for?"*

5.17 Mary and her husband, Joseph Tavares Correira, shortly after their marriage. *"I met him, it was ... right near the mill."*

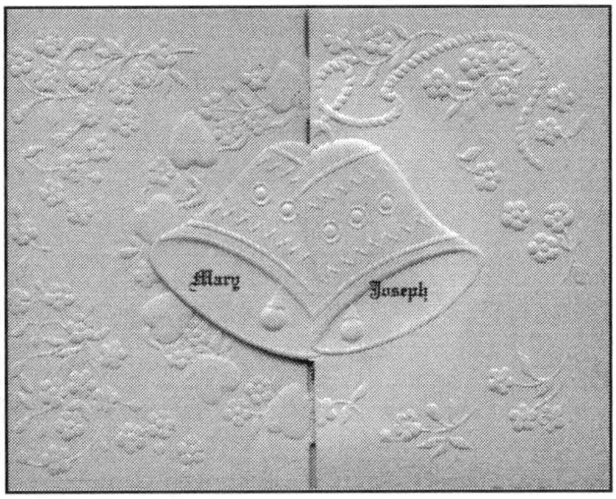

5.18 Mary and Joseph's wedding invitation, 1949. *"Mr. and Mrs. Joseph V. Arruda request the honor of your presence ..."*

5.19 Mr. & Mrs. Joseph Tavares Correira on their wedding day, November 24, 1949, posing with their wedding party. Back row, left to right: Lorraine Paradis, a friend of the bride; the groom's niece, Patricia Ann Estrella; the bride's sister-in-law, Hazel H. Arruda; the bride's father, Manuel Vincent Arruda, Sr.; the bride; the groom; the bride's brother, Manuel Vincent Arruda, Jr.; the bride's brother, John Vincent Arruda; and the groom's nephew, Antonio Estrella. Front row, left: Laura Dispirito, the groom's niece, as flower girl. Front row, right: the bride's brother, David Vincent Arruda, as ring bearer. Mary to her father: *"I don't want to go to Portugal. You are not going to marry me off out there."*

5.20 Mr. & Mrs. Joseph Tavares Correira on their wedding day, November 24, 1949; the couple were married at Espirito Santo Church in Fall River, Massachusetts. *"You know, Ma, Joe is going to give me a ring. I am not going to keep going out with him. We are going to get married."*

5.21 Mary's mother-in-law, Mrs. Manuel Tavares Correira, née Evangelina Soares-Farias, circa 1940s; the strong-willed woman was devoted to her only son, Joseph Tavares Correira. *"Okay, my mother-in-law had it all planned ... I had to move in with her. And let me tell you, I went through hell. I paid for my sins."*

5.22 The newlywed Mr. & Mrs. Joseph Tavares Correira, with their parents, and Mary's maternal grandmother, in the parlor of the Arruda residence, 85 Cash Street, Fall River, Massachusetts, November 24, 1949. Left to right: the groom's mother, Mrs. Manuel Tavares Correira, née Evangelina Soares-Farias; the groom; the bride; Mary's father, Manuel Vincent Arruda, Sr.; Mary's mother, née Maria Souza; Mary's grandmother, Mrs. Manuel Carreiro de Souza, née Senhorinha Moniz Borges. *"I was married from Cash Street."*

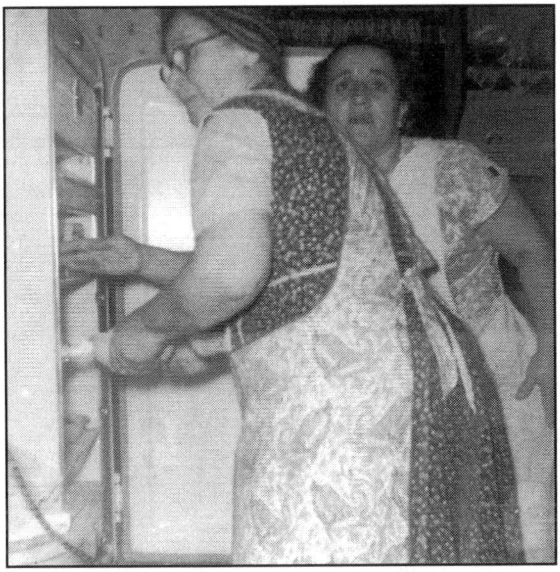

5.23 Mary's mother-in-law and sister-in-law in the kitchen of the family residence, 262 Pitman Street, Fall River, Massachusetts, early 1950s. Left to right: Mary's mother-in-law, Mrs. Manuel Tavares Correira, née Evangelina Soares-Farias; Mary's sister-in-law, Mrs. George Vallee, née Francelina Correira. Tenement kitchens in Fall River were compact, but despite their small size, women managed to cook for large families. *"And uh, she did the cooking."*

5.24 The bust of *Senhor Santo Cristo,* resting on its elaborate palanquin, photographed while ensconced in Espirito Santo Church, Fall River, Massachusetts, 1940s; it was considered a high honor to be one of the four men chosen to carry the bust during Holy Ghost Procession. *"My* [father] *... he'd carry the bust of Christ."*

5.25 *Below:* Mary's father, Manuel Vincent Arruda, Sr. participating in a Holy Ghost Procession from Espirito Santo Church, Fall River, Massachusetts, 1940s. One of the four men selected to carry the palanquin containing the bust of *Senhor Santo Cristo,* he traditionally occupied the front right. *"My* [father] *was very involved in the Espirito Santo procession."*

5.26 Mary's father, Manuel Vincent Arruda, Sr. participating in a Holy Ghost Procession from Espirito Santo Church, Fall River, Massachusetts, 1940s. He is second from the left, carrying the bust of *Senhor Santo Cristo*. *"He used to collect at the churches; he collected the money … if there was anything to be done, he would be right there."*

5.27 Mary's parents and youngest siblings, 1953. Back row, left to right: Mrs. Manuel Vincent Arruda, Sr., née Maria Souza; Manuel Vincent Arruda, Sr.; and Irene Vincent Arruda. Front row, left to right: David Vincent Arruda; Rita Vincent Arruda; and Leo Vincent Arruda. *"On, no, another one."*

5.28 Mary's three youngest siblings, participating in a Holy Ghost Procession from Espirito Santo Church, Fall River, Massachusetts, circa 1949. Left to right: David Vincent Arruda; Rita Vincent Arruda; Leo Vincent Arruda. *"I looked forward to that."*

5.29 Mary's parents posing with friends, 1950s; among the group are Mr. & Mrs. Manuel Farinha, neighbors who owned Farinha's Restaurant, 160 Alden Street, Fall River, Massachusetts. Standing, left to right: unidentified woman; Mary's father, Manuel Vincent Arruda, Sr.; Mary's mother, née Maria Souza; unidentified woman; unidentified man. Kneeling, left: Mrs. Maria J. Farinha, the wife of Manuel Farinha; kneeling, right; Manuel Farinha. *"'Maria,' she says, 'Go to work for me ... just at noontime. You work for me, you get free meal.'"*

5.30 Mary's father, Manuel Vincent Arruda, Sr. posing with a group of his fellow workers at Berkshire Fine Spinning Associates, Inc., Fall River, Massachusetts, late 1950s; Mary's father is standing, third from the left. *"My father was a* [weaver] *... in the mill."*

5.31 Mary's husband, Joseph Tavares Correira, constructing a new residence for his family in Westport, Massachusetts, circa 1956; a very talented carpenter, he built the house himself. *"My husband built this house. He did it himself."*

5.32 Mary's daughter, Joanne Correira (center), marching in a Holy Ghost Procession from Espirito Santo Church, Fall River, Massachusetts, 1959. *"We were in that every year."*

5.33 The former Wampanoag Mills, Fall River, Massachusetts, 1980s. The buildings housed Shelburne Shirt Company, Inc., and Bomark Manufacturing/Klear-Vu Corporation; Mary worked for both companies, and retired from the latter. *"Yeah, I went from Shelburne, I went to ... Bomark."*

5.34 Jacob "Jack" Mintz, president, Bomark Corporation and Klear-Vu Corporation, Fall River, Massachusetts; well-liked by his employees, he would habitually deliver ice cream, candy bars, and cold drinks to his employees. *"He was a good boss. 'Thank you' ... he put $100 in my hand."*

5.35 Mary and her husband preparing for an Espirito Santo Church Holy Ghost Feast, 1992. The crown, a Correira family heirloom, is a replica of the crown of the 13th century Queen St. Elizabeth (Isabel) of Portugal, who founded *the Festas do Espirito Santo. "We have the crown ... a sterling silver crown. So we carry our own crown."*

SIX:

MARIE LILLIAN DESCHENES

Personal Statistics

Name: Marie Lillian Deschenes

Date of Birth: July 8, 1926

Place of Birth: Fall River, Massachusetts

Father: François Xavier Deschenes (1882-1972)

Mother: Albertina Boursier Martin (1886-1957)

Siblings:

Marie Blanche Irene Deschenes (1908-1996)
---(Mrs. Aime Horace Bouchard)
Joseph Albert Octave Deschenes (1909-1980)
Joseph Leo Pierre Deschenes (1911-1926)
Joseph Henri Deschenes (1913-2003)
Marie Dorille Rita Deschenes (1914-2003)
---(Mrs. Joseph Ovila Roy)
Joseph Lionel John Deschenes (1916-1995)
Marie Rita Deschenes (1918-1945)
---(Sister Marie Xavier)
Marie Alice Deschenes (1920-2010)
---(Mrs. Joseph Armande Cote)
Joseph Deschenes (1921-2010)
Marie Lillianne Deschenes (1923-1999)
---(Mrs. George Noël Petrin)
Marie Anita Deschenes (born 1924)
---(Mrs. Joseph Pineau)
Joseph Arthur Albert Deschenes (1927-1972)
Marie Theresa Deschenes (1929-1930)
Marie Gracella Deschenes (1931-2013)
---(Sister Marie Albert)

Employment history:

Har-Lee Manufacturing Company, Fall River
Louis Hand, Inc., Fall River

EDITED TRANSCRIPT

Interview with Marie Lillian Deschenes

Interviewer: (JR) Joyce B. Rodrigues, Fall River Historical Society

Interviewee: (LD) Marie Lillian Deschenes

Additional Commentary: (CN) Claire Marie (Petrin) Norfolk, Lillian's niece

Date of Interviews: August 22 & August 29, 2015

Location: Deschenes residence, Fall River, Massachusetts

Summary by Joyce B. Rodrigues:

Marie Lillian Deschenes was born in Fall River on July 8, 1926.

Lillian, who never married, comes from a family of fifteen: six boys and nine girls. She is twelfth in line. Her story is one of family, church, and work.

Work Years:

Lillian worked a total of forty-six years for two world-class manufacturers in Fall River, Massachusetts. For twenty-six of those years, she was employed in the packing department at the Har-Lee Manufacturing Company, a union shop. "The Har-Lee," the largest cotton dress manufacturer in the United States, closed in 1957.

She was then similarly employed for twenty years by Louis Hand Inc., also a union shop, and the nation's largest curtain and drapery manufacturer. In the 1950s and 1960s, Fall River ranked first as a curtain manufacturing city with up to twenty-three manufacturers and sales outlets. She retired in 1988 at the age of sixty-two with a Social Security and ILGWU pension.

Louis Hand, Inc.:

Louis Hand, Inc. was located at 847 Pleasant Street in the former Pilgrim Mills. The mill was built in 1911 from red brick and was the first mill in Fall River to be powered entirely by electricity provided from the local grid. It produced cotton cloth.

By 1945, Louis Hand, Inc. had acquired the building and was employing 600 workers. The company changed hands at least two more times between 1979 and 2000. The plant closed in March 2008.

The Deschenes Family and the Catholic Church:

Lillian's father, François Xavier Deschenes, and mother, Albertina (Boursier) Martin, emigrated from Canada to Fall River in 1892 and 1896 respectively. They met in Fall River and were married in the Church of the Blessed Sacrament in 1907.

In 1888, Blessed Sacrament began as a mission of St. Anne's Church, the first French-speaking church in Fall River dating from 1869. The church was built in 1902 as a national parish to serve the French-Canadian working population who lived in the south end of Fall River near the Tiverton, Rhode Island, line. The parish had a school and a convent of religious teaching nuns, the Sisters of St. Joseph du Puy.

As members and attendance later dwindled, Blessed Sacrament held on to celebrate its 100th anniversary with a final Mass on June 2, 2002. The church was later demolished in 2008.

All of the Deschenes children were born at home. They were educated in French-speaking Catholic schools and then went to work to support the family: "They quit school and went to work, and that was what you did….We had no choice."

Their pay was turned over "to the house." Family members received spending money and lived at home until marriage.

Lillian's immediate family of fourteen brothers and sisters also included paternal and maternal extended families. Her narrative describes family life: the day-to-day running of the household, the work experiences of her brothers and sisters, her brothers' service in World War II, and post-war life in Fall River.

Growing up meant plenty of sharing, family entertainment, and family outings. Growing up also meant that older siblings took care of younger siblings. This commitment continued into adult years as Lillian's older sister, Marie Dorille "Dot," who had cared for all of her younger brothers and sisters, also cared for their mother who passed away in 1957.

Lillian and two sisters inherited the family home after their father remarried in 1962. Francois Xavier Deschenes passed away in 1972.

Today, Lillian is the matriarch to the next generation of Deschenes family members, and is cared for by her niece and family historian, Claire Marie (Petrin) Norfolk.

Note: This interview has been slightly edited for continuity and readability; in order to preserve the integrity of the conversation, the phraseology remains that of the interviewer and interviewee. Italicized information in square brackets has been added for the purposes of clarification and context.

JR: So, I want to get started. This is quite a story. Lillian lives on Detroit Street [*and*] is from a large family … from the French community background in Fall River, so there is plenty to talk about. And I am going to start by asking her about her family. How did they come to Fall River? How did your family settle in Fall River? Why did they come to Fall River?

CN: Where did they come from?

LD: They come from Canada.

CN: And why did they come here, what do you think? Why did they come to Fall River?

JR: Did your father [*François Xavier Deschenes*] and mother [*née Albertina Boursier Martin*] come together, or did they come separately?

CN: Mémère [*grandmother*] and Pépere [*grandfather*] came from Canada and they met here....

JR: So, they, your mother and father, met in Fall River.

CN: Yes.

LD: Yes.

JR: And they got married in Fall River?

LD: Yes.

JR: Where did they get married?

LD: They got married in the Blessed Sacrament Church [*Church of the Blessed Sacrament, 2460 South Main Street.*]

CN: In what year, do you remember?

LD: [*September 23,*] 1907.

JR: 1907. And where did they live when they, after they got married? Did they live here on Detroit Street or somewhere else?

LD: No, they lived in ...

CN: They lived everywhere ... the Martins was my ... great grandfather's family.

JR: M-A-R-T-I-N-S?

CN: Yes, without the 'S,' [*Jean Baptiste Martin and his second wife, née Philomena Côte, and their children immigrated to Fall River in 1896*] and then there were the Deschenes; they immigrated here in [*1892*] when my grandfather François Xavier Deschenes was 10 years old, and ...

LD: She will know more.

CN: I do, because I have done all the research.

JR: Well, Claire had done the genealogy.

CN: So, that's why I can give her a background.

JR: There are a lot of details.

CN: A lot of background here. And the Martins ... came [*to Fall River*] in [*1896*]. They came from Acton, Bagot, Quebec, Canada, and the Deschenes came from Rimouski, [*Bas-Saint Laurent region, Quebec,*] Canada, [*in 1892*]. They came down separately.... They lived, they both lived in the Blessed Sacrament [*Church*] community [*in the south end of Fall River*]. The church was built in 1902. [*The cornerstone was laid in 1902; the building was dedicated in 1904*]. So, they were there before the church was built. I am thinking there must have been a small community before that. I don't remember ... but they met; how they met, we don't know. But they must have met in the community.

JR: When they came to Fall River, did they work in the mills?

CN: All, the whole family did. My great-grandfather [*Octave Miville Deschenes*] worked in the mills.

LD: I don't think my mother [*Mrs. François Xavier Deschenes, née Albertina Boursier Martin*] ever worked; my mother never worked as far as I know.

CN: Maybe before they got married?

LD: With fifteen kids, she didn't have time.

JR: I think that is true....

CN: So, I don't know, maybe Mémère might have worked before she got married, she might have. That, I bet, is a strong possibility. We don't know a lot.

JR: Maybe they met in the mills? Because that was often a very common story.

CN: Or at the church, somewhere like that. My great-grandmother [*Mrs. Octave Miville Deschenes, Sr., née Delvina Charette*] came here with my great-grandfather ... in [*1896*], and they had [*several*] kids that they brought with them. [*The children of Octave and Delvina were: Francois Xavier Deschenes; Octave Deschenes, Jr.; Joseph Octave Deschenes; Jean Baptiste Deschenes; Marie Louise Deschenes, later Mrs. Eugene Roussin; Flavie Deschenes; Paul Deschenes; Malvina Deschenes; Adelia Deschenes, later Mrs. Thomas Stephen Heron; Joseph Deschenes; and Martha Deschenes, later Mrs. Garant.*] And he [*Octave*] died [*on January 8,*] 1898, from ... typhoid fever.... And, um, my grandmother was a widow after that. So, Pépère [*François Xavier Deschenes*] was born in 1882, so ... he was sixteen years old when his dad died. And my great-grandmother's story is, is that she was a medicine woman in [*the*] Blessed Sacrament area. She would ... help all the people who were sick ... she would have her home remedies to, um, help the neighborhood and the whole community. Uncle Joe [*Joseph Deschenes*] was sick one time and his grandmother came to the house and gave him like a half of teaspoon of turpentine, and he was better the next day. So, we are not really sure how that happened....

JR: Well, you didn't have a lot of doctors. And I don't think you had a lot of money go to doctors.

LD: No, no, they – no.

JR: You say she was widowed. Left with how many children?

CN: Well, my grandfather was sixteen, so there must have been younger ones. I am not sure where in the family he falls – if he was the oldest or not – I don't remember. My guess is that he wasn't the oldest, but I'd have to look at the dates for that. Anyway.

JR: How did they manage after that? How did they manage to support themselves?

CN: So, all of the kids went to work in the factories. So, Pépère [*François Xavier Deschenes*] went to work in the factories, and his whole family was there and they are the ones that supported their mother and their apartment. I believe it was an apartment on Last Street. [*The widowed Mrs. Deschenes and her family resided at 81 Last Street, Fall River, circa 1902 – 1904; and at 134 Last Street, circa 1905 – 1908. From circa 1909 – 1910, they resided at 519 Summit Street, Fall River.*] And then [*circa 1911*] they moved to [*382*] Bay View Street as well. They had a couple of different places where grandmother lived. Um, but anyway, that was way back. So Aunt Lil [*the interviewee, Marie Lillian Deschenes*] didn't remember any of that stuff because that's stuff that I researched. That is stuff I found online, and I looked in all the [*Fall River City*] *Directories*, and their names are in the directories, and where they worked. So we know that Pépere [*François Xavier Deschenes*] worked in all those factories, and ... had lots of different jobs to support his family here [*after he married*], and moved around a lot, as they had [*fifteen*] children. Aunt Irene [*Marie Blanche Irene Deschenes*] was the first born, she was born in ... 1908.... So, they had gotten married [*on*] September [*23,*] 1907 and Irene was born right away. And, um, then all of the brothers, you know, three boys [*Joseph Albert Octave Deschenes; Joseph Leo Pierre Deschenes; Joseph Henri Deschenes*], and then Aunt Dot [*Marie Dorille Rita Deschenes*].

JR: So, Irene was the oldest?

LD: Irene was the oldest, yes.

CN: Followed by [*Joseph Lionel John Deschenes; Marie Rita Deschenes; Marie Alice Deschenes; Joseph Deschenes; Marie Lillianne Deschenes; Marie Anita Deschenes; Marie Lillian Deschenes; Joseph Arthur Albert Deschenes; Marie Theresa Deschenes; and Marie Gracella Deschenes*].

JR: So, Lillian, you're the fourth from the youngest. Okay, so your date of birth would be?

LD: July 8, 1926.

JR: Just to get an idea of how the family grew up, can you give me an idea … where they were working when they became of age? You know, as they grew up and as they moved along, what kind of jobs did they have in Fall River?

LD: They had dress shops and curtain factories.

JR: And your sisters and brothers, where did they work?

LD: Well, one sister [*Marie Alice Deschenes, later Mrs. Joseph Armande Cote*] worked at Shelburne [*Shirt Company, Inc., 111 Alden Street, Fall River*]. Another [*Marie Lillianne Deschenes, later Mrs. George Noel Petrin*] worked in Har-Lee [*Har-Lee Manufacturing Company, dress manufacturers, 426 Pleasant Street, Fall River*], and … my brothers worked at Thomas French.

JR: Thomas French?

LD: Thomas French [*& Sons, Ltd., Stevens Street, Fall River,*] yeah, that was down there, not too far.

JR: What kind of a company was that?

LD: I don't know what they did there [*cotton goods manufacturers*], but my two brothers [*Joseph Henri Deschenes, and Joseph Lionel John Deschenes*] worked there.

JR: Thomas French, where were they located?

LD: On [*Stevens Street*] somewhere, because it wasn't too far from me. They used to walk to go work.

CN: And Aunt Dot [*Marie Dorille Rita Deschenes, later Mrs. Joseph Ovila Roy*], where did she work?

LD: Aunt Dot worked, uh, Anderson Little [*Company Inc., men's clothing manufacturers, Stevens Street, Fall River*]. Anderson Little.

JR: Anderson Little, very good. Do you know what she did there? What kind of work she did at Anderson Little?

LD: She was a cutter.

JR: That is a very demanding, very exacting job; it's very dangerous, too.

LD: Al [*Joseph Albert Octave Deschenes*] worked at Shelburne [*Shirt Company, Inc., Fall River.*] Her [*the interviewee's niece, Mrs. John Barry Norfolk, née Claire Marie Petrin*] mother [*Marie Lillianne Deschenes, later Mrs. George Noel Petrin*] worked at Har-Lee, just like I did. And one of my sisters [*Marie Alice Deschenes, later Mrs. Joseph Armande Cote*] worked at, uh, Arkwright [*Corporation*] on [*Lewiston*] Street, [*Fall River*].

JR: Yes, the Arkwright Mill. Do you remember what she did there? What kind of work she did at the Arkwright?

LD: Some kind of curtains or something.

JR: It was curtains as well?

LD: I think it was curtains. [*Chace Mill Curtain Company, Lewiston Street, Fall River, was located in the former Arkwright Mill.*]

JR: I know Fall River had quite a number of curtain factories at one point, and also shirt factories. And we'll go back a second – you were telling me that two of your sisters went into the convent. Tell me about that.

LD: My sister Rita [*Marie Rita Deschenes, later Sister Marie Xavier of the order of Sisters of St. Joseph*] was the oldest one that was in the convent [*St. Thérèse of Lisieux Convent, New Bedford, Massachusetts*]. She was in there about – she died [*in*] 1945 … yeah, yeah. [*The cause of death was an 'acute sore throat with septicemia,' which was being treated in-house by the Sisters and advanced at an alarming rate; by the time medical attention was sought, it was too late.*] Then, Grace [*Marie Gracella Deschenes, later Sister Mary Albert of the order of Sisters of St. Joseph*] went in. She went in [*St. Thérèse of Lisieux Convent in*] 1950; she [*relinquished her vows*] in … 1960.

JR: Where did you all go to school? I mean, you had fifteen.

LD: We went to school at St. Jean's [*St. Jean Baptiste Parochial School, 65 Stockton Street and 364 Field Street, Fall River*].

JR: All the children went to St. Jean's?

LD: Yup. And Sister Mary Joseph [*Order of Sisters of St. Joseph du Puy*] taught most of my brothers and sisters. Sister Mary Joseph.

JR: She was your favorite teacher?

LD: She taught everybody.

JR: Very good. Did any of the children go past St. Jean's? Did they move any of your sisters and brothers go to high school?

LD: Yes, one of my sisters [*Marie Gracella Deschenes*] went to, uh, down the Flint [*section of Fall River*]. Jesus Mary [*Jesus Marie Academy, 138 St. Joseph Street, Fall River*], yes.

CN: She went there, she also went to Diman [*Vocational High School, Girl's Division, 45 Morgan Street, Fall River*] one year.

LD: She went to Diman, too. Yeah, yeah.

JR: And what was going on at Diman? I know Diman had power stitching classes.

LD: I don't know what she did there.

CN: I think that's what … just a little bit of background to that. Aunt Irene [*Marie Blanche Irene Deschenes, later Mrs. Aime Horace Bouchard*], who is the oldest in the family, was eighteen when they moved here to 47 Detroit Street [*in Fall River*]. So, prior to that, they lived [*at 145*] Baird Street [*in Fall River*]. So, for eighteen years, the family was transient, but they did stay on Baird Street for quite a while. [*The Deschenes family resided on Baird Street from circa 1912 -1920; prior to that, the family resided at 301 Flint Street, Fall River, and 134 Last Street, also in Fall River.*] But I don't know who lived on Baird Street or why they ended up in that house; all I can say is that it's very, very small. And then they moved from Baird Street to somewhere else. [*The Deschenes family moved to 548 Brayton Avenue, Fall River, circa 1921.*] But my mother [*Marie Lillianne Deschenes, later Mrs. George Noel Petrin*], who was [*the*] tenth born – she was born [*at 548*] Brayton Avenue in 1923, and she was the first baby to come into this house … all of the babies after that were born in this house.…

JR: All born in this house. Home-delivered. Home-delivery.

LD: Yup.

CN: Right there. And that is where Aunt Grace [*Marie Gracella Deschenes*] died a couple of years ago [*in 2013*].

JR: Did you have a midwife, or did your Mom know what was going on?

LD: No. She knew what was going on.

CN: Someone must have come here; who must have come here to help her? You don't know who delivered the babies? That's a very interesting thing.

JR: That is a very interesting question. You think maybe the neighbors knew what was, how to deliver children?

CN: That would be a great question to have asked Aunt Dot [*Mrs. Joseph Ovila Roy, née Marie Dorille Rita Deschenes*]. She was the one who lived in this house with Aunt Lil [*the interviewee*] and Aunt Grace [*Marie Gracella Deschenes*] for years since 1960.

1962 when Pépère [*François Xavier Deschenes*] moved away with Kay [*the widowed Kathleen May O'Neil, née Bean*] to get married. So … my grandmother died in 1957, Albertina Martin, who raised all those children in this house. And he remarried five years later, and left the house to Aunt Lil and the rest of the family.

JR: When those children were being born, did you know what was going on or did you have any idea?

LD: No, I was too small, I don't remember.

JR: So you moved into this house in what year again?

CN: 1923.

JR: 1923, you have been here …

CN: She was born in 1926.

JR: Born in this house and [*the Deschenes family*] moved in 1923, so you were really on Detroit Street and this house [*all your life*]. It must have been kind of a farm area at the time. It's a little rural, don't you think, because all of these homes that I see out there [*now*] are kind of modern homes. They were built later.

CN: How many houses were on this street when you were little?

LD: All these houses weren't here and there was nobody here. [*In 1926, the year of the interviewee's birth, there were twenty-four residences on Detroit Street; the figure was the same two decades later.*]

CN: Across the street [*at 48 Detroit Street*] was the Perrons' [*Joseph Leo Henri Perron and his wife, née Marie Rose Laura Rochon*].

LD: And then a few houses down there. There were houses down there, but no houses past this house.

JR: Did you have electricity?

CN: 1934.

JR: 1934 – electricity came to Detroit Street? But before that, uh, that would have…

LD: We had lanterns.

JR: Gas lanterns? You think it was gas lanterns? Was it gas or oil?

LD: I think it was gas.

JR: And how did you heat the house?

LD: We used to have an old fashioned stove. We used to put in wood and coal stove.

JR: Did you have a brother who chopped the wood?

LD: We used to buy the wood.

JR: Oh, you bought the wood. Did you have to buy the coal, too? And the coal was delivered to the house, and went down the chute into the cellar?

LD: Yeah.

CN: Where was the chute, do you remember?

LD: Near the window. There.

CN: The basement is still unfinished – it's a dirt basement.

JR: Now, how about cooking? How did you do your cooking, on that stove?

LD: On that stove, yeah, yeah.

CN: Where was the bathroom?

LD: Upstairs.

CN: With the old fashioned tub; it's still up there – cast iron.

JR: Cast iron, with the [*claw*] feet, on the tub.

CN: It's still up there.

JR: So how about marketing, groceries? Did you do any growing of vegetables out in the …

LD: We had a garden. All that was a garden. We had potatoes, tomatoes, sweet corn.

JR: And who did all of the gardening work?

LD: My father did.

JR: Your father did it?

LD: When we used to work, we would come in from work and help him out. We would have to go out and take the bugs out of the potatoes.

JR: Was it more brothers? Did the brothers do more than the girls?

LD: No, everybody pitched in. Yeah, yeah.

JR: How about cooking?

LD: My mother did all the cooking, and one of my sisters [*Marie Dorille Rita Deschenes, later Mrs. Joseph Ovila Roy*].

JR: I can't, I can't imagine, I am trying to figure out how you can buy things and cook for fifteen people.

CN: Where else did you get your food from?

LD: There was a place [*probably a food assistance program*] down [*in*] the Flint. We used to take a barrow, we used to have to take a barrow ...

CN: Wheelbarrow?

LD: And walk down the Flint and pick up some food.

JR: Groceries, or was it vegetables?

LD: Groceries, or welfare, I guess you might call it.

JR: Was it during the [*Great*] Depression?

LD: Yeah.

JR: So that was in the Flint, you had to walk all the way down to the Flint to get that?

LD: Yeah.

JR: That must have taken all day.

LD: That I remember, yeah. Yeah.

CN: In the Hurricane [*September 21,*] of 1938, my mother [*Marie Lillianne Deschenes*] was fifteen [*years old*], and she remembers going down there with her mother, and they didn't know it was the hurricane, and she was walking by the water and her hat flew off; she lost her hat in the wind. But someone came by and offered to take them back here to the house. But they would often go down there weekly to get the food. What kind of food did you get? Must have been like flour and rice, things that you used for cooking.

LD: Flour and rice, bananas, potatoes, yeah.

CN: Aunt Dot [*Marie Dorille Rita Deschenes, later Mrs. Joseph Ovila Roy*] … was born in 1914, I believe. She was one of the older sisters and she was like [*one of*] the ones who went to work first. So, she took care of all of her younger brothers and sisters. And after the mom, her mom, my grandmother died [*in 1957*], she was the caretaker, too, mostly. Always was the responsible one. What did Aunt Dot buy for you, like, when you were little? What did she bring home for you? Did she?

LD: Paper dolls, we had paper dolls when we were kids.

JR: Paper dolls?

LD: Paper dolls. Yeah.

JR: And you could buy those?

LD: We used to buy a book with all paper dolls and we used to cut them up. We used to have pictures of girls and boys and they had clothes that we would put together. We had coloring books, and chalk.

JR: How about games?

LD: Oh, dodge ball, we used to play break a can; put our feet on the can, and walk with the cans.

JR: Walk with the cans on your feet?

LD: Yeah, yeah, we used to smash the cans and walk. That's what we did when we were kids. We played hopscotch, too. We used to play ... um.

CN: Jacks?

LD: With a little ball with a …

CN: Jacks?

LD: Yeah, jacks.

JR: How about chalk? I remember, I remember seeing kids making hopscotch on the sidewalk with chalk.

LD: Yeah, white chalk. Yeah. I still got some of those.

JR: Marbles?

LD: Marbles, yeah, yeah.

JR: Could you do all this playing in the Catholic school? Did they let you play in the Catholic school?

LD: No, when we come home.

JR: What did you do in the Catholic school for recess?

LD: Recess, just play tag. Yeah.

CN: So, like you went to school. When you came home, there wasn't any TV, clearly, right? So what did you do for entertainment? What did your family do? Did you have a radio?

LD: We used to have a radio.

JR: So, do you remember when you got the radio?

LD: 1920s, I guess. We used to watch Amos and Andy [*Amos 'n Andy, a wildly popular radio show set in Harlem, New York, aired 1928 - 1960*].

JR: Oh, you listened to Amos and Andy on the radio?

LD: Yeah, and The Lone Ranger, [*a popular radio western, aired 1940 - 1957*].

JR: On the radio?

LD: We didn't get no TV – when my folks were living, we never had TV.

JR: I'm trying to think about the 1930s and you were born in 1926, so ... you would have only been six years old when [*President*] Franklin [*Delano*] Roosevelt was elected [*in 1932*], because he was well known for speaking on the radio.

LD: Oh yeah, yeah.

CN: Do you remember him talking on the radio?

LD: Yeah, yeah, I think so. Yeah, yeah.

JR: Yeah, he made a great impression on the American people by speaking on the radio. And he was, one of the, well I think he was the first president to take an airplane to the convention, the Democratic Convention in 1932. So, a lot of things were going on. A lot of things were going on during that period of time.

CN: And that brings me to, like, um, so in the 1940s, you had, your brothers. Who went into the service? Into World War II.

JR: That brings you right back to Franklin Roosevelt, would bring you to 1941, when the United States entered the war. What was going on with your brothers?

LD: They were all in the service: my brother Henry [*Joseph Henri Deschenes*] was in the Army [*enlisted January 31, 1944*]; my brother Tommy [*Joseph Lionel John Deschenes*] was in the Army [*enlisted November 30, 1942, discharged December 23, 1945*]; my brother Joe [*Joseph Deschenes*] was in the Army; [*and*] my brother Albert [*Joseph Albert Octave Deschenes*] was in the Navy [*during World War II*]. And my brother Pete [*Joseph Arthur Albert Deschenes*] was in the Army [*during the Korean War*].

JR: How many is that? Were they drafted or they enlist?

LD: They must have been drafted.

JR: How many is that now that was there in the war?

LD: Four. [*Henry, Tommy, Joe, and Albert, were in World War II; Pete was in the Korean War.*]

JR: Did you know where they were assigned? Did you know what part of the world they were in? Were they able to tell you anything about where they served?

LD: I had a brother, Joe [*Joseph Deschenes*], that was in Germany, and I don't know where the others were.

CN: He was in Germany; he was in the Battle of the Bulge [*the Ardennes: Belgium, Luxembourg, December 16, 1944 – January 25, 1945*]; he also went to the Philippines. He was wounded in, um, one of the fights, was brought back to the tent – and this was in Germany – he got shot in the leg. He didn't feel it at first, looked down, saw the blood. Got brought back to the tent. They were going to send him home, and he refused to go. He went back onto the lines. He wanted to stay in it and fight for our country, and, um, that is what we know about Uncle Joe.

JR: Did all of these brothers make it back?

LD: Yes, they all came back.

JR: Your mother must have been very worried about them.

LD: Oh, yeah.

JR: Did she write a lot of letters to them?

LD: Yes, she used to write to them, yeah. And they would write back to her.

JR: What do you remember about the war? I'm thinking about rationing. Did you have to sacrifice during the war?

LD: Well …

JR: It was the same in this house? You know, the same kind of food? The same kind of things that you were doing [*before the war*]?

LD: We always had the same, yeah. We used to have American Chop Suey, and on a Friday, of course, was fish. Fish every Friday, yeah. [*Devout Roman Catholics traditionally abstained from eating warm-blooded meat on Fridays as a penance imposed by the Church to commemorate the day of the crucifixion of Jesus Christ.*]

CN: So what was a meal like, what would your mom put out on the table for supper?

LD: Um …

CN: Potatoes and …

LD: Potatoes, and hamburg, and American Chop Suey once in a while.

JR: That was a lot of cooking.

CN: Did you have … pancakes in the morning or at night for supper?

LD: Morning.

CN: What about French toast?

LD: French toast for supper.

JR: How about French meat pie?

LD: My mother made pies.

JR: Was your mother pretty good at that? Because that is a delicacy, that's the French meat pie recipes, it's very famous.

LD: Yes, we used to have meat pies [*tourtiere*].

CN: Did Mémère make pies, like blueberry pies or anything like that from the garden? Did she? You don't remember?

LD: No, no.

CN: Do you remember … any drills at school that you did in case of, because of the war? Did you have to have a drill, a fire drill or like an air [*raid*] drill?

LD: We used to have fire drills. I remember that.

CN: Yeah, so Aunt Lil, [*the interviewee, Marie Lillian Deschenes*] you were telling me the other day that it was the end of the war, and what did you do? When you heard about the end of the war? What did you do?

LD: I went dancing downtown …

JR: Where, where did you go dancing?

LD: On South Main Street …

JR: Where did you go on South Main? Tell me, was it a restaurant or a dance hall?

LD: No, it was just in the street. In the street, yeah, yeah.

CN: And then you said when it was the end of the war you did go down; you remember going down there when … they surrendered, or when it was the end of the war?

LD: I remember going downtown, yeah, with my sisters, we used to go downtown. Just that, this one time, I guess. It was on South Main Street, and everybody was dancing in the street. [*Victory in Europe Day, aka V-E Day, May 11, 1945.*]

JR: Dancing in the streets, that's good. Speaking of dancing, did you go dancing as a teenager? Was that an activity that girls in your family were able to do?

LD: We used to go dancing at Lincoln Park [*Ballroom, State Road, Westport, Massachusetts*].

JR: How did you get to Lincoln Park?

LD: We took the bus.

JR: The bus from downtown?

LD: Yeah, yes.

JR: And this is when you were a teenager?

LD: Yeah, yeah, yeah.

JR: Okay, so let me figure this one out. What years would that be?

CN: So '42 is when she graduated [*from eighth grade at St. Jean Baptiste Parochial School, Fall River.*]

JR: Something like 1942 to '46, you were taking buses to Lincoln Park? I think there were a lot of service men up there.

LD: Yeah, that's, I used to go dancing with my niece [*Marie Lauretta Deschenes, daughter of her brother, Joseph Albert Octave Deschenes, and his wife, née Marie Bermande Lemieux*] out there in Lincoln Park.

JR: So you met a lot of boys?

LD: Yeah, yeah, yeah.

JR: I can see you had a lot of fun at Lincoln Park.

LD: Yeah, it was nice....

CN: And then you went to New York City one time, right? In your twenties. Yeah, in her twenties.

LD: Went to New York City, [*to*] Times Square. I went there with my niece [*Marie Lauretta Deschenes*], and we were supposed to go on a radio, we were supposed to go on the TV ... the following day, but we were at the Times Square for so long, that when we got back we fell asleep. We were supposed to go on TV at ten o'clock, but we woke up at eleven o'clock.

JR: What program was that going to be? You were supposed to be on television.

LD: I forgot what, what program we were supposed to be on. But we were going to be interviewed on TV.

JR: Did you do a lot of other traveling? Have you traveled quite a bit?

LD: When we were kids, I used to, uh, we used to travel a lot together, on vacation, the whole family with my mother and father. We used to go to New Hampshire all the time. Then with my other sister [*Marie Alice Deschenes*] and [*her*] husband [*Joseph Armande Cote*], we used to go to New York [*City*] quite a bit, too.

JR: How about Cape Cod, [*Massachusetts*]? I know that was a ...

LD: Cape Cod – we went there a few times.

JR: It's a familiar place for us.

CN: And Uncle Armande used to take you to Boston. What did you do in Boston when you went to Boston?

LD: We used to go to the park. And go drinking.

JR: Oh. Did I hear that? I don't know if I heard that.

CN: And what else, go ahead.

LD: I'm not going to tell about that. No, no, no.

JR: Okay, I guess we hit a story. We hit a story she don't want to tell us about.

CN: Something that she doesn't want to be put in the papers.

JR: We will let that one go.

LD: Yeah, yeah. [*She is referring to the so-called Combat Zone in Boston, Massachusetts, known in its heyday during the 1940s – 1950s for its suggestive burlesque shows and jazz clubs.*]

JR: I am going to ask you to just kind of conclude a little bit, because we have so much family and so many things to talk about, that I think, um, I will come back.... And then we will talk about the work years. ... We're looking at the work years in Fall River and the kinds of manufacturing companies that made this city famous again.

LD: Yeah, uh-huh.

JR: I mean the [*cotton*] mills were [*mostly*] gone by the '20s, but all of the [*needle trade*] factories came in, in the '30s and '40s and '50s....

LD: I worked in two shops, though. I worked in Har-Lee [*Manufacturing Company, dress manufacturers, 425 Pleasant Street, Fall River*] and Louis Hand [*Inc., sash curtain manufacturers, 847 Pleasant Street, Fall River.*]

JR: Louis Hand and ... Louis Hand at the time was curtains. Was it always curtains at Louis Hand?

LD: Yes. Yup.

JR: Okay.

CN: And Aunt Grace [*Marie Gracella Deschenes*] worked there with you, when she left [*the convent*].

JR: Let's leave it at that – when I come back, we're going to be talking about working at Har-Lee.... Thank you so much, Lillian. Thank you, Claire.

CN: You're welcome.

Interview resumes August 29, 2015

JR: So let me … get started with, um, graduating from school. What school was that? What school did you graduate from?

LD: St. Jean de Baptiste [*St. Jean Baptiste Parochial School, Fall River, in 1942*].

JR: St. Jean Baptiste, okay. And when you graduated, did you have any idea what you were going to do as a – as a career?

LD: No, I knew that I had to go to work to help the family, so.

JR: Was there any idea that, in your, in your own mind, what you would like to do?

LD: No, I … I just went to work, that was it; I went to work. I enjoyed my job. It was a nice job.

JR: So, how did you get, how did you get into that factory? How did you get that job?

LD: I went down to apply. The following week I started to work.

JR: Now, at what factory was that?

LD: Har-Lee.

JR: That was the Har-Lee.

LD: Yes, on Pleasant Street.

JR: On Pleasant Street.

LD: Yeah.

JR: Can you describe that factory? I heard it was quite big. I heard it had something like two thousand employees.

LD: It was a big place, yeah. What can I say?

JR: Well, where about did you work? And what were you doing?

LD: I was a packer. I was packing dresses, putting them in a box, and put the cover on a box. And we would put them on a conveyer belt, and ship it; someone was at the other end, to pick it up.

JR: Okay, so the dresses came down a conveyer belt.

LD: Yup, and we packed them in a box.

JR: Did you have to fold them?

LD: We had to fold them and put them in a box.

JR: So, when they came down the belt, were they flat on the belt or hanging up?

LD: They were flat, it was, uh.

JR: And you had to fold them.

LD: Yeah.

JR: And then you put them in. How many in a box?

LD: Just one in each box.

JR: One in each box.

LD: Yeah.

JR: How many did you have to do per day? Or per hour?

CN: Were you on piecework or were you on …

LD: On timework. On timework – everything was timework.

CN: So you had to do so many every hour?

LD: No, we just kept on going, whatever we did.

CN: So, um, where did the dresses come from?

LD: Oh, I don't know.

CN: Another floor?

LD: The second floor.

CN: And what did they do up there? It must have been, that must have been …

LD: It was the sewing, I guess.

JR: But did you get any training at Har-Lee? Or how did you learn this job?

LD: No, I didn't need no training because it was easy to do.

JR: Well the, the sewers, I think the machine operators had to be trained. I know I was reading about a training school on Pleasant Street that prepared women to work at Har-Lee on the sewing machines.... So, you know there were places in Fall River at the time that would train young women, you know, for jobs in the, in the factories.

CN: I remember one thing my Mom [*Mrs. George Noel Petrin, née Marie Lillianne Deschenes*] saying about being a sewer, because we used to shop at Arlan's [*of Fall River, department store, 440 Rodman Street.*]. We used to go there. I remember when I graduated from eighth grade [*from St. Mary's Cathedral School, 468 Spring Street, Fall River, in 1972*], we went to Cherry & Webb [*Company, women's clothing & misses' clothing, 139-149 South Main Street, Fall River*] to look at dresses – after we had gone to Arlan's. We went to Arlan's and we picked out my dress, and bought it, and then we went to Cherry & Webb, and my Mom said, 'Claire, come look', and it was the same dress that I had bought at Arlan's, but it was twice as much money.

JR: In Cherry & Webb.

CN: Yeah, and she said ... I remember her telling me this, that the clothes that went to Arlan's were seconds – something was wrong with it or it had the wrong size tag on it. She said sometimes the dresses, when she was sewing, they would run out of labels for a dress. If it was like a size, say the dress was really a size ten, well, they couldn't put a size twelve label on it; they would have to go down a size to size eight. And all of those dresses would have eight on it, and they would be seconds. So then you went to Arlan's and took your dress. I am pretty sure that's the way it was; it could have been the other way around. I'm not sure now – I'm doubting myself. Maybe, if it was a ten, they went up to a twelve, I don't remember. But they would send all the, um, and so there was really nothing wrong with the dress, it was just a different label, a different size, and therefore it was called a second. And they would sell those at Arlan's or Kerr Mill [*Bargain Center, department store, 18 Martine Street, Fall River*] or Globe Mills [*Discount Department Store, 460 Globe Street, Fall River*].

JR: I remember all of that kind of thing, too. My mother was at the Shelburne [*Shirt Company, Inc., 111 Alden Street, Fall River*] and seconds there might have been maybe an imperfection in the fabric. It wasn't going to sell in a top store, so they would put that in the factory store, and call it as a second.

CN: Yup, and a lot of times, there was really not, you know, it was something you couldn't see. Maybe the hem was unfinished. Or, yeah.

JR: So, how many years were you at Har-Lee, Lillian?

LD: About twenty years.

JR: And did you stay in the packing department?

LD: Yeah, the same place all the time.

CN: In the same job? You had the same job?

LD: Yeah, for twenty years.

JR: Did they ever want to move you around?

LD: No.

CN: How many other people were with you doing that job?

LD: Oh, quite a few. There was a lot of people.

CN: The same job.

JR: Were you standing up?

LD: Standing up. Yeah.

CN: When did you get a break?

LD: Only at twelve o'clock when it was time for lunch, we had a half hour break.

JR: Did you get a break in the morning for restroom?

LD: No.

JR: How did you get a break to go to the restroom? Could you do that in the morning?

LD: Oh, I could go to the restroom, yes.

JR: How did you do that? How did you get off the, um?

LD: Someone would take my place so I could go.

JR: Someone would take your place and was there a floor lady?

LD: Yes, it was, but I don't remember her name.

JR: You don't have to remember her name. But I guess you had to alert the floor lady before you were leaving.

LD: Oh, yeah. When we left our post, we had to tell her that we were going.

JR: And then she could find a backup.

CN: No cigarette breaks. They didn't have cigarette breaks.

LD: I don't think so.

CN: You never smoked cigarettes anyway, did you?

LD: Nope, nope.

JR: Okay, so how long was this? When did you start at Har-Lee and when did you leave?

LD: I was sixteen [*years old, in 1942*]. I left at twenty-six, I guess.

JR: Okay, so sixteen plus twenty years would be thirty-six. I think you were about thirty-six, maybe?

LD: Um, I was there. I was one place for twenty years, and the other place twenty-six years, at Louis Hand. Twenty-six years. Or vice versa. I am not sure now.

JR: Okay. So when you left Har-Lee.

CN: Yup, she's right.

JR: When you went to that place [*Louis Hand, Inc.*]

LD: They [*Har-Lee Manufacturing Company*] closed down [*in 1957*].

JR: They were closing down. What happened then? How did you find out that things were not working out there?

LD: They just told us that the place was going to close down.

JR: Did they give you a timeline as to when it was going to close?

LD: No. I can't say too much. I don't remember.

CN: Did you wait until it closed down to go to Louis Hand?

LD: Yes.

CN: And did a lot of those other people, do you remember anyone else going with you to Louis Hand?

LD: There were a few people that went to Louis Hand with us.

JR: Now, Louis Hand obviously was hiring, and is that what they told you? To go to Louis Hand? Har-Lee told you that?

LD: Yeah, I don't know, unemployment.

JR: The unemployment office?

CN: So, Aunt Grace [*Marie Gracella Deschenes*] started to work, did she start working at the same time?

LD: No, she started to work after, a few years after me.

CN: After you were already at Louis Hand?

LD: Yeah.

CN: So, what did she do before that? Do you remember what she did before she worked at Louis Hand? You don't remember? So, that is interesting.

LD: She was in the convent. When she came out [*in 1960*], that is when she went to Louis Hand.

JR: That was a big change [*for you*], because you are going from dresses to curtains.

LD: Curtains, yeah, yeah.

JR: So when you got to Louis Hand, were you also in the packing department?

LD: Louis Hand, I was an, an order picker, which means they had bins, and we had to go in a bin and pick up so many curtains and put them in a box. Then we drive the, we have a truck – a hand truck to push it, and we put so many curtains on there, and then we go to one place, and we drop it off there. And they would pack it.

JR: So, when you were picking …

LD: In other words, I was an order picker, it's coming back to me now. I used to pick curtains and I used to, there were all these guys over here checking. We used to give these curtains to these guys and they used to check them out. And a guy that would check them, and after they checked the curtains that we picked, they'd give them to a packer, and the packer would pack them, and then they went out.

JR: So the floor lady or the supervisor would give you a list.

LD: And then we take it from there …

CN: So, that was your job down there. And Aunt Grace was on the second floor, right?

LD: No, she was on the same floor with me – Grace went down to the first floor after … we all worked the office downstairs.

CN: Aunt Grace worked in the office?

LD: Aunt Grace worked in one office, and I was in the other office. Yeah, because there was a girl who came downstairs to give us some papers or something. So she came to my office first. Then she went to the other office. So, no, she went to Grace first, then she came back to me. She says, 'What are you doing here? I just saw you in the other office.' Because we looked alike, you know? She thought she was seeing double. My sister was there and I was there, different office.

JR: How did she end up in the office?

LD: Well, the same thing as me. How did I end up in the office? Eventually they put me in the office.

JR: What were you doing in the office?

LD: In the office, I was giving out the work. I had a machine … and I had a machine that was giving out the work. My table, my desk was here, and the window was here. I gave out the work, and when they come back, I'd have to write down how long it took them to do it.

JR: It sounds like you would like that job, handing out the work. Did you like to do that?

LD: Yeah, that was a nice job. I enjoyed it.

JR: Did it pay more?

LD: No, a couple of dollars more, not much.

JR: And your sister was doing the same thing?

LD: She was doing something different. She worked in the office, but then there was kind of a conveyor belt. And when there was so much, so much work on the conveyor belt, she had to go out there. She would leave the office. That was her job to go out there and take care of the, whatever it was she was doing then.

JR: When did you retire?

LD: I retired at sixty-two.

JR: At age sixty-two. What year, what year was that? Do you recall what year that was?

LD: 1988.

CN: So, one of the interesting things is, she worked at Louis Hand, but there were so many nieces and nephews …

JR: In the same factory.

CN: That Aunt Lil [*the interviewee*] would get ...

LD: I get the work to them.

CN: So my whole family, my brother [*Ronald Arthur Petrin*], my sister [*Diane Marie Petrin*], I ...

LD: The four of them.

CN: And my brother Roger [*Arthur Petrin*] all worked at Louis Hand in the summer, because she would be there, and she would get us a job for the summer.

JR: There you go, so you didn't have a resume, you didn't have to write a resume.

CN: And Cousin Louise [*Louise Pineau, daughter of Mrs. Joseph Pineau, née Marie Anita Deschenes*] was there.

CN: So, there was a lot of our Bouchard cousins [*the children of Mrs. Aime Horace Bouchard, née Marie Blanche Irene Deschenes*] that worked there, right? Years and years. So it's, like, it was a way of life.

JR: Yes, it certainly was ...

CN: For our family. Because our family, that was what they did, you know? They quit school and went to work, and that was what you did.

LD: We had no choice.

JR: How did you manage your paycheck?

LD: I gave all my money to my mother.

JR: All your money went to the house?

LD: Yeah. And we didn't get too much spending money.

JR: So, you got an allowance after that? You got spending money?

LD: Not too much. She couldn't afford it.

JR: Did it ever increase as you got older and did you ask or need more money?

LD: As I got older, I got more. I got more spending money. And when my mother died [*in 1957*], it was the same thing; I gave my pays to my sister [*Marie Dorille Rita Deschenes*]. I gave all my paycheck, and she would give me spending money. But then I would get a little bit more spending money.

JR: So, at that point you were sharing the expenses in the house?

LD: Yeah.

JR: After your mother died and you had your sister living here.

LD: Yeah, there were three of us living here [*Marie Dorille Rita Deschenes, the interviewee, and Marie Gracella Deschenes*].

JR: Three sisters were living here, and you were sharing the expenses.

LD: Yeah.

JR: I am going to jump ahead a little bit and ask you about unions, because the unions were important in Fall River, and I think I will go back to Har-Lee. Do you remember joining the union?

LD: ILGW [*International Ladies Garment Workers Union, Local 178, Garment Workers Square, 38 Third Street, Fall River.*]

JR: ILGW.

LD: Yeah.

JR: Was there a recruiting for that? Or were they, did they expect you to join the union? How did that happen?

LD: We had to join the union.

JR: To work at Har-Lee you had to join the union?

LD: Yeah.

JR: Now when you went to Louis Hand …

LD: Louis Hand, the same union. Yeah.

CN: You had no choice? You had to do it?

LD: Yeah. Everybody joined that union. Every worker.

JR: So, fortunately, you had, when you retired you had Social Security, and you had ILGW.

LD: ILGW.

JR: That was good, that came in handy.

LD: Yeah, yeah, yeah. It wasn't too much though, I was on timework a lot of time. I didn't make too much money.

JR: I think that was true of a lot of factories in Fall River. I think if you weren't on piecework then you had minimum wage. Were there any strikes at Har-Lee or Louis Hand? Any strikes for higher wages?

LD: No, not that I remember.

JR: Did you get laid off from time to time?

LD: No, no, I was lucky.

JR: It was always steady work?

LD: Yup, $40 a week.

CN: So, that's really good. Never had to worry about losing your job....

JR: How about ILGW, I recall that they had a health center ... in back of what is today [*the*] City Hall. Were you able to go to that health center?

LD: I never went there, no.

JR: That was part of your union benefits, you could go there if you needed to. I still have to go through some of the technology questions ... about the period of time that you were living in. When did you ... get your radio? The first radio?

LD: Our first radio? I don't know.

JR: Your mother and father would have been still living.

LD: Yeah.

JR: And they bought the radio maybe?

CN: I will think it's in the [*nineteen*] thirties because they didn't have electric, but it could have run on battery, huh?

JR: I'm not sure. I heard that the first ones were, I remember those, but like crystal radios, I think they were almost like wireless. But I'm not sure how the first ones operated. I would think you would need electric.

CN: Yeah, so they got electric here in 1934.

JR: And how about television?

JR: When did television come?

LD: We didn't have television when my father was living. [*He died in 1972.*]

CN: So, not when my grandmother was alive ... she died in 1957, so that means they didn't have television until after that.

JR: How about the telephone?

LD: Telephone, we got a telephone in before 1950, telephone.

CN: Where was the telephone?

LD: It was in the parlor.

JR: You probably had a four-party line?

LD: Oh, we did, yeah. We kept because of the little woman [*Rose Cabral, wife of David F. Cabral*] who lived on the corner [*at 92 Detroit Street.*] She used to be talking on the phone all the time my mother was on the phone, because when she hung up, she used to call me. She was on the phone and that woman kept interrupting her on the phone all the time. So, you [*were*] on the phone and someone else is on the phone with you.

CN: Listening to your conversation.

CN: Why don't you tell them about the card playing? That was a big thing for the family and it always has been.

LD: We play cards every Sunday.

CN: That is for entertainment. So, go ahead and tell them about that.

LD: We used to play ... we played bingo for peppermints.

CN: And what about the, there was another one – there was another game. Michigan Rummy?

LD: Michigan Rummy, yeah.

CN: But you used to play cards with all of your brothers and sisters for entertainment.

LD: We used to play cards all the time [*when*] my mother and father were living. We used to play cards all the time.

CN: It was always cards around this table, and, on New Year's Day, the women stayed here and the men went upstairs.

LD: The men gambled upstairs. Now we are just down to my sister [*Mrs. Joseph Pineau, née Marie Anita Deschenes*] and I on a Sunday. I have her over for dinner.

JR: Someone told me, too, that if you play cards it really keeps your mind sharp. So you don't have to worry about that, Lillian.

LD: I play solitaire a lot, too. So, thank goodness for cards and for TV.

CN: And so family has always been important, family has always been important.

LD: And I don't want too much …

JR: I am going to finish with that, I feel we have plenty to work with. And I thank you so much …

LD: I wasn't that much help, but, hey.

JR: No, it was wonderful. It just gives you an idea of what family life was like in Fall River and that's so important, because it's disappeared, Lillian. You know? It really has disappeared, family life is very different today.

LD: Yeah, oh yeah, yeah. There is no more family now.

PHOTO GALLERY

6.1 Lillian's father, François Xavier Deschenes, as a young man. *"They immigrated here … from Acton, Bagot, Quebec, Canada … in* [1892] *when* [he] *was ten years old."*

6.2 Lillian's paternal grandmother, Mrs. Octave Miville Deschenes, Sr., née Delvina Charette. *"She was a medicine woman in* [the] *Blessed Sacrament area. She would … help all the people who were sick … she would have her home remedies to, um, help the neighborhood and the whole community. Joe was sick one time and* [she] *came to the house and gave him like half a teaspoon of turpentine, and he was better the next day."*

6.3 *Left:* Lillian's father, François Xavier Deschenes, and her mother, née Albertina Boursier Martin, on their wedding day. *"They got married on September 23, 1907."*

6.4 Aerial view of the Church of the Blessed Sacrament, 2460 South Main Street, Fall River, Massachusetts, 1960s. *"They lived, they both lived in the Blessed Sacrament community. The church was built in 1902."*

6.5 Lillian's father, François Xavier Deschenes, and her mother, née Albertina Boursier Martin, in the 1920s. Lillian's mother, who was pregnant in this photograph, gave birth to fifteen children in a span of twenty-three years. *"All born … home delivered. Home delivery. She knew what was going on."*

6.6 The Deschene family residence on Detroit Street, Fall River, Massachusetts, 1940s; the family purchased the house in 1923. "[I was] *born in this house."*

6.7 A "Solace Art" card for Lillian's brother, Joseph Leo Pierre Deschenes, who died on August 15, 1926, from a ruptured spleen incurred during an accidental fall at Maplewood Park in Fall River, Massachusetts. *"May Jesus Have Mercy on the Soul of Leo Deschenes."*

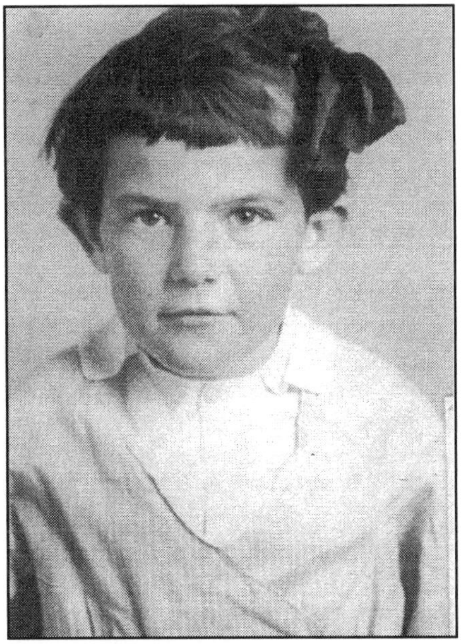

6.8 Marie Lillian Deschenes, called Lillian, as a child, circa 1932. *"We used to buy a book with paper dolls … we had coloring books, and chalk … we used to break a can; put our feet on the can, and walk with the cans. Yeah, yeah, we used to smash the cans and walk. That's what we did when we were kids. We played hopscotch, too."*

6.9 R.A. McWhirr Company window display at 85 North Main Street, Christmas 1931; Lillian's mother cooked for a very large family consisting of her husband and their fifteen children. *"My mother did the cooking, and one of my sisters."*

6.10 Lillian and her brother, Joseph Arthur Albert Deschenes, called "Pete," dressed for the Sacrament of Confirmation, circa 1938. *"Sister Mary Joseph taught most of my brothers and sisters. She taught everybody."*

6.11 Lillian's parents, Mr. & Mrs. François Xavier Deschenes, August 2, 1941. *"I don't think my mother ever worked ... with fifteen kids she didn't have the time."*

6.12 St. Jean Baptiste Parochial Grammar School, 364 Field Street, Fall River, Massachusetts, 1970s; the school operated under the direction of the Sisters of St. Joseph du Puy, a religious order from Haute Loire, France. Lillian graduated from this school in 1942, which had been constructed four years earlier, to replace the old building. *"We went to school at St. Jean's."*

6.13 Lillian's graduating class from *École St. Jean Baptiste*, Fall River, Massachusetts, 1942; Lillian is standing in the second row from the front, second from the left. To her right is her brother, Joseph Arthur Albert Deschenes, called "Pete." Following graduation, she immediately went to work, securing a position at Har-Lee Manufacturing Company, dress manufacturers, 425 Pleasant Street, Fall River. *"I knew I had to go to work to help the family, so."*

6.14 A listing for Har-Lee Manufacturing Company, Fall River, Massachusetts, from the *Fall River City Directory,* 1942 edition, the year Lillian started working there; the firm employed 2200 people in its factory on Pleasant Street. *"I knew I had to go to work to help the family. I just went to work, that was it; I went to work. I was a packer. I was packing dresses ...* [I was there] *for twenty years."*

Hargreaves Ernest (Lillian) beamer Superba
Towel h 90 Lafayette
—Fred R died May 19, 1939
—John R (Sarah W) police sta 2 h 351 Langley
—Wm (Lucy) uphol h 46 Talbot
Harkin Anna A trimmer Luther r 56 Marsh
—Catherine A r 56 Marsh
—Ida N opr Small Bros r 56 Marsh
—John F hlpr r 56 Marsh
—John P r 480 Bradford av
—Thos F master mech Luther h 56 Marsh
—Thos F jr, hlpr James F Derrig Engraving Co Inc r 56 Marsh
—Wm H lab r 480 Bradford av
—Winfred A h 480 Bradford av
Harkins Edwd T r 102 Palmer

Har-Lee Mfg Co
Division of Wentworth Mfg Co Benj Sopkin pres Harry Lee treas dress mfrs 425 Pleasant tel 5842

Harley Emma Mrs clk r 620 N Main
—Wm T h 615 Middle
Harlow Mabel tchr B M C Durfee High sch h 106 Highland av
Harmon Saml R (Ethel M) clk h 969 Locust
Harnett see Hodnett
—Edwd r 322 Mott
—Edwd J (Alta L) h 322 Mott
—Geo C (Nora A) loomfixer h 611 Walnut
—Helen L insp r 611 Walnut
—Robt A (Bertha A) firemn h 229 Linden
—Thos F (Catherine) clk h 322 Mott
—Wm V (Eliz V) carrier South Sta PO h 99 Rockland
Harney Clarence E (Alice) shipper r 183 Denver
—Eliz A opr r 87 Cambridge

6.15 Three of Lillian's brothers depicted in a composite novelty photograph produced during World War II; top: Joseph Albert Octave Deschenes, called "Albert", United States Navy; bottom left: Joseph Lionel John Deschenes, called "Tommy," United States Army; bottom right: Joseph Deschenes, called "Joe," United States Army. *"They were all in the service."*

6.16 Lillian's brother, Joseph Henri Deschenes, called "Henry," at camp during World War II. *"My brother Henry was in the army."*

6.17 Lillian during World War II, wearing one of her brother's uniform jackets and hat. *"They* [were] *drafted."*

6.19 Lillian posing in a friend's garden, circa 1943.

6.18 Lillian in the mid-1940s.

6.20 Lillian's sister, Marie Rita Deschenes, following the Ceremony for Veiling and Profession or Final Vows in the order of Sisters of Saint Joseph; she received the religious name Sister Marie Xavier. She died at St. Anne's Hospital in Fall River, Massachusetts, at the age of twenty-six, due to "acute sore throat, with septicemia"; the nuns had attempted to treat her condition in-house, before transferring her to the hospital. She entered the convent at age fourteen, and was teaching at St. Joseph's Parochial School in New Bedford, Massachusetts, at the time of her death. *"She died in 1945 ... yeah."*

6.21 Lillian parents, Mr. & Mrs. François Xavier Deschenes, on an Easter visit to their daughter, Sister Marie Xavier, at St. Thérèse of Lisieux Convent, New Bedford, Massachusetts, early 1940s. *"My sister Rita was the oldest one that was in the convent."*

6.22 Lillian, her sisters, and a family friend on an Easter visit to their sister, Sister Marie Xavier, at St. Thérèse of Lisieux Convent, in New Bedford, Massachusetts, early 1940s. Standing, left to right: Marie Lillianne (Deschenes) Petrin; Sister Marie Xavier, formerly Marie Rita Deschenes; Marie Gracella Deschenes; Eva Perrault, a family friend. Kneeling, left to right: Marie Alice (Deschenes) Cote; Lillian.

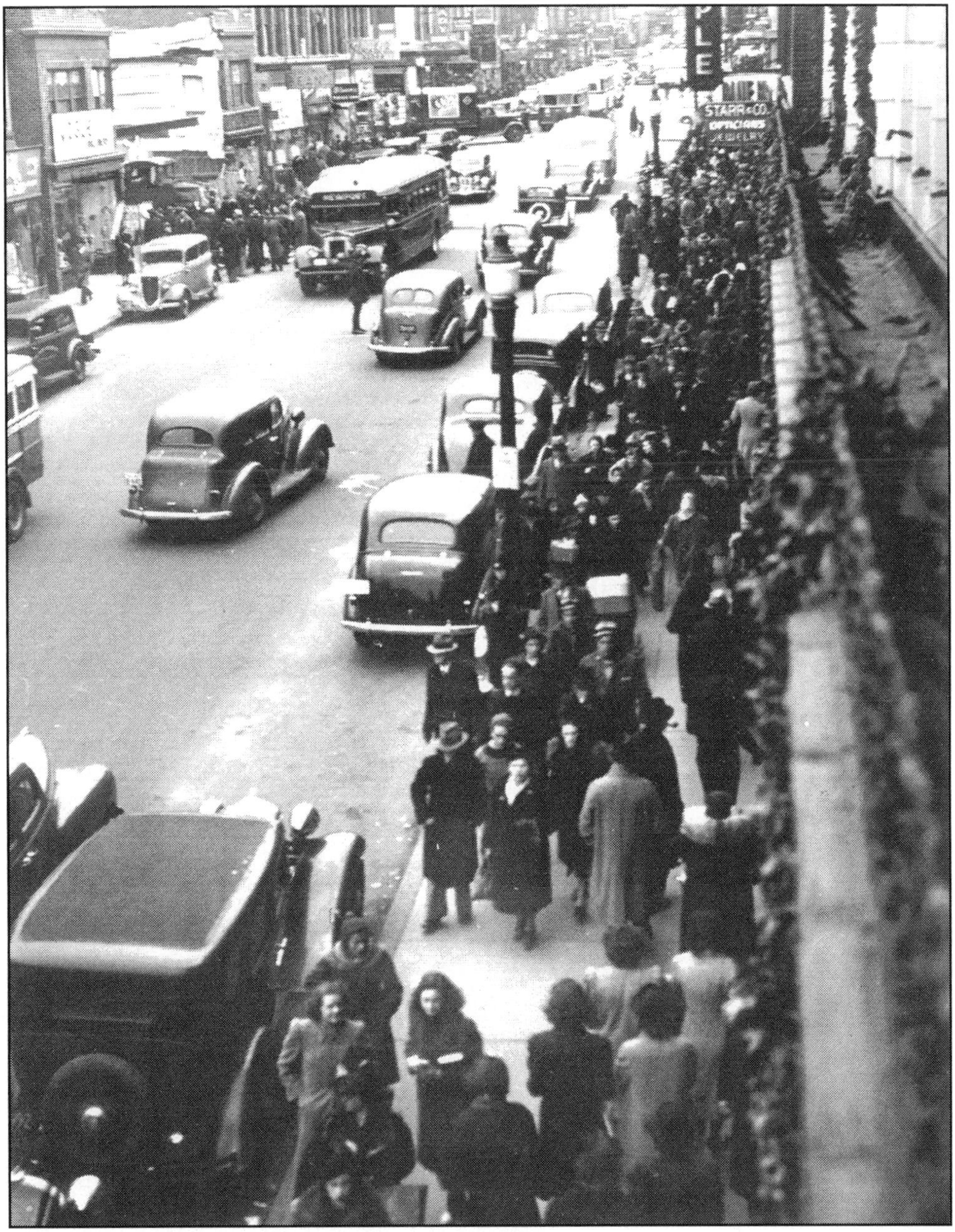

6.23 South Main Street, Fall River, Massachusetts, looking south, 1940s. *"I remember going downtown, yeah, with my sisters, we used to go downtown."*

6.24 Lillian's brother, Joseph Arthur Albert Deschenes, called "Pete," posing in uniform, with his parents, Mr. & Mrs. François Xavier Deschenes, circa 1947. *"Yes,* [my mother] *used to write to them, yeah. And they would write back to her."*

6.25 Lillian, with two of her sisters, outside the family home on Detroit Street, Fall River, Massachusetts, circa 1947; the three sisters would later live together in the family home, sharing expenses. Standing, left to right: Marie Gracella Deschenes; Marie Dorille Rita (Deschenes) Roy; Lillian. *"Yeah, there were three of us living here."*

6.26 Interior of a Fall River, Massachusetts, bus, 1940s; Lillian often used this form of transportation to get to the Lincoln Park Ballroom in Westport, Massachusetts, to go dancing. *"We took the bus, I used to go dancing … out there in Lincoln Park. Yeah, it was nice …"*

6.27 Lillian's sister, Marie Lillianne Deschenes's wedding party, April 10, 1948. Left to right: Marie Gracella Deschenes; Irene Petrin, the sister of the groom; Joseph Arthur Albert Deschenes; the bride; George Noel Petrin, the groom; Paul Berube, the best man; Lillian.

6.28 Lillian, circa 1950.

6.29 A Deschenes family portrait, 1952. Standing, left to right: Lillian's father, François Xavier Deschenes; her mother, née Albertina Boursier Martin; Lillian; her sisters: Marie Alice (Deschenes) Cote; Sister Mary Albert, formerly Marie Gracella Deschenes; Marie Lillianne (Deschenes) Petrin; Marie Dorille Rita (Deschenes) Roy; Marie Blanche Irene (Deschenes) Bouchard. Seated, left to right: Joseph Albert Octave Deschenes; Joseph Lionel John Deschenes; Marie Anita (Deschenes) Pineau; Joseph Deschenes; Joseph Arthur Albert Deschenes. Lying down: Joseph Henri Deschenes. Lillian's sister, Gracella, joined the Sisters of St. Joseph in 1950 and, as Sister Mary Albert, resided at St. Thérèse of Lisieux Convent, in New Bedford, Massachusetts; she relinquished her vows in 1960. *"Then Grace went in ..."*

6.30 Lillian with her niece, Marie Lauretta Deschenes, circa 1955. *"*[We] *went to New York City,* [to] *Times Square. I went there with my niece, and we were supposed to go on a radio show … the following day, but we were at the Times Square for so long … that we fell asleep."*

6.31 Louis Hand, Inc., sash curtain manufacturers, 847 Pleasant Street, Fall River, Massachusetts, 1970s; Lillian was employed here for twenty-six years. *"Louis Hand, I was an, an order picker, which means they had bins, and we had to go in a bin and pick up so many curtains and put them in a box. I retired at sixty-two."*

6.32 Lillian's father, François Xavier Deschenes, posing with his daughters on the occasion of his 80th Birthday, June 1962. Four months before this photograph was taken, he had married his second wife, the widowed Kathleen May (Bean) O'Neil; Lillian's mother had died in 1957 following a stroke. Left to right: Marie Alice (Deschenes) Cote; Lillian; Marie Dorille Rita (Deschenes) Roy. Standing: Marie Anita (Deschenes) Pineau; Marie Lillianne (Deschenes) Petrin; Marie Blanche Irene (Deschenes) Bouchard. Seated, to the right of their father: Marie Gracella Deschenes. *"He remarried five years* [after his first wife died] *and left the house to … his family."*

6.33 Lillian and her sister, Marie Gracella Deschenes, with their Petrin nieces and nephews, December, 1964; they are the children of Mrs. George Noel Petrin, née Marie Lillianne Deschenes. Left to right: Diane Marie Petrin; Marie Gracella Deschenes; Lillian; Claire Marie Petrin; Ronald Arthur Petrin. As young adults, their "Aunt Lil" found them summer jobs at her place of employment, Louis Hand, Inc., sash curtain manufacturers, 847 Pleasant Street, Fall River, Massachusetts. *"I get the work for them."*

6.34 Lillian and her sister, Marie Gracella Deschenes, with their fellow employees at Louis Hand, Inc., sash curtain manufacturers, 847 Pleasant Street, Fall River, Massachusetts, 1970s. Lillian is standing in the third row, eight from the left. Her sister, Grace, is standing in the same row, twelfth from the left. *"Grace worked in one office, and I was in the other office."*

6.35 Cherry & Webb Company, women's and misses' clothing, 139 - 149 South Main Street, Fall River, Massachusetts, 1940s. Although the upscale store was considered one of the city's finest, its stock in the early 1970s also included inexpensive first-quality dresses made in Fall River's garment factories, which were retailed at highly inflated prices. *"It was the same dress that I bought at Arlan's* [of Fall River, department store], *but it was twice the money."*

6.36 Lillian and her fellow employees at her retirement party from Louis Hand, Inc., sash curtain manufacturers, 847 Pleasant Street, Fall River, Massachusetts, in 1988; Lillian is seated at the right, second from the front. Her sister Grace is seated at the right, fourth from front. *"I retired at sixty-two."*

6.37 A Deschenes family reunion, held at Blessed Sacrament Church Hall, 2470 South Main Street, Fall River, Massachusetts, 1995. *Back row, standing left to right:* Lillian; her brother, Joseph Henri Deschenes; her sister, Marie Dorille Rita (Deschenes) Roy. *Second row, standing, left to right:* her sisters, Marie Alice (Deschenes) Cote; Marie Lillianne (Deschenes) Petrin; Marie Anita (Deschenes) Pineau; Marie Gracella Deschenes. Seated: Marie Blanche Irene (Deschenes) Bouchard. *"Now we are just down to my sister* [Anita] *and I."*

6.38 Lillian and her niece, Mrs. John Barry Norfolk, née Claire Marie Petrin, at the Clam Chowder festival in Newport, Rhode Island, 2014; Claire is the family genealogist. *"She knows more than I do."*

SEVEN:

MARITA FRANCES HARNETT, NÉE VOKES

Personal Statistics

Name: Marita Frances Vokes
(Mrs. Thomas Edward Harnett)

Date of Birth: November 17, 1921

Place of Birth: Lawrence, Massachusetts

Father: Reginald Arthur Vokes, Sr. (1901-1965)

Mother: Alma M. Latraverse (1899-1974)

Siblings: Reginald Arthur Vokes, Jr. (1926-2010)
Alice Marie Vokes (1929-1997)

Spouse: Thomas Edward Harnett (1920-1990)

Children: Robert William Harnett (1944-1994)
Katherine Mary Harnett (1947-2011)
Christine Harnett

Employment history:

Red Mill Café, North Westport, Massachusetts
F.W. Woolworth & Company 5 & 10 Cent Store, Fall River
The Boston Store, Fall River
Mell's Jewelry Company, Fall River
Firestone Rubber & Latex Products Company, Fall River
S & S Manufacturing Company, Massachusetts
Henry's Latin Quarter - Showbar, Fall River
Har-Lee Manufacturing Company, Fall River
Kerr Thread Mills (American Thread Company),Fall River
White's Family Restaurant, Westport, Massachusetts
Edgar's Department Store, Inc., Fall River

EDITED TRANSCRIPT

Interview with Mrs. Thomas Edward Harnett, née Marita Frances Vokes

Interviewer: (JC) Joseph J. Conforti, Jr

Interviewee: (MH) Marita Frances (Vokes) Harnett

Additional Commentary: (JR) Joyce B. Rodrigues, Fall River Historical Society

Date of Interview: December 3, 2014

Location: Catholic Memorial Home, Fall River, Massachusetts

Summary by Joyce B. Rodrigues:

Marita (Vokes) Harnett was born in Lawrence, Massachusetts, on November 17, 1921.

Marita's story is rooted in the textile centers of Lawrence and Fall River. Her father, Reginald Vokes, immigrated to the United States from England in 1904 with his parents and sister. The family settled in Lawrence. Her paternal grandfather was a car inspector for the Boston and Maine Railroad.

Marita's mother and maternal grandparents were born in New England of French-Canadian descent. The Latraverses lived in Lawrence and were operatives in a cotton mill. Her parents met and married while working in the mills in Lawrence.

Marita's father, as an enterprising young man, worked in retail, managing McLellan's, a 20th-century chain of five-and-dime stores. His work took the family to Maine, New York, New Jersey, Pennsylvania, and finally to the two McLellan stores in Fall River. There were three children in the Vokes family: Marita the eldest, a younger brother, and a younger special-needs sister.

Marita's husband's family, the Harnetts, emigrated from England to the United States in 1862. They lived in Fall River and occupied positions as weavers, mule spinners, doffers, loom fixers, and speeder-tenders in the city's booming textile industry.

Marita's narrative describes her teen and young adult years in Fall River from 1935 to her marriage in 1942, a period from the height of the Great Depression to World War II.

The impact of the New Deal:

Reginald Vokes worked for the Works Progress Administration (WPA) in Fall

River. He had been a Republican until the enactment of Social Security in 1935. From then on he voted as a Democrat for the rest of his life. He tried the restaurant business and finally settled in the 1940s and 1950s on managing a Socony gas station and later owned an auto parts business.

Life during the Great Depression:

The Vokes family lived with both sets of grandparents in the same house. Marita recalls sharing meals with other families in their Orchard Street three-decker home, attending dish night at the Strand Theater, and competing for a title in a beauty contest at the Empire Theatre in 1940.

Marita attended high school for two years (1935-37). She then worked alongside her mother operating a power stitching machine in the sewing factories of Fall River. Among the places her career took her to were: S & S Manufacturing Company, Har-Lee Manufacturing Company, Kerr Thread Mills (aka American Thread Company), and Firestone Rubber & Latex Products Company.

She married Thomas E. Harnett in 1942 and had one son and two daughters. After marriage, Marita worked as a waitress, as an office clerical, and a retail sales worker.

Note: This interview has been slightly edited for continuity and readability; in order to preserve the integrity of the conversation, the phraseology remains that of the interviewer and interviewee. Italicized information in square brackets has been added for the purposes of clarification and context.

JC: Mrs. Harnett, let's begin. Your name, your first name, Marita, very unusual. Can you tell me about it?

MH: I've got a long story about that.

JC: You have? Tell us.

MH: I wondered too where I got that name. Because I had nothing to do with it. When I was born, I was born at home, in the old days, you know? A featherbed, I think. My grandmother's house … my mother [*née Alma M. Latraverse*] and father [*Reginald Arthur Vokes*] were living with [*his*] parents [*Arthur Vokes and his wife, née Amy Balderson*] at the time. And the doctor's name was Nevins [*Dr. Harry Hill Nevers*]. [*He*] delivered me. And my grandmother and mother were debating what to name this new baby, you know, me. And she happened to say to the doctor, 'What is your daughter called?' He says, 'Marita.' They decided there and then. That is how I got that name. So they stole it from the doctor.

JR: Interesting.

MH: I had to live with it, and I've got different pronunciations, but you said it correctly. I have had Maritta, Maratta, Marrita, all different versions of Marita.

JC: When and where were you born?

MH: I was born in Lawrence, Massachusetts. 238 Farnham Street in … Lawrence … second floor tenement house. The landlady's name was Mrs. Svensco [*Blanche Svenconis, the wife of August Svenconis*]. I can't spell that.

JC: What year was that?

MH: [*November 17,*] 1921.

JC: 1921. Your father worked in the Lawrence Mills?

MH: Well, as a young man I suppose he did. But, after he was married, he got into the retail as a manager. He worked from stock boy up to manager. I guess you must remember the five-and-tent-cent stores. [*F.W.*] Woolworth's [*Company*], [*J.J.*] Newberry [*Company*]. Well, he was in charge of McLellan's [*5 Cent to $1.00 Store, 281 South Main Street*]. I don't know if you know that … there was a McLellan's in Fall River. And we traveled quite a bit because he must have been good with figures … because when a chain store was in the red, they would say, 'Send Vokes … Send Vokes, he will get us in the black.' So we moved quite a bit. And the way I came to Fall River was through moving from … Gloversville, New York. He was sent [*from New York*] to govern a store on Main Street at that time, called McLellan's. It was a five-and-ten. And we stayed here. My mother said, 'I'm sick of moving every few years. I've lived in Maine, New Jersey, New York,' … she said, 'I am sick of it, you know … I just get the window treatments all set in one house and then I have to go to another one, get all new drapes and curtains.' So we stayed in Fall River. And he started to try a business of his own [*Red Mill Cafe in Westport, Massachusetts*]. And that little menu I brought was one of the businesses he had. The date is on it. It's a menu of what they served. And they used to have a three-piece band Friday night [*for*] dancing, you know? And they served food, not big food, but French fries and pitchers of beer.

JC: In what year did he begin this?

MH: Let me see, that's '41. It must have been in '39.

JC: The Depression was still on? Yes?

MH: Yes. I think I had just come out of [*B.M.C. Durfee*] high school…. My father said, 'Now, you have to help me out the weekend. It's a holiday, you know? And I need a girl to serve table.' I said, 'Oh, no, I can't do that, I want to go to Lincoln Park.' If you wanted any news about Lincoln Park, I could stay here for a month talking. But we will forget about that right now. I said, 'No I don't.' He said, 'You can keep your tips and I will pay you the same as the other girls get.' 'Oh, well. Alright,' [*I said*]. Well, I wasn't of the age to put down a pitcher of beer. So, I had to put down the food like

French fries or potato chips or something like that. So, who do you think got the tips? The other girls, they were of age. And I would say, 'Oh,' and he said, 'You go home and make out the payroll and give yourself the same pay as the other girls. No tips, though.'

JC: So was this successful?

MH: He had that for a few years and then he branched out....

JC: We would like to hear about your father.

MH: He had two, do you remember the Socony Gas [*Socony – Vacuum Oil Company*], the flying red horse [*logo*]? You remember that, huh? He opened up, and leased two gas stations, [*Standard Oil Company of New York, 2211 Pleasant Street, Fall River circa 1935, and Socony – Vacuum Oil Company/Vokes Friendly Service at the same address circa 1935-1940*]. And my grand ... everyone took their grandparents in in those days; there was no Social Security. I can remember two sets of grandparents in the house with us. So my mother went to work. She had two people to cook and two grandmas there to look after us. So, [*my father*] opened two gas stations.... And he kept it open twenty-four hours. There was no other stations in Fall River that did that. So my grandfather [*Arthur Vokes*] worked the night shift, my father went in during the day. That was pretty good.

JC: Did he, did he?

MH: When the war came [*World War II*], my brother [*Reginald 'Reggie' Arthur Vokes, Jr.*] went to war, [*United States Navy Airman, Gunner, enlisted on October 14, 1944*]. He got the Purple Heart, by the way. My brother went to war and my father went to work at, was there a Camp Devens [*Fort Devens, United States Army, Ayer and Shirley, Massachusetts*]? He worked nights as a bartender and days painting the barracks at Fort Devens. So, he was working two jobs. So I was free to work, so I worked two jobs ... I did like my father. The second job just gave me enough money to pay room and board at home, and buy what I needed, and my first, the job at Firestone [*Rubber & Latex Products Company, Inc., Fall River*], paid bigger. My father and I didn't take our pay. We took it in War Bonds. So, when the war was over, we had a few bucks, you know? To start off, because there was a big depression. So my father used his money and the G.I. Loan [*Servicemen's Readjustment Act of 1944, aka G.I. Bill*] when my brother got out to start another business. And that was in Tiverton, Vokes Auto Parts [*R.A. Vokes & Son, 2127 (later 2137) South Main Street, Fall River, from circa 1946 to 1951*].

JC: So that was the last business venture?

MH: Yes, he retired from that. They did very well with that; they both went to [*Oakland Park,*] Florida, except me. That's okay, I went down when they needed me.

JC: Your mother was a stay-at-home mom?

MH: Yes, but she [*also*] worked in the sweat shops. The power machines when we were younger and the grandmas were home. And I did, too.

JC: In Fall River?

MH: In Fall River. Now, you want to talk about where I worked?

JC: Before we get there, let's talk about your family. How many children in the family?

MH: Myself, my brother, and sister [*Alice Marie Vokes*]. Three. And my mother and father.

JC: Where was your place?

MH: I was the eldest of three.

JC: Okay. Can you tell us a little bit about your family origins?

MH: Yes. My descent: my father was born in [*Sculcoates, Yorkshire*] England, and my mother was of French descent [*and born in Maine*]. My grandparents on my mother's side [*Charles Latraverse and his wife, née Alice Boulanger*] were Canadian French. But my father was really English. He came over with his mother and father [*in 1903*] when he was four years old.

JC: Alright.

MH: And I don't think he went more than the eighth grade. But he evidently was good with figures.

JC: Your mom and dad came from different religious backgrounds?

MH: Yes, they did.

JC: Tell me about it.

MH: Well, my mother was a [*Roman*] Catholic, brought up Catholic, [*a*] staunch Catholic, I would say. My father was brought up Episcopalian. But when they went to be married [*in Lawrence, MA, in 1921*], in the old days, the priest said, 'Well, you have to convert. Become a Catholic.' [*My father*] said, 'No.' He says, 'Well, you can't be married in the church. I can marry you in the rectory. But you can have a nice church wedding if you convert....' And my father said, 'No, I won't do that, because if something happens to my wife, and there's children, I would be forced to bring them up my way, that is all I know.' So, that was his excuse. So they were married, not at the church, but in the rectory. It never caused any trouble in any way. But my mother became a luke-warm Catholic.

JC: I see, ok. So, it was never a problem in the home?

MH: Not until I got married and had children.

JC: You want to tell us about that?

MH: Sure. In the old days, there was prejudice between the Catholics and the Episcopals. And I married a Catholic fella [*Edward Thomas Harnett, aka Thomas Edward Harnett*], his mother [*née Catherine L. Barry*] and father [*Thomas F. Harnett*] were Catholic, they were sort of staunch Catholics, never miss Mass, go to confession and all that. And I had two children, my boy and girl [*Robert and Katherine*]. And it came time to enter them into school; my mother-in-law was whispering in my husband's ear, 'Make sure they go to St[*s*]. Peter and Paul [*Parochial School, 240 Dover Street, Fall River*]. You know they may end up at St. Luke's [*Episcopal Church, Warren Street, corner Oxford Street, Fall River*].' And I said, 'Well, I got to please them all, I have got to live in this house with all the Catholics, well, all right, and it won't do no harm.' I told the kids that if they ever say anything, those nuns say anything about the Episcopal faith, [*that*] they are black Catholics or something, or black Christians. You don't take notice of that. I brought them up in the Catholic school.... It's come in handy. It's come in handy.

JC: Yes. And you have been an Episcopalian? Or you were brought up as a Catholic as well?

MH: Luke warm, I went to both churches. I used to like to go to the evening Mass at the [*St. Luke's*] Episcopal church because they all used to sing and I could sing. And the Catholic church, I liked that too, because I had friends there. I was broadminded in that way.

JC: Did you father have any political convictions?

MH: He was a staunch Republican until [*President Franklin Delano*] Roosevelt brought in that Social Security [*in 1935*]. And he thought that was the best idea that ever happened. He turned and he voted Democrat the rest of his life.

JC: You have any stories you would like to share with us about your brothers and sister?

MH: They were good kids. My brother went to war. He was a gunner. You know the planes that take off from the ships? And underneath there is a ball; he rode that turret, I think they call it, a turret. And he used, he used to shoot down the Japs. He got the Purple Heart though.

JC: He survived the war?

MH: Yes, thank God. His ship got hit one time. My father was down. I never saw my father down on his knees at his bed praying for his son. You know? It was the first time. My father was a good man. And [*that was*] the first time I actually saw him on his knees praying for his son. I remember those things so well, indelible in my mind.

JC: You were born in Lawrence. How long did you live in Lawrence?

MH: I went to the first grade [*at Rev. George Packard School, Parker Street*] in [*South*] Lawrence, because my father had to been transferred to Maine for a chain store [*circa 1927*]. And I was already enrolled in the school, so to finish out the year, I stayed with my grandparents. And my mother had a little boy, my brother; they took the baby because he needed more care. And I was safe with my grandparents. So, then we went, several places we lived. But I do remember when I came to Fall River.... We lived in a tenement.... I could walk to the [*Hugo A.*] Dubuque [*Elementary*] School. I could walk from that down Locust Street. I can't remember the number on the house, but if I went on the street I could point it right out. I could see it all. So I went to the Dubuque School. At recess the kids liked to get me in the corner, because I still spoke with that New York accent. And they thought it was funny. They would say, 'Talk, talk.' Kids. Fourth grade.

JC: Your father was very enterprising, so I imagine the family never suffered any real economic hardships.

MH: Yeah, when he was out of work. He worked for the WPA [*Works Progress Administration, instituted in 1935*]. Sure, he dug ditches.

JC: Wow.

MH: We were poor. When the Depression was on. But that is what made him save all his money when he worked, knowing his son was going to come home from the war and there would be another depression. We were on what they called food stamps [*ration books*]. But everyone was on stamps, if you remember, during that war [*World War II*]. And you could only [*get*], I think three eggs a week. Something like that. And we used to stand in line [*at 211 South*] Main Street, Fall River, to get the butter from Kennedy's [*Kennedy & Company, Inc.*]. It used to be in a bucket and they used to cut the butter. And we stand in line. Do you remember that?

JR: My mom told me a lot of that. You are saying exactly what she experienced.

MH: And we had [*ration*] stamps. We had lots of money, mind you. But you couldn't buy anything. Everything, cigarettes, oh God, and everybody, all the guys smoked in those days. The women too. But I can remember that one cigarette you could buy, not that I did, Raleighs. Yeah, and they sent all the good cigarettes; good cigarettes, there are none that are good. But the Chesterfields, Lucky Strikes, all went over to our boys overseas. They got the best of everything and we had to [*ration*], we didn't starve, but we had a lot of money. When the people didn't rob you, but you couldn't buy anything.... Everything was rationed.

JC: What work was your father doing when the Depression began?

MH: Oh, twenty-nine, he'd be, [*in*] 1929.... They went to work in the mills at fourteen, you know.

JC: So he wasn't working for the five-and-ten [*Cent Store*].

MH: No. I would be eight years old, that must be when he was starting and went to Maine. So I saw the first grade.

JC: Yes, did he lose his job with the five-and-ten?

MH: No, he left of his own accord.

JC: He left of his own accord?

MH: My mother badgered him, I bet.

JC: Okay.

MH: That was when he started his own, trying to get going in his own business. He was his own boss.

JC: What brought him to the WPA? He must have lost work?

MH: Let me see. We were on [*15*] Orchard Street, off Pleasant Street, Fall River.... He worked for the WPA. It must have been before he got into that, before the Red Mill and before the gas stations. He worked, it was hard times then.

JC: Yes, how long was he on the WPA?

MH: I don't know, it wasn't a long time. I don't remember really.

JC: Do you remember what he did? On the WPA

MH: He dug ditches.

JC: He dug ditches?

MH: A lot of the men did. And remember we were keeping the old folks, too. Everybody had grandparents in their home.

JC: So you had to scrimp and save at home? Yes?

MH: Yes, but we never felt hungry. I remember we used to, the neighbors were always bringing in food. My grandmother sending food - when she made a bunch - she would send it upstairs. When the Italian lady [*Mrs. Benardo Caruso, née Maddalena Do Nardo, who lived on the third floor*] would make her spaghetti, she would send a big bowl down to us. It was a different kind of life back then. You know? People were generous to each other. Everyone was in the same boat. And that was the way it was.

JC: Fall River in those days was a collection of ethnic groups. And in some cases they didn't get along. But you are telling me in the Depression they pulled together.

MH: Oh, absolutely. Absolutely. I can remember neighbors, Italian upstairs [*Mr. and Mrs. Caruso*], French over there [*Mr. Moise Gamelin on the first floor*], oh yeah, they all pulled together.

JC: Yes.

MH: It was a different world than it is now.

JC: So you have mentioned a few neighborhoods, Orchard Street. Is that where you were living during the Depression?

MH: I was in the fifth grade. You know, that was when it was, my father was working on the WPA. Now I'm trying to remember, was he out of work? Because I hadn't graduated from eighth grade yet. I went in the fifth grade. There is a [*Samuel*] Watson [*Elementary*] School up there [*935 Eastern Avenue, Fall River*].

MH: We made our graduation gowns [*in home economics class*]. Dotted white muslin. Yeah. And we would bake cupcakes.... And I would have to walk from Bedford Street to that school and be on time.

JC: Can you tell us what you saw on your walk to the Watson School?

MH: There was, it depends on what route you took. But Mark You [*Chinese Restaurant, 1236 Pleasant Street, Fall River*]. And if you had a nickel you could go in there and get a, they wrap it in paper, French fries, and take them out and eat them on the way.

JR: On the way to the Watson School?

MH: Or on the way back.

JC: Any other?

MH: Yes, I can remember the Strand Theatre [*1363 Pleasant Street, Fall River*], where they would give you a dish if you go on a Wednesday with your girlfriend [*so called "Dish Night"*] and your mother would say, 'Don't come home without the dish.' I still have pieces of that stoneware. Oh, I could give that to the Smithsonian. And I have other antiques, too. But, they end up in the trash.

JC: Do you have any other memories of your school days in Fall River?

MH: Oh sure. Sure.

JC: Something you would like to share with us?

MH: I'm thinking, I'm thinking. I remember in the eighth grade, making our own dresses, going up to the uh, the uh, what is that school I said, Watson?

JC: Yes.

MH: I remember it took all year to make the dress. But you only had an hour a day and you were learning. I remember that and ...

JC: How about your friends?

MH: I had friends, yeah.

JC: When you weren't in school, what did you do together?

MH: Jacks.

JC: Jacks?

MH: Jump rope—French style, hide-and-seek. I liked to play. You know Potterville [*School*] at all, in Somerset, [*Massachusetts*]? You know that school.... I think the handbars are still in the yard. I used to swing from them when I was in the fourth and fifth grade. See, we lived in Somerset for a short while, too.... You know? It's down the hill a little bit.

JC: You moved?

MH: There used to be a post office [*United States Post Office, Pottersville Station, Riverside Avenue, Somerset*] way down, you had to walk for your mail when I was a kid. Yeah. Maybe. I am wracking my brain, trying to think. Some memories, most memories, are very vivid.

JC: Your school days ended with ...

MH: High school.

JC: You graduated from high school?

MH: No, I didn't. I went to work.

JC: After how many years of high school?

MH: Two [*B.M.C. Durfee High School, circa 1936-1937*].

JC: Okay. That was the norm in those days?

MH: Oh, yeah. Well, yeah, a lot of the girls had more than I had, as far as dressing up. You know, when you are that age, nice sweaters and we weren't that poor. It was just teenagers got to want nice things. I went to work. That is when I started working on the power machines. With my mother. When they came within the working age, what was it, sixteen back then?

JC: I think so.

JR: I think it was sixteen.

MH: Well, summer vacations from school, [*B.M.C.*] Durfee, I used that vacation … to go with my mother and we worked on the power machines. Side by side. And then I would go back to school … the first job I ever had was in the summer vacation in the five-and-ten [*Cent Store*]. All the girls worked the five-and-ten, right? Weekends, nights, and whatever in high school. And [*F.W.*] Woolworth's [*& Company, 95 South Main Street*] was one of them.… The first power machine I ran was in S & S Manufacturing [*379 Pleasant Street, Fall River*].... I was a side joiner on ladies' dresses. Women didn't wear slacks in those days. They wore dresses. And I used to [*do piecework*]; the faster you go, the more money you could make. And you would have a wooden horse here and a wooden horse here. And the floor lady would put a pile to be done on this side. They had to be joined on the side. Tops were together. And then when you finish and throw them on there. When I think of it. That was the first power machine. Then the Har-Lee [*Manufacturing Company, 425 Pleasant Street*]. Those buildings are still standing on Pleasant Street…. I did piecework, the collar and the hems. Wouldn't be fast.

JR: That was a big place. I heard that was a really big.

MH: Har-Lee was big. Bigger than S & S.

JR: I heard that. I heard it was two thousand employees there.

MH: Probably so. There was a lot. Yeah.

JC: Now, your mother was working side by side with you?

MH: Not in the Har-Lee, in the S & S, the first one.

JC: Yes. She went to work because of the Depression?

MH: No, we needed the money. She always wanted to help.

JC: She wanted to?

MH: She had two grandmas in the house. It wasn't like she was neglecting us.

JC: She hadn't worked before then?

MH: Of course she worked when she was younger in the mills….

JC: Yes, before she married?

MH: Yes. Before she married, she worked [*as an operative*] in the mills [*in Lawrence*].

JC: Yes.

MH: I can remember the stories they used to say. I would say, 'How did you meet Dad?' She said, 'I hit him with a bobbin in the mill.' They were young. She must have thrown a bobbin at him. That's what I grew up with. And then, [*I worked in*] the Har-Lee, piecework, a collar and hem maker. Then the Kerr [*Thread*] Mill[*s, American Thread Company, Martine Street, Fall River*]. Remember the Kerr Mill? It's down now, it's gone. I was a yarn inspector. And, uh, I worked in The Boston Store [*women's dresses, 80 South*] Main Street. If you remember, coats and dresses? You are too young, you are all too young. It's nice to be young. The Boston [*Store*], Mell's Jewelry [*Company, 74 South Main Street*] on the corner. I worked in the office there. And I left that office job, to go to work for the war effort. That was when I went to Firestone and left my pay into War Bonds and took my second job waiting tables for necessary things. Just necessary things. I lived at home with my mother and father, I wasn't married. And then, [*later, after I married and had my children*] ... I was working to help out with the tuition. I worked as a waitress at White's [*Family Restaurant, North Westport, Massachusetts, owned by Roland Aime LaFrance and his wife, née Rita Fallon*]. Yeah. I worked there for twelve years. I kept my tips.

JC: Which job did you enjoy doing the most?

MH: I liked retail. I loved waiting on people, I worked at Edgar's [*Department Store, Inc., 109 Mariano S. Bishop Boulevard, Fall River*], the last job I had. Edgar's, everyone, you know, went to Edgar's. I could work in any department. Because I loved selling stuff. I don't like buying. I like saving.

JC: The power machines in the mill, were fun or not so much fun?

MH: They were all right. I knew nothing else at the time. They were all right. But I couldn't go as fast as some of those people.

JC: The supervisors treated you well?

MH: Oh yes. I was friends with them.

JC: Now, you were an attractive young lady then. And so the young men must have ... had their eye on you.

MH: Oh, come on. I used to like to go dancing.

JC: Where?

MH: Lincoln Park [*State Road, Westport, Massachusetts*]. The Grand Ball Room. I liked to go dancing.

JC: Were there sailors there?

MH: Sailors?

JC: Sailors, from Newport.

MH: You're too young. No, they weren't in uniform when I was going to Lincoln Park.

JC: Okay. So you would take a street car to Lincoln Park?

MH: Sometimes the trolley. The tracks are still there under the tar. And the bus. You would have to walk down from … Lafayette Street and Barnes Street [*in Fall River*]. We used to walk down to get the bus or the trolley, way down.

JR: To take you to Westport?

MH: To Lincoln Park. And then when I married, we always took the children there all the time….

JC: How did you meet your husband?

MH: I'm trying to remember now. Oh, I think there were four of us, I was introduced to him by another girl.

JC: What did you find attractive about him?

MH: I don't have to tell you that.

JC: No, you don't.

MH: He was a redhead. An Irish redhead. But it wasn't that carrot red. It was gold and blond hair. Tall. Good looking.

JC: I didn't get your maiden name. What was it?

MH: Vokes. A lot of people say it's German, but I don't know about that. [*The Vokes surname is said to derive from an old Germanic personal name translating to 'people.'*]

JC: Have you looked into your ancestry? Do you have any Germans in your family tree?

MH: I never looked into that. I never looked into that, my dear.

JC: How long did you date your husband before you got married?

MH: I don't think about those things. I don't know. Not years and years. But I don't remember exactly. During the war.

JC: The lunches at the mill. When you worked at the mill, what did you do for lunch? You carried it?

MH: From home ... sandwich, piece of fruit. You know, you could buy a drink. I remember with my mother, way back, she used to buy me a bottle of coffee milk. Both of us have a coffee milk with our lunch. We would bring it from home. And on Friday, when you get paid, if you had time you would sneak out to buy something, and sit in a restaurant and eat. When you had a bit of money. We used to bring our pays home, too. And hand them over to Daddy. You remember that?

JC: You were given spending money?

MH: Oh, yeah.

JC: Yes, what did you do with the spending money?

MH: Saved it.

JC: What year were you married?

MH: Oh, I don't know.

JC: Was it before the war? During the war?

MH: Just after when the war was ending.

JC: 1945?

MH: Around, maybe a little later. I don't remember that one exactly.

JC: Okay. Do you remember when your first child was born?

MH: No. I don't. [*Robert W. Harnett, born in 1944.*] He died at fifty [*in 1994*]. Heart attack. My son. He went like that. He was with me the night before....

JC: No matter what the age, you never get over losing a child.

MH: That is what the priest said to me. He put his hands like that, said, 'No mother should bury her child.' I lost my other girl, too. I lost Katherine Mary [*in 2011*].... My other daughter [*Christine*] has had a stroke. Kathy died. Bob died. My husband died....

JC: When your children were young. Were you a working mother?

MH: I worked part-time most of the time. Because I had an eight room house, and the three kids, and a husband. You know, I was kind of particular about my home, too.

JC: What would you say was most satisfying and most difficult about those years?

MH: Oh. You won't print it? No, I won't say it.

JC: Okay. Alright. Your children were well behaved? They didn't give you much trouble?

MH: Absolutely, not a bit. Once my son hid a six pack of beer under the lilac bush in the yard. He was only a teenager. And I found it. And I said to my husband, 'Look at this. That darn kid. Him and the boys must have got it somehow. And hid it under the lilac bush.' He said, 'That's good, I like that, bring it in. Put it in the fridge.' And he enjoyed it.

JC: We seem to have passed over the [*beauty pageant*] story. [*The "Big Hollywood Bathing Beauty Contest" was held at the Empire Theater, 116 South Main Street, produced in cooperation with Republic Pictures Corporation, August 19, 1940.*]

MH: Oh, that is so long ago, who is going to believe that baloney. I was second runner up. My daughters always said don't talk about it. I'm an old lady with two great-grandchildren. Don't say that. It spreads like wild fire up here. They have nothing else to talk about anyway.

JC: Who persuaded you to?

MH: Nobody. Did you know Rose [*M.*] Boulas?

JR: Yes.

MH: She was in it with me.

JR: She is dynamic.

MH: Oh, absolutely, she brought all these [*people from the*] east end up on Pleasant Street, Quequechan Street. She brought the whole gang with her. Very vivacious. Very vivacious.

JR: Remember her shop on Main Street?

MH: Klose [*By*] Rose. Spelt with a K. Klose [*By*] Rose.

JR: She pushed you into the competition?

MH: Oh, no, but she was in there. I thought she would come out first. I don't remember who came out first. But every time I went to the movie way back then ... there was a William [*Samuel*] Canning … William [*S.*] Canning Boulevard is named for that man. Well, he was in charge of the Empire Theatre [*116 South Main Street, Fall River*]. Remember the Empire Theatre?

JR: Yes, I do, I do.

MH: We had [*in Fall River*] the Durfee [*Theatre, 28 North Main Street*], the Empire, and the Capitol [*Theatre, 309 South Main Street*], the Plaza [*Theatre, 381 South Main Street*], and the big Bijou [*Theatre, 162 North Main Street]* way down, and the Strand [*Theatre, 1363 Pleasant Street*], up the Flint [*section of the city*], where they gave the dishes. Yeah, well, he was in charge at that time. And he wanted me to go to Atlantic City, [*New Jersey*]. And my father said … Of course, way back then, you didn't know [*who*] William Canning was. He was mad at something to do with the theatres, and my father said, 'Oh no, no, no, the wolves will get you.' Imagine that. The silly things you do and say when you are young like that.

JC: He was very protective of his little girl.

MH: Yeah.

JR: So, what was the competition like?

MH: Well, it was in the Empire Theatre, and the seats were like they were for the movies. But they run a walkway over the seats around to up the aisle. The stage was here, and they had a runway that way. Yeah. But I didn't tell anybody. Only my father said to my mother, 'You and her friend, you go. Be in the audience. At least she will have someone.' Because I didn't tell anybody.

JR: What did you wear?

MH: I wore a bathing suit.

JR: You had a bathing suit?

MH: Not a bikini. I remember I bought it at McWhirr's [*R.A. McWhirr Company, department store, 165-193 South Main Street, Fall River*]. It was a Black Jantzen. The one that had the red swimmer on the logo. They were good. I think I got it in Cherry's [*Cherry & Webb Company, women's and misses clothing, 139-149 South Main Street, Fall River*] or McWhirr's. High heels, black patent leather high heels. No makeup, and I had brown hair.

JR: Did they have a talent competition?

MH: Good thing they didn't.

JC: Do you have any other memories that you would like to share with us about those years?

MH: Do you remember Lincoln Park? Everybody does. Well, some cousins on my husband's side used to manage that park, it's gone now, I know—the McConnell family. 'Slim' [*Everett A.*] and Shirley [*L.*] McConnell, [*née Cachia*] used to manage Lincoln Park.

JC: I hope we are not tiring you.... You have had an interesting life.

MH: Well, I never thought of it that way. But it's normal.

JC: What would you say was the most satisfying thing you've done in life?

MH: I'm not finished yet!

JC: So there is something yet to come?

MH: Yes, but I can't tell you. What? What?

JC: Do you have any regrets?

MH: No, I haven't. I wonder about a lot of things: why, how, how come?

JC: Mrs. Harnett, we thank you very much for sharing your stories, your life story with us.

PHOTO GALLERY

7.1 McLellan's 5 Cent to $1.00 Store, 281 South Main Street, Fall River, Massachusetts, 1930. Marita's father, Reginald Arthur Vokes, relocated his family to the city when he accepted a position to manage this store. *"Well* [my father] *was in charge of McLellan's."*

7.2 McLellan's 5 Cent to $1.00 Store, 281 South Main Street, Fall River, Massachusetts, 1930.

7.3 McLellan's 5 Cent to $1.00 Store, 281 South Main Street, Fall River, Massachusetts, 1930.

7.4 North Main Street, Fall River, Massachusetts, looking south, circa 1938; the Socony – Vacuum Oil Company billboard is visible atop the iconic Academy Building. Marita's father operated Vokes Friendly Service, a Socony gasoline station, circa 1935-1940. *"... do you remember Socony Gas, the flying red horse?"*

BIG HOLLYWOOD
BATHING BEAUTY CONTEST
TO BE HELD AT THE
EMPIRE THEATRE
TO SELECT "MISS FALL RIVER"

Applicants Leave Name with the Manager!

Valuable Prizes — Motion Pictures of Each Contestant Will Be Taken. Pictures to Be Sent to One of Hollywood's Leading Producers

7.5 Advertisement that appeared in the *Fall River Herald News*, July 22, 1940. Marita and her friend, Rose M. Boulas, entered the competition. *"She was in it with me. I thought she would come out first."*

7.6 Empire Theatre, 116 South Main Street, Fall River, Massachusetts, 1924. Marita was a contestant in a "Big Hollywood Bathing Beauty Contest" held in this theatre with the cooperation of Republic Pictures Corporation on August 19, 1940. *"My father said, 'Oh no, no, no, the wolves will get you.' Imagine that. The silly things you do and say when you are young like that."*

7.7 Interior of the Empire Theatre, 116 South Main Street, Fall River, 1924; the theater was specially outfitted by Republic Pictures Corporation for the "Big Hollywood Bathing Beauty Contest," held on August 19, 1940. *"It was in the Empire Theatre, and the seats were like for the movies. But they run a walkway over the seats around to up the aisle. The stage was here and they had a runway that way."*

7.8 "By the Sea Shop," R.A. McWhirr Company, department store, 165-193 South Main Street, Fall River, 1936. *"I remember I bought it at McWhirr's. It was a black Jantzen ... that had the red swimmer on the logo. High heels, black patent leather high heels. No makeup, and I had brown hair."*

7.9 Mell's Jewelry Company, in the Academy Building, 74 South Main Street, Fall River, Massachusetts, 1940s. *"I worked in the office there. And I left that office job, to go to work for the war effort."*

7.10 A glamorous Marita in the 1940s.

7.11 Marita flanked by two military buddies of her brother, Reginald Arthur Vokes, Jr., outside the family residence at 30 Lafayette Street, Fall River, Massachusetts; in keeping with the war effort, the Vokes family did their part entertaining 'the boys' during World War II. *"When the war came, my brother went to war. He got the Purple Heart, by the way."*

7.12 Durfee Mills, Fall River, Massachusetts, depicted in an early 20th century postcard. Marita was employed at S & S Manufacturing and Har-Lee Manufacturing Company, both of which operated from this location in the 1940s. *"The first power machine I ran was in S & S Manufacturing … I was a side joiner on ladies' dresses. Then the Har-Lee … I did piece work, the collar and the hems."*

7.13 Woman workers inspecting gas masks during World War II at Firestone Rubber & Latex Products Company, Fall River, Massachusetts, 1942. *"I went to Firestone, and left my pay into War Bonds."*

7.14 Henry's Latin Quarter - Show Bar, 289 Central Street, Fall River, Massachusetts; one of Fall River's most popular night clubs, Marita was employed at this establishment in the late 1940s.

7.15 Waitresses at Henry's Latin Quarter - Show Bar, 289 Central Street, Fall River, Massachusetts, circa 1948; Marita was employed at this establishment, which was one of Fall River's most popular night clubs. Marita, wearing knotted pearls, posing with her mother, Mrs. Reginald Arthur Vokes Sr., née Alma M. Latraverse, flanked by two unidentified women.

7.16 Kerr Thread Mills, American Thread Company, Martine Street, Fall River, Massachusetts, where Marita was employed as a young woman. *"I was a yarn inspector."*

7.17 *Left:* Marita serving a buffet at White's Family Restaurant in the early 1960s. *"I worked as a waitress … I worked there twelve years."*

7.18 *Right:* Marita's mother, posing with her daughter and three grandchildren in Tiverton, Rhode Island, circa 1963. Left to right: Mrs. Reginald Arthur Vokes Sr., née Alma M. Latraverse; Christine Harnett; Marita; Katherine Mary Harnett; and Robert William Harnett.

7.19 *Below:* An architectural design for Edgar's Department Store, Inc., 109 Mariano S. Bishop Boulevard, Fall River, Massachusetts. *"I worked at Edgar's, the last job I had. Edgar's, everyone, you know, went to Edgar's."*

EIGHT: Eva Rochefort

MARIE EVA ROCHEFORT, NÉE GAGNON

Personal Statistics

Name: Marie Eva Gagnon
(Mrs. Rene Joseph Arsene Rochefort)

Date of Birth: March 25, 1916

Place of Birth: Fall River, Massachusetts

Father: Joseph Arthur Gagnon (1893-1961)

Mother: Marie Eva Turgeon (1896-1968)

Siblings: Marie Rita Gagnon (1918-1993)
---(Mrs. Raymond H. Payer)
Joseph Arthur Armand Gagnon (1921-1992)
Marie Helene Yvette Gagnon (1923-2013)
---(Mrs. Rene Ovila Peladeau)

Spouse: Rene Joseph Arsène Rochefort (1907-1991)

Date of Marriage: February 22, 1936

Children: Doris Eva Rochefort
---(Mrs. Robert Louis Bernier)
---(Mrs. Raymond James Thibault)

Employment history:
Gorin's Inc., Department Store, Fall River
Charlton Mills, Fall River
Made Rite Potato Chip Company, Inc., Fall River
Bonnie Products Corporation, Fall River
Elbe File and Binder Company, Inc., Fall River
Shelburne Shirt Company, Fall River

EDITED TRANSCRIPT

Interview with Mrs. Rene Joseph Arsene Rochefort, née Marie Eva Gagnon

Interviewer: (AS) Ann Rockett-Sperling

Interviewee: (ER) Marie Eva (Gagnon) Rochefort

Additional Commentary: (JR) Joyce B. Rodrigues, Fall River Historical Society

(DT) Doris Eva (Rochefort) Bernier Thibault, Eva's daughter

Date of Interview: July 29, 2015

Location: Rochefort residence, Fall River, Massachusetts

Summary by Joyce B. Rodrigues:

Marie Eva (Gagnon) Rochefort was born in Fall River on March 25, 1916.

Her parents, of French-Canadian descent, were born in Fall River and met and married in 1915 at the Notre Dame de Lourdes Church. Eva's paternal and maternal grandparents, the Gagnons and Turgeons, immigrated to the United States from Quebec, Canada, in the 1880s, met in Fall River, and were also married at the Notre Dame de Lourdes Church.

Notre Dame was established in 1874 to serve the growing French-Canadian population located in the city's east end — "the Flint Village." At its peak, the parish served a population of over 10,000. In 1900, 40 percent of Fall River's population of over 100,000 claimed French-Canadian ancestry.

Throughout the New England states, French-Canadian immigrants developed their own churches, schools, newspapers, cultural and political organizations, and social clubs. In Fall River, entire sections of the city were French-speaking. The Flint neighborhood, in particular, was a stronghold of French culture.

There were four children in the Gagnon family. Eva was the oldest, followed by a younger brother and two sisters.

Eva started working in 1931 at the age of fifteen at the Charlton Mills, a historic textile mill, built in 1911 with Earle P. Charlton as president. Charlton was a successful businessman who had established a chain of 53 five-and-dime stores and in 1912 merged with F.W. Woolworth.

The Charlton Mill was the last granite mill constructed in Fall River.

Eva met her husband at the Charlton Mills. They married in 1936 and lived in the south end of Fall River in former mill housing originally owned by the King Philip Mills. They had one daughter.

Eva's career took her to factories in Fall River: Charlton Mills, Shelburne Shirt Company, Made Rite Potato Chip Company, Bonnie Products Corporation, Elbe File and Binder Company, Inc., and Gorin's, Inc. (department store).

Eva's story begins during the French-Canadian cultural ascendancy in Fall River and continues through the boom and bust years of the textile industry, the Great Depression, the rise and fall of Fall River's garment, manufacturing, and wartime industries, and the striking social and technological changes that followed.

In this interview, Eva said the best thing about her life is her family. Her family was close and even as it grew, remained close. In March 2016, Eva celebrated her 100th birthday surrounded by family, friends, grandchildren, step-grand-children, great- and great-great-grandchildren, and received well wishes from the City of Fall River, the State of Massachusetts, and the White House.

Note: This interview has been slightly edited for continuity and readability; in order to preserve the integrity of the conversation, the phraseology remains that of the interviewer and interviewee. Italicized information in square brackets has been added for the purposes of clarification and context.

AS: So, could you tell us, Eva, when and where you were born?

ER: Well, I was born [*at 130*] Barnes Street, [*Fall River, Massachusetts, on March 25, 1916*]....

AS: Were you born in the house?

ER: Oh, yeah, I was born in the house. I had [*my daughter, Doris Eva Rochefort*] in the house, too. In those days that is what, no hospitals. And in my days I had her [*at*] home [*at 431*] Kilburn Street.

AS: So what did your parents do for a living?

ER: My father [*Joseph Arthur Gagnon*] ... he done a couple ... he was selling insurance [*circa 1927*], but he had a wagon and a horse, and he delivered some milk, you know, bottles of milk [*for the Fall River Dairy Company, 840 Bedford Street, circa 1922-1924 and 1928-1933; and Guimond's Dairy, 359 Robeson Street, Fall River, circa 1935-1941*]. I used to live around there. And my uncle [*Jean Baptiste Couture*] had a little store there, too [*Central Ice Cream, 781 Eastern Avenue, Fall River, managed by his wife, née Marie Berthe Turgeon, circa 1939-1940*]. We lived on Eastern Avenue. [*The Gagnon family relocated to 774 Eastern Avenue circa 1926.*]

AS: So, what school did you go to?

ER: I don't remember; it was on Eastern Avenue.

AS: Oh, the Watson maybe.

ER: Okay, well, the [*Samuel*] Watson [*Grammar School, 935 Eastern Avenue, Fall River*] is further up, I think. That was when I was older....

JR: I'm thinking that maybe that school isn't there anymore.

ER: No, it's not there. That was when I was like a young kid.... I went to Notre Dame [*Parochial School, 34 St. Joseph Street and 226 Mason Street, Fall River, circa 1921-1925*]. I lived around there. Notre Dame [*de Lourdes*] Church and school.

AS: Did your parents, did they work in the mills?

ER: My mother [*née Marie Eva Turgeon*] did, just for a little while, not that much, you know? Because she had two kids. I was the oldest one. But, she had some time off, and then she knew ... someone to take care of us. And she went to work. But not that long.

AS: What did you have for brothers and sisters? You were the oldest, who else did you have?

ER: I had another sister [*Marie Helene Yvette Gagnon*]. She was eight years younger than me. I had a brother [*Joseph Arthur Armand Gagnon*], so I was the first one. Then I had another sister [*Marie Rita Gagnon*].... So we were four.

AS: Four.

JR: Were your parents from Canada, maybe?

ER: Yes, some of the [*grand*]parents were. But [*my parents*] were [*born*] here.

AS: So your grandparents were from Canada [*and*] your parents were from Fall River?

AS: Canada. That was said, it was 'Cana-daw.'

JR: 'Cana-daw?'

AS: 'Cana-daw.'

JR: But your mother and father were from Fall River?

ER: Yeah, [*both were born in Fall River*].

AS: Now, how about the house where you grew up, what was that like? Do you remember? What the house was like?

ER: On Eastern Avenue ... the house is still there.

AS: So, what floor did you live on?

ER: The second floor. [*The house was a three-family tenement.*]

AS: Do you remember anything about it? Did you have like a stove?

ER: We had a big belly stove, you know? We must have burned some wood. And coal.

AS: When you were young, did you have to do anything in the house?

ER: No.

AS: Your parents did everything?

ER: That's why I'm okay. I didn't do no work.

JR: You mean you didn't cook with your mother? You didn't try to cook?

ER: No, in our days, they didn't do that. But later on, I made up for it.

AS: How about your family, did you do things together, like on a weekend when your parents weren't working?

ER: Not much ... you know, yeah. We stick around the house.

AS: Did you play outside?

ER: Yeah, and I used to play baseball with ... Loretta [*Marie Lorette Lilianne Turgeon*]. Is that my cousin, my niece? [*In fact, 'Loretta' was Eva's aunt, born to her maternal Turgeon grandparents on August 7, 1916. Thus, Loretta was slightly less than five months younger than her niece, Eva.*] And we used to play ball in the yard. And this was my bat. You see? They throw the ball, that is all they had. Back then, they had nothing.

AS: Right, you didn't play marbles or any of that?

ER: Oh yeah, I would win sometimes ... I would lose. I go home with a bag full, the next day it was empty, you know?

JR: How about hopscotch?

ER: I done all that. I jumped rope.

AS: Now how about on the holidays, like Thanksgiving. Was it just your family? Or did other people...

ER: In our days, it was just the family, and then as we got older, we went to the in-laws and all that. I was still young, but good enough to go to them.

AS: You went to visit relatives?

ER: That was what it was like.

AS: So, on Christmas, did you hang up stockings, or did you not do that?

ER: We had nothing.

AS: Not like the other kids?

ER: No, we had nothing.

AS: But you must have gotten some little presents for Christmas.

ER: Yeah.

AS: You were happy with what you got, I'm sure.

JR: Did you speak French in your house?

ER: All the time. And when we went to Notre Dame [*Parish*], they went English. You know? But, I was better at French than English, but it didn't take me long to get back at it.

AS: But you still speak French, I'm sure. Can you read French also? Can you read it? Or just speak it?

ER: I can read better than speak it. I still know my French, I look at that and 'di-di-di-di-di.' I'm slow though. But I am better … yes.

JR: The nuns? [*Roman Catholic religious congregation, Religieuses de Jésus-Marie.*] You had the nuns at Notre Dame? Your grandparents, were they in Fall River?

ER: They were around. Yeah.

AS: And so … your family, what did you do for fun? Did you do anything? Did you go anywhere?

ER: Not that much … I am going to bring my uncle [*Joseph Alfred Gagnon*] in…. I am in a [*buggy*]; he had the buggy. What do you call the horse and buggy, and I [*will*] get the picture of that. I am sitting next to my uncle [*circa 1920, he was a clerk for Lussier Brothers, meats & groceries, Elzear and Gaudiose Lussier, proprietors, 1395 and 1572 Pleasant Street, Fall River*]. See, that's all. And then … we played in the yard, and there was, um, a hill, two or three houses from us, and then we go down there when there was snow, we go down there. Very simple. Very simple.

AS: Life was simpler then, wasn't it? So much simpler.

ER: Yeah, it was. I feel as though I'm rich now. You know?

AS: Because you have a beautiful home, with relatives. How about school? You said you went to …

ER: Notre Dame [*Parochial School*].

AS: And you remember anything about it?

ER: Notre Dame? Um … let me see. No, Notre Dame was all right. Then I went to, and I had to change when I moved, to [*Samuel*] Watson [*Grammar*] School.

AS: Oh, you went to the Watson school?

ER: Yeah, and I went, um, what is the name of that one … it was like a high school. Which one was it, I don't know? It was a high school, and I didn't like the gang that was there. They used to hang in the corner…. But, so I didn't like the place, so, I stayed home.

AS: So you didn't go to [*B.M.C.*] Durfee [*High School*]?

ER: No.

AS: No. You stayed home?

ER: No, I left Durfee and came home. And I didn't go back. So the truant officer in those days come and get me. One man comes over and says, 'Why you aren't in school?' He was nice though, you know? I told him, 'Well, my mother is sick,' you know. 'She is super sick,' and I says, 'that is why I stayed home for her.'

AS: Was that true?

ER: Yeah, I mean, you know, that was … for him. That was for him.

AS: Oh, for him?

ER: So, he must have seen my mother, and she looked okay. He looks at me and says, 'I think you should go back to school.' I said, 'Okay.' So my uncle [*Jean Baptiste Couture, the husband of her mother's sister, née Marie Berthe Turgeon*] had, he was a first [*hand, a section hand in the*] … Charlton Mill[*s, 109 Howe Street, Fall River*]. And he was working there, my uncle. He says, 'You want a job?' I says, 'Yeah.' He said, 'Go get your school card.' So I went to get my school card and I started to work.

AS: How old were you?

ER: I was fifteen or sixteen. So he gave me a job. And then I met my boyfriend [*Rene Joseph Arsene Rochefort*]. After so many years of working there.

AS: And is that who you married? Was that your husband?

ER: Hmm.

AS: Oh, so you met him when you were young.

ER: Yeah, well, see in those days, you know … you either worked or you don't work, or you just hang around or you go work in a store. But today, they all go to college.

AS: It's different.

ER: So, it's a different age.

AS: Right, and times are different. But I'm sure in those days, all your friends worked.

ER: And they had no money. They couldn't, you know.

JR: How about your clothes in those days. Did you make your own clothes?

ER: No, my mother bought that. And a man would come around the house. $1.00 each time he come. And we bought some of that. But, no, I just had enough.

AS: Enough?

ER: A cotton dress, and this and that.

AS: And how about in the mill. Did you bring your own lunch … when you worked there?

ER: No, because I was working from six in the morning to noontime. So I go and come back home. And the week after, I was working at noontime to six. Six to twelve, and the other one was noontime to six.

JR: So you had different shifts.

ER: Two shifts.

AS: So you didn't have to take a lunch, because you would be home for lunch. Now how about your friends? Do you remember any of your friends when you were young?

ER: Well, we didn't go out, we didn't do anything, but we had neighbors.

AS: In the neighborhood.

ER: Across the street, so we made friends there. And so I, I was there until I got married and moved away from there.

JR: How did you get to the mill ... did you walk to the mill?

ER: No, we started with the [*trolley, Eastern Massachusetts Street Railway Company*], on Eastern Avenue, downtown, get out downtown. Get one going to the south end. Because that was pretty far. Yeah. And then the next week we would be twelve to six. See, six in the morning. So I used to get up early in the morning. And now, when I see them do that, I say, 'Oh my God, you get up early!' Then I think, you did the same thing! You know?

DT: That is what has kept you the way you are.

ER: I don't know.

AS: Now your husband worked in the same mill eventually?

ER: Yeah, that's where he met me. He was lucky.

AS: Now what did you do on dates?

ER: We went to the movies. Capitol [*Theatre, 390 South Main Street, Fall River*] show downtown. Yeah. I went there. And then we would go and eat. And I was so bashful; you wouldn't think so today. I was so bashful, and he looks at me and says, 'Aren't you going to eat?' So I am bashful. I think we had ordered pie and ice-cream. So I say, he says you know, 'Look at me.' He said, 'All you do is take a bite.' And that's all you have to do, you know? After I was married, I woke up.

AS: Before you married, you don't want them to think you eat too much.

ER: Everybody is so surprised. 'You were bashful?' And then they see me now, they say, 'YOU?' I says, 'Yes!'

AS: How old were you when you got married?

ER: Almost nineteen.

AS: So you were young.

ER: I was in those days.

AS: And so were you married at the church or at the house?

ER: Notre Dame [*de Lourdes Church, February 22, 1936*].

JR: In the old Notre Dame? The one that burned down [*on May 11, 1982*]?

ER: Yeah, I was at the Stop and Shop [*Supermarket Company, 933 Pleasant Street, Fall River*] ... and I could see a lot of smoke. Someone come in and I says, 'Wow, there must be a big fire over there.' She says, 'Notre Dame is all on fire.' I looked at her and I says, 'Not the church?' I was angry. It was the church. It was the church.

AS: After you got married, did you go on a honeymoon?

ER: Yes, we went on a big trip; we went to Boston [*Massachusetts*].

AS: In those days that was a big trip.

ER: And then he used to get some money, the work he was doing. And he says, 'You want to call up?' And he says, um, 'We can stay maybe a week longer, you know?' I says 'No, we can go home. We will be okay.' So we didn't stay there. We come home and the money, he bought a chair with it. A rocker.

JR: What did you do in Boston? What kind of fun did you have in Boston?

ER: We had some, um, it's not the movies ... it was the real people.

AS: A play?

ER: Yes, we see quite a few of those. We went shopping at [*F.W.*] Woolworth's. And I bought some earrings. And a little boy, when we come home, he says to his mother, he says, 'What she got there?' They didn't even know I had the earrings. You know? So he looks at me, so I says, 'Hey, that's it. I bought some earrings.'

AS: So did you stay there a few days?

ER: Yeah, I think maybe a week.

JR: Now, how did you get there? How did you get to Boston?

ER: His brother [*Joseph Roland Victor Rochefort*] had a car and brought us to downtown [*to the bus station*].

JR: And you had to stay in a hotel?

ER: Yeah. Yeah.

JR: Was that the first time you were in a hotel?

ER: The first time for everything, yeah.

AS: We are not going to go there, Eva.

ER: No, but what I, I knew. I knew way up not that long ago, where it [*the hotel*] was. And uh, I think it was $11 or something like that. Anyways, I forgot that one.

DT: You had your reception at the Eagle [*Restaurant, 33 North Main Street, Fall River*] downtown.

AS: Oh, you had the reception at the Eagle? Your wedding reception was at the Eagle?

ER: Yeah.

AS: That must have been nice.

ER: It was nice.

JR: I think that was the place to go in those days.

ER: That's it, yeah, yeah.

JR: That was pretty classy.

ER: They did that. [*In 1936, the restaurant advertised 'A special banquet hall, apart from the main dining room ... reserved for Parties, Bridge, Teas or Socials.'*]

AS: So after you were married did you go back to work in the mill while you were waiting before [*your daughter*] was born?

ER: Yeah, I worked on [*South*] Main Street. [*Later on,*] I was working with the chip man ... potato chip [*Made Rite Potato Chip Company, Inc., 1853 South Main Street, Fall River*]. I was filling those [*containers*] up. I [*had*] worked downtown at Gorin's [*Inc. Department Store, 281 South Main Street, Fall River*]. And there was a knick-knack [*department*], and I wanted more hours and they couldn't give me that, so I let go. And ... people come in and they wanted certain things. That was me. I says, 'I will go check in the back, see if there is something there.' Some people [*other clerks*] said, 'That's all I've got because I've been there.' So I went in the back, and I would tell them, 'I am sorry,' you know, I couldn't give it to them. So I had that, a knick-knack [*department*]. Yeah. I was busy.

[*Eva was also employed as an assembler at Elbe File and Binder Company, Inc., 649 Alden Street, Fall River.*]

AS: You didn't work in one of the fabric mills?

ER: No.

JR: Jump back a little bit, Eva. When you were at the Charlton Mills, what kind of work did you do in the Charlton Mills?

ER: That's a funny one. They bring me a little container, they had a bobbin, wooden bobbin, and you put it in that machine, press a button, and you turn it. And it fills it up. When it's full, they take it off. Put it in that container. When that is full, someone picks it up. So that is what I was doing. [*She worked as a 'filler.'*]

AS: So you filled bobbins all day. All different colored threads like black and brown.

ER: Yeah, and my husband was working in the other room. He was making, putting the thread on a big roll, you know? And that went on another machine. [*The position was known as a 'drawing-in operator.'*] So that is how he knew me. Yeah. He was lucky he met me.

AS: He was lucky he met you.

JR: So what did the Charlton Mills make?

ER: It was all cotton stuff [*cotton goods manufacturers*]. And when I was living [*at 431 Kilburn Street, Fall River*] across the street [*from Berkshire Fine Spinning Associates, Inc., 372 Kilburn Street*] after I was married ... you hear those machines make a lot of noise, you know?

AS: So they didn't make dresses or coats. They made the cloth.

ER: Yeah.

AS: So when did you stop working there? When [*your daughter*] was born?

ER: No, before that. Because that is when I wasn't going to school, remember? My uncle says, 'You want a job?' I says, 'Yeah,' so he gave me a job. I went to work. Yeah. That was my job. Now I got a better job.

AS: So when you married ... you cooked every night. I'm sure different things for dinner.

ER: Oh, everything.

JR: And did your mother and father like your husband?

ER: I guess so, but in those days, they didn't talk like that, you know? They don't make such big things.

JR: Did they know each other? They know the families?

ER: No, they met them when we, you know. I had a nice beautiful mother-in-law [*Mrs. Arthur Rochefort, née Alphonsine Dufresne*].

AS: Oh, that's nice.

ER: A lot of people, you hear them, 'Oh my god, my mother-in-law, blah, blah, blah,' and I listen to that and I couldn't [*relate to*] that because I didn't have that.

AS: Where did he live when he was younger?

ER: On Kilburn Street [*circa 1936*]. And they were living in the house near the water. [*Prior to the move to Kilburn Street, the Rochefort family resided on Tripp, Dwelly, Benjamin, Penn, and Kay Streets in Fall River.*] My husband then, he was a carpenter [*beginning circa 1943*], so he was all over. He had a truck ... you know, that was his work.

JR: I think, on Kilburn Street ... the houses were owned by the mill.

ER: Yes.

JR: The Berkshire Mills?

ER: Yeah, yeah.

JR: So you were living in Berkshire property?

ER: My husband's father [*Arthur Rochefort*] lived there. [*He purchased the former Berkshire Fine Spinning Associates, Inc. property.*]

AS: Did you have a radio when you were younger? When you were first married?

ER: That's all we had.

AS: No TV.

ER: No.

AS: But you were happy?

ER: Yeah, hey, that's all we had.

AS: So how about in the mill, do you remember like, did it smell of anything? Or was it just ... noisy?

ER: We went to work, it was fine.

AS: Was it noisy?

ER: Yeah, well further up, you hear 'boom, boom, boom.'

AS: How about the men that were in charge? Were they all nice?

ER: It was just my uncle [*Jean Baptiste Couture*] for that part of the place.

AS: So you worked for a relative?

ER: He was good.

AS: He was good to you, because you ...

ER: He married my mother's sister [*née Marie Berthe Turgeon*].

AS: Right, so you were lucky that you worked with someone you knew.

ER: I was lucky all the way.

AS: How about safety? They were careful about making sure you weren't hurt?

ER: No, it was an easy thing. You just put the [*bobbin*] over there. And turned it. Nothing hard. No. Oh, then I worked with the powder puffs [*Bonnie Products Corporation, 126 Shove Street, Fall River*]. I worked [*as a powder puff stuffer*] in those [*mills*] there, [*the former Shove Mills*]. You take the puff ... because one girl makes that. She sews. We have to turn the puff to put [*it*] on the right side. And we ... we have a pick ... it's not pointed. You put that in there and there is a lining in there. You know, the powder puff?

[*Between the years 1949 and 1964, Fall River, Massachusetts, was called the 'Powder Puff Capital of the World'; Bonnie Products Corporation, the world's largest manufacturer of powder puffs, produced 350,000 puffs on a weekly basis. An undated contemporary newspaper clipping from the 1950s describes Eva's occupation: 'Rows and rows of women take the cover, inside out, and the stuffing, either sponge or cotton, put the stuffing on a tool, put the cover over the stuffing, push and arrange. In one motion, these hurried women turn the cover, fit the stuffing, and reach for another.'*]

JR: Satin?

AS: A powder puff like makeup?

ER: You put that in there. I worked in there.

AS: They had a whole mill that made powder puffs?

ER: And I worked ... with the...

DT: [*Potato*] chips.

ER: Yup, I was trying to forget him [*Anthony Salvo, President, Made Rite Potato Chip Company, Inc.*]. Yeah, yeah, yeah. I worked there.

AS: They used to come to the houses and bring tins of chips.

ER: That I wouldn't know. I wouldn't go [*do that*].

AS: So you worked there.

JR: Where was that chip place?

ER: [*1835*] South Main Street … before Charles Street.

ER: And one time, I get my check, you know, they had a check then for my pay. And I looked at that, and says, 'Oh. Something wrong here, there is too much,' you know? But there was a girl watching me all the time, because I knew later on. She must have said she works hard … she did that, and told the boss. The boss gave me a little bit extra.

AS: That was nice.

ER: So, I went to him, and I said to him … I made on purpose to go. I says, 'You gave me too much.' I says, you know, 'I think it's about three times.' I said it, you know? 'You gave me too much.' He looks at me and says, 'Have you got enough?' Then I woke up, and says to myself, you know he wants me to, I says, 'Yeah.' So he looks at me, so I thanked him. Five cents an hour more. Five cents. Big deal.

AS: So, do you remember what you made a week?

ER: $15

AS: $15 every week, and you went every day? Five days?

ER: Yeah, yeah.

JR: Now, how about the rents in those days? … What kind of rents did you pay … did you own your own home or did you pay rent?

ER: No, we paid rent, because [*my husband's*] mother and father owned it.

AS: So you paid it to them.

ER: And then they had the … first floor, [*and on the*] second floor [*was*] my husband's … sister [*Mrs. Joseph Noel Omer LeBoeuf, née Marie Rosilda Rochefort*]. So, it was the mother, the sister, and then upstairs it had rooms where they put different things. So, they cleared that all up. And my husband was a carpenter, too, [*as was his father*]. So they cleaned it all up on the third floor, that's where they put me [*after I was married*]. On the third floor.

AS: So that was nice; it was all family in the house.

ER: Yeah.

AS: So, when you worked at the potato chip factory and the powder puff [*factory*], did you take your lunch then? Did you take a lunch pail or did you eat at home? Or did you buy it there?

ER: No, we didn't buy things. We had no money, you know? I don't remember. I guess it was the hours were different. That is why I started at six to twelve. I go home at twelve, so I didn't have to bring a lunch.

AS: So, you could eat at home.

ER: And then the other one, the other [*shift*] started earlier, but I guess I ate before I left.

JR: Did you do a lot of cooking … did you make meals in advance?

ER: Me? I only had [*my daughter*], so.

AS: You probably made gorton [*French-Canadian pork spread*]. Did you make gorton?

ER: Oh, yeah. Gorton. Yeah.

AS: Takes a long time to make that.

ER: I had it, though.

AS: And meat pie [*French-Canadian tourtiere*]. Did you make meat pie?

ER: No, I wasn't good at pies. But cakes, I was always making cakes. For this one, that one, and then when my husband's brother [*Joseph Albert Rochefort*] come out of the army [*circa 1945*], I made him a cake, and I decorated it with little flags and this and that. But then when I met [*Raymond James Thibault, my widowed daughter's second*] husband, he had a bakery [*Poirier's Bakery, 1524 Pleasant Street, Fall River*]. I used to take his. I didn't make no more.

AS: So you stopped working when you were ready to have [*your daughter*]? Is that when you stopped working at the mills?

ER: Yeah.

AS: And then you didn't go back?

ER: I went [*to Shelburne Shirt Company, Inc., 69 Alden Street, Fall River*] I was doing, folding … it was the shirts I was folding.

AS: Shelburne Shirts?

ER: Yeah, I was working there I had to fold that, [*by*] size, you know?

AS: So that is what you did at Shelburne? You folded the shirts to put into the bag?

ER: Yeah, we had to fold that a certain size, you know and all that.... If I had known I was going to have this [*interview*], I would have wrote it down in a book.

AS: You are doing great.

JR: Do you remember Social Security coming in? 1935, I think. And you had to put your money into the Social Security Fund.

ER: I must have. That I don't remember. I can't say, because I don't remember.

JR: So, then you got a pension when you retired? Did you get a pension?

DT: No. She didn't work long enough.

AS: So, where was [*your daughter*] Doris born?

ER: In the house [*at 415 Kilburn Street, Fall River*]. They didn't have hospitals for that then. But you know, later on, then they do it at the hospitals. But not in my time.

JR: Did you have a nurse there? Was your mother with you?

ER: Yeah, I had a nurse. When I was having [*my daughter*], I was on [*the*] third floor. She [*the nurse*] done all the work. So, she calls the doctor [*Joseph Arthur Archambault*], it's about, you know, she is doing this – blah, blah, blah, blah – so after she gets through with him, he told her, 'Well, it's not time yet. A little bit.' You know? So he waited. She done all the work. Then he gets paid. And she got all the work. You can't win with them. So, she was on the third floor. It was hot! Someone was there. They opened the window. I had no air-condition there.

AS: So, do you remember the Depression?

ER: I was in it.

AS: Right.

ER: I used to go to the store.... I had to go and get some butter, but you had to stand in line. It was very rare ... the butter and the coffee, and this and that. I stayed in line to get it. You know? I go, I think it was, it starts with an 'F.' It was on Main Street.

DT: First National [*Stores, Inc., 1788 South Main Street, Fall River*]?

ER: Yeah. That is where I went, because it was [*near*] Kilburn Street. And I went and see. The girl said, 'Go see the man in the back.' So when I went in, he says … 'Are you going to shop?' I says, 'Yeah.' He said, 'When you are all done shopping … come over.' When I came over, he had a pound of butter in a bag. So I went, and I had the cash.

AS: That was nice. So you had to stand in line for all that?

ER: And then I went and I bought, you never know, I bought some horse meat. But I took the best part of the horse. I didn't know how good everything was, but I did. I had to. You know?

AS: If that was all you had, then …

ER: When my mother had it, oh my God, that was so good. And when I said what it was, oh my God. Yuck. I said, 'Yeah, but I took the best part of the horse.' You know? I'll tell you.

JR: How many times did you do that … buy horse meat?

ER: That was the only time with the horse. I let go of the horse.

AS: Your mother didn't want you buying horse meat.

ER: I'm lucky I just had one. Oh, what a life, you know? When you talk about all those things from way, way back, you know? And people today, and the kids are so smart today. But, compared to us, we had nothing. We didn't go nowhere. I never complained, you know.

AS: How about the hurricane? Do you remember the Hurricane of 1938? Or do you remember any of the hurricanes from when you were younger?

DT: You were on Kilburn [*Street*].

ER: Yeah, I would have to be there. 1938. Yeah. And then [*my husband*] had to …

DT: He had to walk home during that storm. Because they walked.

ER: Everything, yeah. And they had to put something in the window, you know, so it wouldn't break. Because we were in front of that mill [*Berkshire Fine Spinning Associates, Inc., Plant E*].

JR: The bricks were flying from the chimneys?

DT: From the roof.

ER: I know it was….

JR: I am going to jump back a little bit to the Twenties, to the Depression. Were, was everyone working in your house … was there a lot of unemployment?

ER: I know my husband was, I don't know if the others were, too. Yeah. Because that's a long time ago.

DT: Was your father working in the Twenties? You weren't married then.

ER: I don't remember that, that is way back. [*Eva's father was employed throughout the Depression years.*]

AS: So, do you remember when you got your first car? Do you remember? After you were married, I'm sure.

ER: I was forty-two. Not like today, they are seventeen and on the road. And then the first thing you know, they are underneath the road. No, but, um, my husband one time. I never asked for anything. So one day he says, 'If I buy a car … would you learn how to drive?' I looked at him and I says, 'Where did that come from?' I never asked for that. 'Well,' I says, 'okay.' So I learned how to drive. And I got a car. He got me a car. It was green and beige. I still remember. So I was driving.

AS: Do you remember anything about the war [*World War II*]? Do you have any memories about that?

ER: No … we didn't have no this or that.

AS: Just that you had to stand in line.

ER: We had some that went in the war though. There was, uh, not my brother … my brother-in-law [*Joseph Albert Rochefort, United States Army, enlisted July 3, 1942*], he went.

JR: Do you remember when the day that Pearl Harbor happened [*December 7, 1941*]? A lot of people remember that day. They listened to it on the radio.

ER: I must have. Because my husband must have put that [*on*]. So, yeah, I must have.

DT: [A*t the end of the war,*] we went out in the truck. The streets were busy. We went around town. Everyone was celebrating. That was the end of the war.

AS: Oh, the end of the war.

DT: Yes, the end of the war. Everyone was celebrating. Everyone was out [*Victory in Europe Day, aka V-E Day, May 11, 1945*].

JR: Now, [*your daughter*] said your husband built this house?

ER: He was smart. He is lucky he got me. He was very smart. He didn't like school. And his mother [*Mrs. Arthur Rochefort, née Alphonsine Dufresne*] would go to the fence, and talk to him at recess. Then she would go back home. But he made himself, he went to night school [*Bradford Durfee Textile School, 64 Durfee Street, Fall River, graduating June 1, 1928*] and this and that. I said she is smart, just like her father. Yeah.

AS: Where did he go to school?

ER: Well … in the South End.

DT: Benjamin Street, there was a school there.

JR: Benjamin Street?

ER: Yeah. It was on a side street [*Blessed Sacrament Parochial School, South Main Street and Benjamin, corner of Tuttle Street, Fall River*].

ER: So, at noon time, he didn't like school. So, at noon time, his mother used to go to the fence, you know? And talk to him a little bit, and then she would go home. But later on, he made himself, you know?

DT: Look at how well he did.

JR: So, he worked in the mill, and then he changed jobs. He went into carpentry. And then, after the war, he built this house?

DT: He built a lot of houses.

AS: Did he work for a contractor?

DT: No, he was Rochefort Brothers [*Carpenters and Contractors, 431 Kilburn Street, Fall River*].

ER: He was the boss.

JR: He was the contractor.

ER: He and his brother [*Roland Victor Rochefort*].

AS: So [*he*] built a lot of houses?

ER: Oh, yeah. He built a lot.

JR: So he was a well-known business man. That's wonderful.

ER: I know because … you tell somebody about a certain thing. Word of mouth, okay? And a lot of people [*said*] they done a job. So the people said … 'Who does it?

Who does it?' So, they get that job. And they get that job. Word of mouth. Yeah. He done alright.

JR: I am going to go back a little bit ... to things that came about during all of these years. The radio. When did you get your first radio?

ER: We were on Kilburn Street. That's a long time ago.

JR: So you were married already? You didn't have a radio growing up?

ER: We had one of these, you know, these...

AS: Phonographs?

ER: Yeah, phonographs. We had one of those.

JR: And you had to crank it?

ER: That is what we had. And then after that, TV came. [*My husband*] bought one [*at*] Mason's [*Mason Furniture Company, Inc. 146 Second Street, Fall River*]. And it was black-and-white, and it was only about this big. That little picture ... that wasn't big. And then, when the other come out, we still went to Mason's, and he got a colored one.

JR: How about the telephone? When did the telephone come in?

ER: I don't know, but we were four on it.

AS: Four families on it?

ER: At least three or four.

AS: That's a real party line.

ER: My husband, they had his business, and then, in the morning, he wanted to call for some material. That woman [*Mrs. Jean Baptiste Gallante, née Marie Alexina Rosanna Bourque*] was always on the phone. He says, 'Every time I take it, I can never get it. She is always there.' She wasn't going to work, so she should have been in bed. But, anyways. So, that's a long time [*ago*], huh?

JR: So you had to, you were already married, to get a telephone. And then you were married when you got the car.

JR: You grew up near Eastern Ave. You went to Kilburn Street. And then back to the East End [*of Fall River*].

ER: Yeah.

JR: And back to the parish, back to Notre Dame [*de Lourdes*].

ER: Yup.

JR: Now, when you were in the Kilburn Street area. Did you go to … St. Anne's Church [*South Main Street, Fall River*]?

DT: When you were on Kilburn Street … do you remember where you went? Blessed Sacrament?

ER: Yes, Blessed Sacrament [*Church of the Blessed Sacrament*].

JR: And [*then*] came back to the East end and back to …

ER: Notre Dame.

AS: So you sang in the choir?

ER: Is that what they call it?

DT: It's not what you call it.

ER: No, I used to sing in the 'chaw-riss.'

AS: The 'chaw-riss?'

ER: Yeah. I did a lot of things [*at church*]. I modeled a coat one time. And it was pink. And after the program was done, I bought it. It was something. I bought that pink thing. Then, what we had, we walked down the aisle…. I was Lydia [*Saint Lydia of Philippisia, aka The Woman of Purple*] and [*my daughter*] was the Blessed Mother.

JR: Really.

ER: So we went down the aisle. So I says, when they told me, 'You are going to be in it?' I says, 'Can I smile?' They says, 'Yeah,' I can smile. I used to have that purple material. I had it and I smiled there. He said, 'Yeah, otherwise we wouldn't give you the job.' You see, it's just a little thing. I could never make it as the Blessed Mother. I was, would laugh too much. [*My daughter*] is more serious than I am. I am cuckoo. So, they gave me the other one.

AS: Seems like you had a lot of fun.

ER: All the time.

JR: Do you have any advice for us, Eva, that you can give us that is going to keep us as beautiful when we are ninety-nine years old?

AS: As happy as you, as pleasant as you?

ER: I wish you all of that.

AS: Thank you. Thank you very much.

JR: Thank you so much.

ER: I like your company.

AS: This has been wonderful. You have got a wonderful memory.

ER: Not all of it. But some of it.

JR: Okay, I am just going to close. I thank you again.

ER: Thank you, that wasn't bad.

PHOTO GALLERY

8.1 Eva sitting beside her uncle, Joseph Alfred Gagnon, in a delivery wagon from Lussier Brothers, meats and groceries, 1395 and 1572 Pleasant Street, Fall River, Massachusetts, circa 1920. Joseph was employed as a clerk at that establishment. *"I am sitting next to my uncle."*

8.2 Eva as a child. *"When I was a young kid … I went to Notre Dame Parochial School."*

8.3 Eva with her parents and siblings, 1924. Standing left to right: Mrs. Joseph Arthur Gagnon, née Marie Eva Turgeon, holding newborn baby, Marie Helene Yvette Gagnon; Joseph Arthur Gagnon; Marie Rita Gagnon; Eva (with large bow); Joseph Arthur Armand Gagnon. *"I had another sister. I had a brother … then I had another sister. So we were four."*

8.4 Interior view of the Charlton Mills, 109 Howe Street, Fall River, Massachusetts, 1930s. Eva can be seen in the front row, fifth from the left, sitting beside her uncle Jean Baptiste Couture, who secured her employment. *"And he was working there, my uncle. He says, 'You want a job?' I says, 'Yeah.'"*

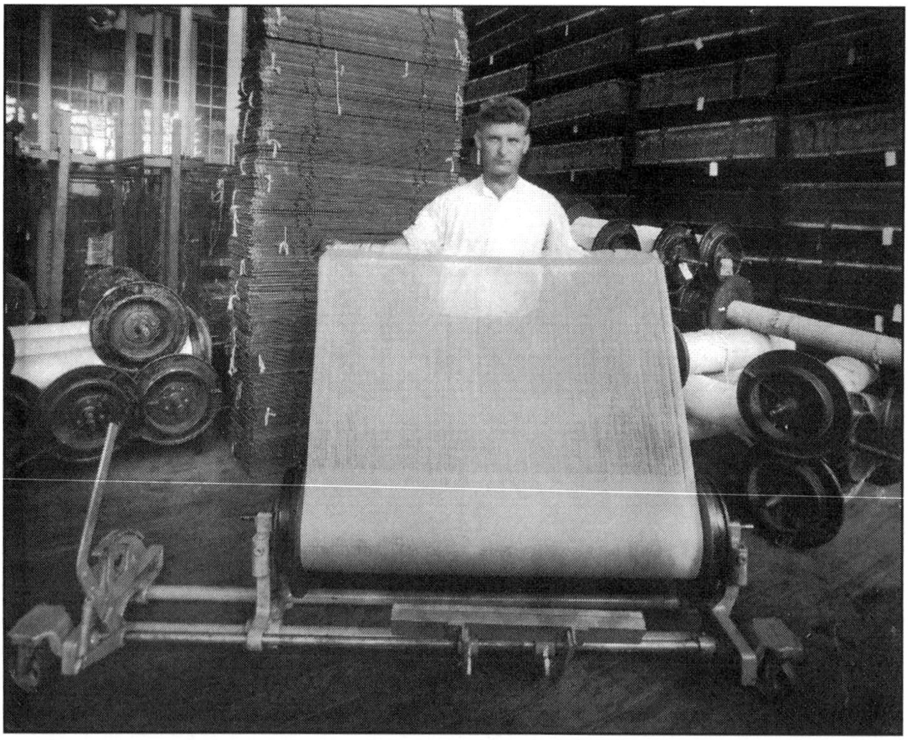

8.5 A worker in the Lincoln Manufacturing Company, Stevens Street, Fall River, Massachusetts, 1925. Eva's future husband, Rene Joseph Arsene Rochefort, performed the same task in the Charlton Mills, 109 Howe Street, Fall River. *"He was … putting the thread on a big roll … and that went on another machine."*

8.6 Gorin's Department Store, Inc., 201 South Main Street, Fall River, Massachusetts, 1940s. *"I worked downtown at Gorin's."*

8.7 The Gagnons posing *en famille.Standing, left to right:* Eva's sisters, Marie Rita Gagnon; Marie Helene Yvette Gagnon. *Seated, left to right:* Eva; her father, Joseph Arthur Gagnon; her mother, née Marie Eva Turgeon; and her brother, Joseph Arthur Armand Gagnon. *"In our days, it was just the family."*

8.8 Eva as a young woman.

8.9 Eagle Restaurant, 33 North Main Street, Fall River, Massachusetts, 1933; Eva's wedding reception was held here on February 22, 1936. *"*[My] *wedding reception was at the Eagle."*

8.10 Interior view of Eagle Restaurant, 33 North Main Street, Fall River, Massachusetts, 1934; the interior of the restaurant was designed to mimic the grand saloon of a Fall River Line Steamship. The restaurant advertised: "A special banquet hall, apart from the main dining room … reserved for Parties, Bridge, Teas or Socials." *"It was nice."*

8.11 Mr. & Mrs. Rene Joseph Arsene Rochefort on their wedding day, February 22, 1936. Eva's father, Joseph Arthur Gagnon is on the right, and Rene's father, Arthur Rochefort, is on the left. *"After we were married we went on a big trip; we went to Boston."*

8.12 Eva and Rene with their daughter, Doris Eva, in the yard of their residence at 431 Kilburn Street, circa 1942. In the background is the Berkshire Fine Spinning Associates, Inc. *"And when I was living across the street ... you heard those machines make a lot of noise."*

8.13 Workers at the Bonnie Products Corporation, 126 Shove Street, Fall River, Massachusetts, enjoying a factory party. Eva is seated, third from the right. The company produced 350,000 powder puffs weekly, earning them the distinction as the world's largest producer of powder puffs. *"Oh, then I worked with the powder puffs."*

8.14 Rochefort Brothers, Carpenters and Contractors. Standing left to right, Eva's husband and her father-in-law, Arthur Rochefort. In the foreground, left to right, are Eva's three brothers-in-law: Joseph Roland Victor Rochfort, Joseph Albert Arthur LeBoeuf, and Raymond Payer. *"So, they get that job. And they get that job. Word of mouth. Yeah. He done alright."*

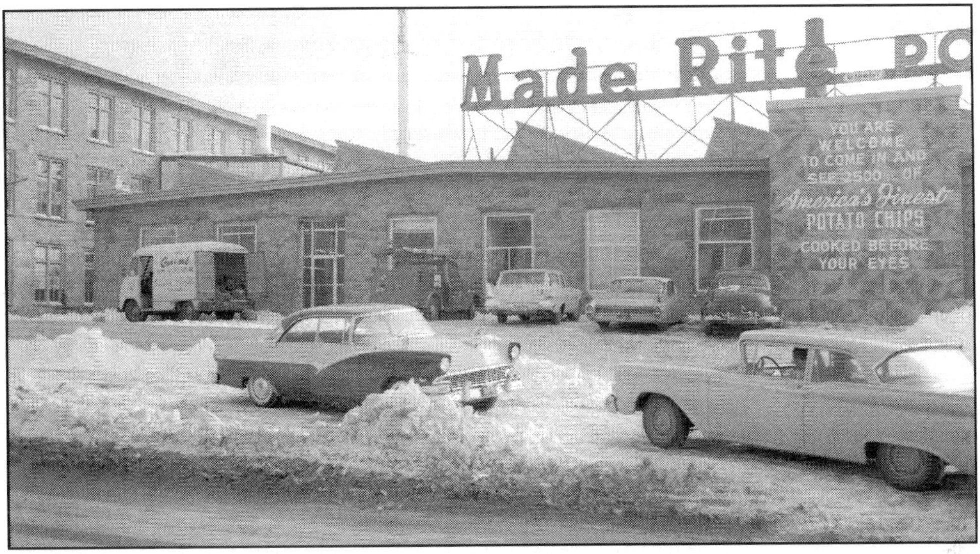

8.15 The Made Rite Potato Chip Company, Inc. plant at 638 Quequechan Street, Fall River, Massachusetts; Eva was employed at the 1853 South Main Street location of that establishment. *"I was working with the chip man … I was filling those* [containers] *up."*

8.16 Eva and Rene with their daughter, Doris Eva Rochefort, circa 1955.

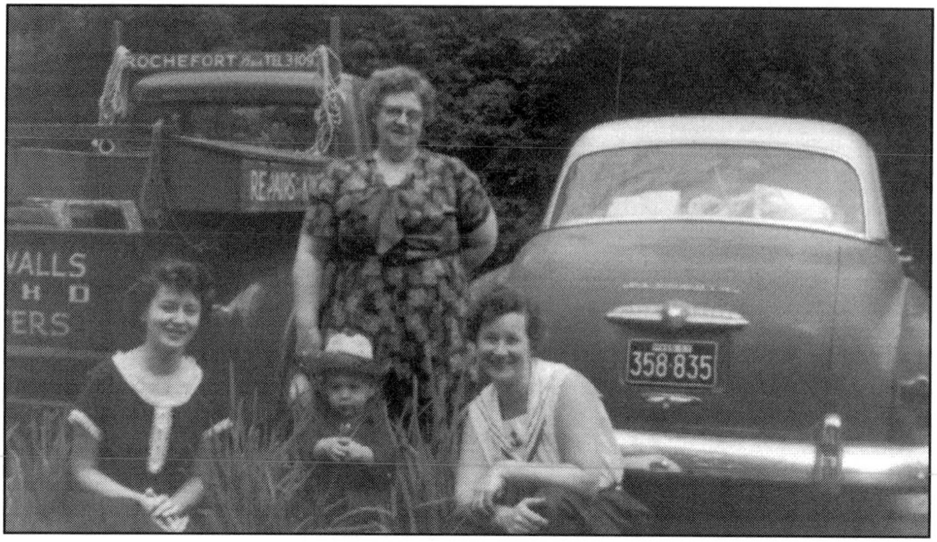

8.17 Eva, seated at right, posing with family members, 1958; in the background is her first car. Standing: Eva's mother, Mrs. Joseph Arthur Gagnon, née Marie Eva Turgeon; seated: Eva's daughter, Doris; and Eva's grandson, Robert Paul Bernier. *"He* [Eva's husband] *got me a car. It was green and beige."*

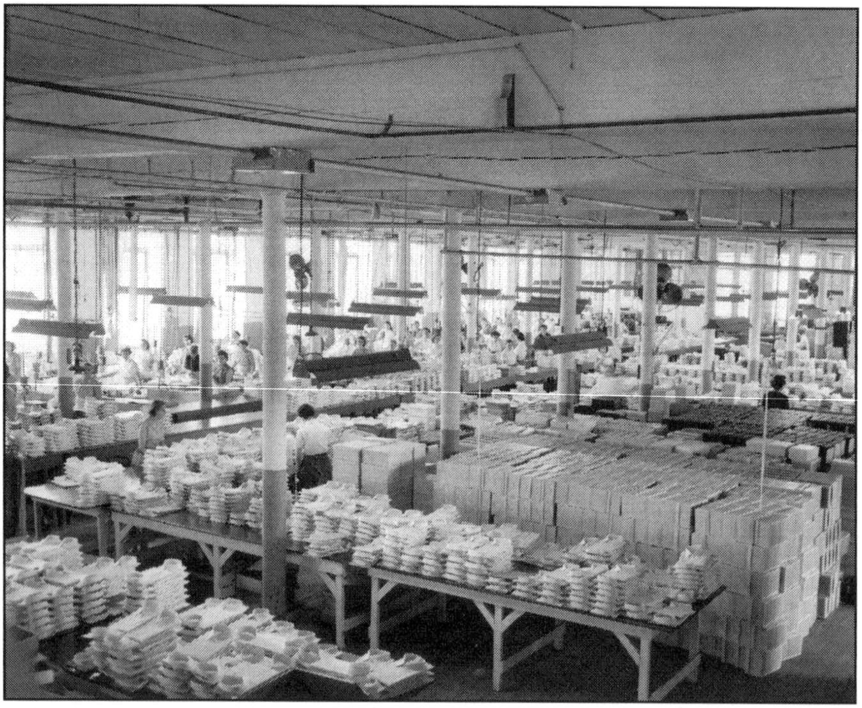

8.18 Workers in Shelburne Shirt Company, 69 Alden Street, Fall River, Massachusetts, late 1960s. *"I was doing, folding ...it was the shirts I was folding."*

8.19 Eva, as Saint Lydia of Philippisia, and her daughter, Doris, as the Blessed Mother in *Women in the Bible*, a program presented at the Diocesan Council of Catholic Women's annual convention, held in Taunton, Massachusetts, in 1980; Eva was an active member of Notre Dame de Lourdes Church, in Fall River, Massachusetts. *"Can I smile?" "Yeah, otherwise we wouldn't give you the job."*

8.20 Eva at the occasion of her 100th birthday, 2016.

NINE:

LEDORA SOITOS, NÉE ISIDORIO

Personal Statistics

Name: Ledora Isidorio
(Mrs. Francis Silveira Soitos)

Date of Birth: May 3, 1921

Place of Birth: Fall River, Massachusetts

Father: Manuel Isidorio, Jr. (1889-1933)

Mother: Anna Emmett (1889-1974)

Siblings: Hilario Isidorio (1911-1911)
Joseph Isidorio (1912-1986)
Mary Lillian Isidorio (1914-1987)
---(Mrs. Elmer Francis Gazek)
Frank Isidorio (1916-1967)
Nora Isidorio (1917-1918)
Vincent John Isidorio (1919-1952)
Irene Alice Isidorio (1923-1993)
---(Mrs. John Gray)
Thelma Isidorio (1925-1995)
---(Mrs. Steve Barabas)
Maria Delores Isidorio (born 1929)
---(Mrs. Wesley Henri Grandmont)

Spouse: Francis Silveira Soitos (1920-1984)

Date of Marriage: : April 18, 1942

Children: Stephen Francis Soitos
Francine Anne Soitos
---(Mrs. William Joseph Aloisa)

Employment history:
Cape Cod Dress Company, Fall River
Monarch Textile Corporation, Inc., Fall River
Superior Laundry, Santa Maria, California
Glenwood Range Company, Taunton, Massachusetts
Narragansett Electric Company, Taunton
Taunton Municipal Lighting Plant, Taunton

EDITED TRANSCRIPT

Interview with Mrs. Francis Silveira Soitos, née Ledora Isidorio

Interviewer: (AS) Ann Rockett-Sperling

Interviewee: (LS) Ledora (Isidorio) Soitos

Additional Commentary: (JR) Joyce B. Rodrigues, Fall River Historical Society

Date of Interview: June 3, 2015

Location: Soitos residence, Taunton, Massachusetts

Summary by Joyce B. Rodrigues:

Ledora "Doris" (Isidorio) Silveria Soitos was born in Fall River on May 3, 1921.

Ledora's story captures the history of the village of Mechanicsville, located in the north end of Fall River, and the struggles and determination of her family to make it through the Great Depression.

Mechanicsville:

The Isidorio family lived and worked for three generations in Mechanicsville. The area was a densely populated, bustling neighborhood that developed after the Civil War during the "era of new mills."

Mechanicsville was dominated by the Mechanics and Weetamoe Mills. Mill housing, churches, schools, and businesses clustered around the new mills. By the 1960s, Mechanicsville would undergo a dramatic transformation, and Ledora's neighborhood would disappear due to urban renewal and the expansion of the Interstate Highway System.

The Isidorio family:

Ledora's maternal grandfather, James Emmett, immigrated to the United States from England in 1884. Her maternal grandmother was born in the United States of French-Canadian ancestry. They met and married in Fall River in 1887 and raised their family in Mechanicsville. He was a spinner; she a speeder-tender (i.e., an operative who sets up, operates, and oversees machines that spin fibers into yarn).

Ledora's father immigrated to the United States from the island of St. Michael in the Azores in 1892, and met and married Ledora's mother, Anna Emmett, in Fall River in 1909. They both worked at the Sagamore Mills, he as a doffer (i.e., an operative who "doffs" bobbins from a spinning frame and replaces them with empty ones), and she as a speeder-tender.

There were ten children in the Isidorio family, four boys and six girls, all born at home with a midwife in attendance. Ledora was the sixth child. An older brother died as an infant of pneumonia in 1911. An older sister died at the age of seven months in 1918 at the height of the worldwide influenza epidemic.

The Isidorio family lived in the Brick Block on Otto and, later, Monte Street; the Brick Block, originally built for workers of the mills on Davol Street. As mills went into receivership and began to close in the 1920s and 1930s, some of these properties were acquired by banks in Fall River and rented out.

Ledora's childhood:

Ledora recounts caring for her younger siblings, coal stove heating, family traditions, neighborhood games, swimming in the Taunton River, dish and bank night at the movies, winning the family's first radio, electric lighting, and bringing lunches to the Sagamore Mills in dinner pails to members of the Isidorio's extended family.

Ledora was twelve years old when her father passed away in 1933 at the age of forty-four, leaving his wife to raise eight children. The family struggled to make ends meet. All of the children went to work as soon as possible and brought their pay home to support the family.

Ledora was able to attend high school. She took the commercial course and graduated in 1938 from B.M.C. Durfee High School. With no office jobs available and no work experience, she took a night course at Bradford Durfee Textile School to learn to operate a power-stitching sewing machine.

The Isidorio family moved to Taunton, Massachusetts, in 1938 to live near Ledora's mother's sisters. Ledora, her sister and brother, and two neighborhood girls commuted from Taunton to work in Fall River.

Ledora worked from 1938 to 1941 at Cape Cod Dress Company, where her sister was the floor lady, and at Monarch Textile Corporation, Inc. making chenille bedspreads and bathrobes. Her narrative clearly describes the factory work processes and the impact of the union on employees.

Ledora met her husband in Taunton in 1939. They were dating when they heard on the radio that the Japanese had attacked Pearl Harbor in December 1941. Francis Silveira Soitos had enlisted in the Army in January 1941. He was immediately called up to active service stateside.

Francis and Ledora married in April 1942. He was sent overseas in 1944, saw action in Europe, and was awarded the Bronze Star. He was discharged in October 1945.

After the war the Soitos made their home in Taunton and raised one son and one daughter.

After marriage, Ledora worked in Taunton at the Glenwood Range Company, manufacturers of the well-known Glenwood cooking stove, and as a supervisor at the Taunton Municipal Lighting Plant.

She retired in 1987 at age sixty-six after forty-nine years of employment. At the time of this interview, she was active in senior centers.

Note: This interview has been slightly edited for continuity and readability; in order to preserve the integrity of the conversation, the phraseology remains that of the interviewer and interviewee. Italicized information in square brackets has been added for the purposes of clarification and context.

AS: Ledora, could you tell us when and where you were born, please?

LS: Yes. I was born at 38 Otto Street in Fall River, Mass[*achusetts*], May 3, 1921.

AS: And how about your parents, where were they from?

LS: My mother [*née Anna Emmett*] was born in Fall River, 1889. My father [*Manuel Isidorio, Jr.*] was born [*in 1889*]. I think [*it*] was [*in*] St. Michaels [*Lagoa, São Miguel, Azores*]. My father.

AS: In Portugal?

LS: Yes.

AS: São Miguel.

LS: Yes.

AS: Oh ... what did your parents do for a living?

LS: Worked in the mills.

AS: Do you remember what mills?

LS: Sagamore [*Manufacturing Company, 1822 North Main Street, Fall River*], was in the Sagamore, down the North End.

AS: Oh, the Sagamore ... How many children were in your family?

LS: My mother had ten children. All born in the second floor cold-water flat in Fall River, with a midwife.

AS: Oh my goodness. How many boys? How many girls?

LS: Uh, four boys and six girls. But one, the first boy, died after birth [*Hilario Isidorio died on January 13, 1911, at the age of one month and one day, from pneumonia*]. And I would have to count down. And one of the girls died at six months [*Nora Isidorio died October 1, 1918, at the age of seven months and twenty-four days, from bronchial pneumonia*]. They were born before me. [*In 1910, the death rate in Fall River for births* *under 1 year of age was 239.5 per 1,000 for cities with populations of 100,000 or over. This rate was the highest in the state of Massachusetts and the highest in the United States. Source: Bureau of the Census, Bulletin 112.*]

AS: Where did you fall in the line?

LS: I fell in, let's see – sixth. I was sixth one down. Fifth one died at six months. [*Hilario; Joseph; Mary Lillian; Frank; Nora; Vincent John; Ledora; Irene Alice; Thelma; Maria Dolores.*]

AS: Oh, that's too bad. Could you describe the house that you grew up in?

LS: Yes, I can. I was born at 38 Otto Street, which is off Lindsey Street in Fall River … the North End. And it was the 'Brick Block' [*Weetamoe Mills Block*]. They were called 'Brick Blocks' because the [*Weetamoe*] mills on … [*1290*] Davol Street, when they were working, people from the mills had to live in the Brick Block. But the mills were closed so they rented them. The bank owned them and rented them. So, we lived on the second floor. We had two tenements on the second floor. A dollar-and-a-half a week for each one because we needed the four bedrooms.... They were cold-water flats. And they had indoor plumbing, but no showers or nothing.

AS: Did you have any duties in the house as a child? Did you have anything you had to do? Did you have to help?

LS: Oh, well, really, yes, we had to help my mother all the time. And, of course, I had to wheel the babe – the two youngest ones [*her sisters, Thelma and Maria Dolores*]. I remember the two youngest ones being born [*in 1925 and 1929, respectively*], but I don't remember that much about them. Just that the midwife told us we had a baby sister.

AS: She came to the home?

LS: Yeah…. My younger sister [*Maria Dolores*] was born … November 1, 1929, and the stock market crashed the night before [*two days before, the Wall Street Crash occurred on October 29, 1929, aka 'Black Tuesday'*]. So my father wouldn't let us go out for Halloween. We didn't know my mother was having a baby in the next room. We didn't know until the morning, when they told us that my mother had something to show us. And it was my baby sister. She is still living; she is eighty-six.

AS: Now did you go trick-or-treating in those days? Did children go from house to house like the children do now?

LS: No, we never did that. We dressed up in old clothes. Grabbed a rag bag and something made ourselves. We would go down the streets singing, yelling, and maybe ring a few doorbells. No candy, not in those days.

AS: But it was still fun, I'm sure.

LS: We had a good time. And we were out. We had a good time in the neighborhood.

JR: How did you heat that home?

LS: Coal stove in the kitchen, the tenement we lived in. And my brothers had to live in the … had to sleep in the other tenement, which was, there was a hallway. The Brick Block was built with a stairway going up two first floors, two second floors, and two third floors. But they were mostly all empty. In fact, our corner house was empty. I remember a man living downstairs when I was small, but he was gone. So, the second floor, my mother rented, a dollar-and-a-half for each side. We had a coal stove. Cold bedrooms. There was no coal stove in the other apartment where my brothers slept. And so, my mother had a little cloth store in the kitchen of the other apartment. She went to the mills, my father brought her to the mills and she bought remnants. And people would come and buy. It was cheap. But I'll tell you, she had a legend that a lot of people owed her. So, that was only until we moved. We had to move in … 1932. We had to move. The bank was after us. We were the only tenants left in two long blocks. We couldn't find a place with eight children. But we did on [*19*] Monte Street [*in Fall River*].

AS: Is that in the North End, also?

LS: Yes, not too far from where we were. Bank-owned. That was a house that had two [*three*] tenements. So, we had the first floor; we rented the first floor. And it had four bedrooms. Till my father died.

JR: Was that also coal stoves?

LS: Yes, always a coal stove. I remember my father standing on the thing, when we'd get up to get ready to go to school, with our clothes in front of the oven door. But, anyway, I can remember him, because he'd build a fire that died during the night, he built it. But then he got sick and died. He died on January 30, 1933. He died in Truesdale [*Hospital, Inc., 1820 Highland Avenue, Fall River*].

JR: How old was he? He must have been a younger man.

LS: Forty-four.

JR: Forty-four?

LS: And my mother is forty-four, a widow with eight children. My oldest brother [*Joseph*] was twenty, I think. So, you know, there was, when you think of it – I was twelve. And the youngest [*Maria Dolores*] was three.

AS: Had he been sick? Your father, had he been sick?

LS: Yeah, he had been sick off and on, and when he went to the hospital, they wanted to operate. See, they didn't know what it was, his stomach. It probably was cancer. [*His* *cause of death was chronic interstitial nephritis, a kidney disorder.*] But, anyway, uh, that is when he died. Of course, my mother never married again. We got by, I don't know how.

JR: How did she get by?

LS: Well, my oldest brother [*Joseph*] worked. Not in an office or anything, he worked in the mill first. He graduated 1930 from [*B.M.C.*] Durfee [*High School*] and he went to work in the mills, Sagamore Mill [*Manufacturing Company*]. I don't know what he did. Something to do with the yarn [*he was a spinner*], it goes up in the things. I think it was about $12 a week then. My sister [*Mary Lillian*] graduated 1931 ... from Durfee and she went to work in the sewing shop right away, down Steep Brook [*section of Fall River*] ... it was the Paroma Draperies [*Inc., Weaver Street, Fall River*]. And it was up on the third floor, I think, and they had to make these bedspreads and draperies. And they were all very heavy work; $9 a week for forty hours.

AS: Was that because she was a woman, or was that because that was the pay for that particular job? She made less than your brother made.

LS: Yeah, and he worked in the mill nights ... I think, he probably made $10 a week, maybe twelve, but they had to bring the pay home, you know, to help?

AS: Help the family.

LS: Yes, and then my other two brothers [*Frank and Vincent John*] went down. They didn't want to go to school. They went to [*James Madison Morton*] Morton [*Junior High School*] and graduated. My father said, 'You have to go to school or you have to go to work.' Frank, he looked all over. Went to all the mills. Wanted to sweep the floors. So my uncle [*Antone D. Medeiros*] in Taunton [*Massachusetts*], that is how we got involved in Taunton; my uncle in Taunton worked in Presbry Factories [*Presbry Refactory Corporation, 600 Somerset Avenue*]. He said to my mother – his wife [*née Elizabeth Emmett*] was my mother's sister – he said, 'If you want to let him come here and stay with us [*at 893 Somerset Avenue*], and we won't [*charge*] anything, and he can bring his pay home ... we will take him in.' Because my aunt [*Elizabeth Medeiros*] ran a restaurant [*at 260 West Water Street, Taunton*] for the workers at Glenwood Range [*Company, 300 West Water Street*]. So, it was no problem.

AS: So he could work for her?

LS: He got the job, so he moved to Taunton. Then my brother, Vincent ... is [*a*] year-and-a-half older than me; we was eighteen months apart. So, he came along. He don't want to go to school. He graduated from Morton. So, he had to look for a job. Well, my uncle took him in and got him a job. So there were two out of the family.

AS: But they were bringing their paycheck home to your mother.

LS: Yes, because they didn't charge them anything for food or anything.

AS: So, they must have been young, about fourteen, maybe?

LS: Well, yeah, because …

AS: Morton.

LS: Yeah, it was Morton freshmen. We went to the ninth grade in Morton.

AS: So the ninth grade, they would have been fourteen.

LS: So I had caught up to my brother and we both graduated at the same time. But I wanted to go to school. They wouldn't let me. I wouldn't stay out of school for anything.

AS: You liked school? Where did you go to elementary school? Before Morton.

LS: Before Morton was Borden [*Grammar School, 501 Brownell Street, Fall River*], I think. Borden school. And before that was Fulton Street School [*160 Fulton Street, corner Wellington Street, Fall River*], which was the North End. And that was first grade and second grade.

AS: How about Christmas and the holidays? Thanksgiving. Do you have any memories of the family with those?

LS: Yeah, well, first, the first Christmas I can remember now, it was in 38 Otto Street. Um. We never had a tree. Never had a tree. But, when I remember that, my father going downtown. We had the trollies then. He came home with two Christmas wreaths. This is my favorite. For a quarter. My mother said, 'Why did you spend twenty-five cents on two Christmas wreaths? You know we need the money.' He said, 'No, we have to have something green in the house.' So they went up in the window, on the second floor. And we strung a string behind the coal stove and we had a stocking with the orange, apple, nuts, and candy. And no toys. No games. We might have had a book or something. But it wasn't much.

AS: Not like today, of course.

LS: No, too much today. But we were happy. We had family. We played games on the kitchen table, a big round kitchen table. And we turned the table cloth over and we had a Parcheesi game. Every night. It was always a baseball game going or softball game going. The kids jumping rope. And summer was swimming down at Weetamoe Yacht Club, down the end of Monte Street. That is gone now.

JR: Yeah.

LS: That was a big club there. People used to drive down Monte Street; it was a dead end at Monte Street. Gold Medal Bakery [*506 Lindsey Street, Fall River*] was at the other end of Monte Street. And we lived … when we finally moved a second time [*in 1935*], we moved in the six-tenement house [*at 1 Monte Street, Fall River*], which was on the banks of the Taunton River, and down below was Weetamoe Yacht Club [*2 Monte Street*]. Only they, the guys that had money or something, belonged to that. Because they had a raft [*dock*]. They had a big meeting room. They had a place where you could swim. It was the Taunton River, but we didn't care, that was where we did our swimming. That's true, everything that was in that beach, we brought down there from our house.

JR: Now they had rides down there? They had rides on Bliffin's Beach [*at Steep Brook*]?

LS: I don't remember rides, but I remember going down [*to Bliffin's Beach*] and you had to have a nickel to get a basket. Because they wouldn't let you in to swim unless you had a basket to go in the bath house. And you couldn't sneak in, because they had a shower going. So, if you had your clothes on, you had to go through the shower. Or if you did get in, you couldn't undress on the beach, because there were all signs and guards. But it was nice, Sunday, it seemed more like the beach.

AS: So you put your clothes in a basket?

LS: Your shoes and everything. They had a boy attendant with a key. And a number, you got that, but that would cost you a nickel. But we walked down there, too, from where we lived.

AS: Now how about your neighborhood? Did you have a lot of friends in the neighborhood?

LS: Yeah, every family had children. So, we always had some games going on. In fact, Charlie [*Charles M.*] Braga [*Jr.*] from Charlie Braga Bridge [*Charles M. Braga, Jr. Memorial Bridge, dedicated April 15, 1966*] was our neighbor [*at 37 Otto Street*] with his three sisters [*Adriene, Agnes, and Delia*], and we were friends. But he was [*two years*] older than me. He graduated from [*B.M.C.*] Durfee [*High School*], [*in fact, he left during his sophomore year,*] and then joined the [*United States*] Navy right away [*enlisted September, 1939*].... Of course, he was the first one killed [*in World War II from Fall River*] at [*the Japanese attack on*] Pearl Harbor [*on December 7, 1941*].... And they lived on the, not the 'Brick Block,' but they lived on the tenements on top of the stores ... on [*96*] Brightman Street [*in Fall River. The stores*] had tenements up there. And that was where the Braga family lived. But ... it's funny I don't remember his mother [*née Maria Figuerido*] and father [*Charles Braga, Sr.*]. I remember his sisters, 'cause Delia and Adriene were friendly, more my age ... but I remember him very well because he sometimes, he would come play baseball or something. But we always had games going. Of course, times were different.

AS: Is that where you shopped? Mostly on Brightman Street at that time? Is that where most of the shops were?

LS: Yeah, they all were there and the Royal Theatre [*277 Brightman Street, Fall River*] was down the road.

AS: You have a good memory. A wonderful memory.

JR: Now you went down to the movies a lot?

LS: It was five cents to go to the movies and we would try to save if we had pennies. Well, like, I used to help my brother with newspapers. Deliver newspapers. And he would give me some money on payday. And I, we would go to the movies Sunday afternoon, a nickel.

AS: Do you remember any of the names of the movies?

LS: Of the movies?

AS: Any of them?

LS: I remember the first talking picture [*The Jazz Singer, 1927*], was that Al Jolson? I'm not sure. The first talking one, was that. And a lot of times my mother would let us, she would go with us … Saturday night was 'Bank Night.' And if you went Saturday night, of course you had two movies [*and*] news; you were in there a long time.

JR: Cartoons?

LS: 'Bank Night,' they would put your name in a box and draw a name in the middle. And my sister Irene's name came out and she won $35.

AS: That must have been amazing.

LS: I don't remember what year it was, because she is younger than me. But that closed [*circa 1956*], I don't know why, but it was still open when I moved away.

JR: It's been closed for quite some time now. There is a business there now.

LS: So, the one who ran it [*Antone Tavares Moniz, Sr.*], I don't think owned it, [*he was the manager*]. Well, he might have owned it. I don't know. It's right near where the cemetery [*North Burial Ground to the east, and St. John's Cemetery to the north*] comes down. See, our entertainment. A friend of mine, in the summer time, spring and summer, at night, she would come to get me and she would say, 'Let's take a walk over the [*Brightman Street*] bridge.' And we would go walk over … to Somerset [*Massachusetts, across the Taunton River to the west*]. Because all the guys were on the bridge trying to get the breezes. There may have been men fishing then. And so that was … the entertainment in the summertime. But we all went to the movies on the weekend. We always managed to find a nickel somewhere and go.

JR: I remember my mother telling me about dishes at the movies.

LS: Yeah, we did, we got dishes, and the Durfee Theatre [*28 North Main Street, Fall*

River], I think, first started it. And then the Empire [*Theatre, 166 South Main Street*], and I remember going way up to, I told you I couldn't remember that name, up to…

JR: The Plaza [*Theatre, 381 South Main Street, Fall River*]?

LS: The Globe [*Theatre, 226 East Main Street, Fall River*]. Yeah, and I was telling her that my neighbor in the six-tenement house [*Roland Rapoza*], we lived on the first floor, one tenement. And he had a girlfriend in Somerset. So, he asked me if I would go to the movies. He gave me his pass to go on the trolley. He gave me the money to go in the movies so I could get the dish for him. So he saved a set of dishes to give to his girlfriend. That was fine. Then my sister had somebody who would pay for hers. So the two of us would go out to the movies for free.

JR: And is that how you got to the movies? On the trolley?

LS: Yeah, the trolley. I loved those trolleys. We moved to Taunton [*in 1938*]. They had already done away with them.

AS: Now, how about a television. Do you remember when you got a television?

LS: My first, can I tell you about my first radio? We didn't have any radio. In 1932, that was before, when we moved to Monte Street. A store opened up on Brightman Street. A grocery store [*Hormisdas Heroux & Son, 177 Brightman Street, Fall River*]. And for opening night, they were giving away a radio. A little table-top radio. And you put your name in. So, all kids and we went in, and we put our name in, put it in the box. They are going to draw it on Saturday night, who could win the radio. And, of course, we had just moved to Monte Street and it had electric. We had gas in the Otto Street [*tenement*] … gas bulbs [*mantles*]. So anyway, we all went down, the kids. All went down to the store to see who was going to win the radio. Well, my friend, one of my friends, went up and they asked her to pull the name. Ledora Isidorio.

AS: Oh my goodness.

JR: Oh my gosh!

LS: I couldn't believe it. So the man says, 'Oh, no, you have to have a grownup. We can't give you the radio. You have to have a grownup.' I said, 'I'll go home and get my father or my mother.' So he said, 'Alright, we will hold it for you.' So, the neighborhood was Brightman Street, and we lived on Monte Street, which was around the corner. Well, my father was out on Brightman Street further down near one of the stores. Just outside. And, I says to him, 'I just won a radio at the store, but I need a grownup with me to get it.' He says, 'They don't give away radios free in this time…. I am not going to that store.' Oh, I started crying, I ran home to my mother. My mother said, 'I'll go with you.' We had that radio and were they glad in my house…. We had electric in that tenement.

JR: Okay, so when did that happen? When did electricity come in?

LS: See, I don't remember when, because ... up until 1932, we lived in the 'Brick Block,' which was gas. All gas. You had ... a flame [*gas light*] that come out of the stairway [*wall*], because we lived on the second floor – at night, so we could see. And up top ... we bought a globe. They called them a gas globe [*mantle*]. In the drugstore for a nickel. When that globe [*mantle*] would burn out, my mother would send us to the store to get a globe [*mantle*]. But, otherwise, it was a lit flame that came out in the hallway, and you had to light it at night. That was [*in*] the 'Brick Block.' But this one, we moved to, I don't know when they got electric, but it must have been ... just before that or something. But not like we have electric now. It was one or two plugs.

AS: Enough for the radio?

LS: But we got the radio. Philco [*Radio Corporation*]. I can see copies. I don't know what happened to that radio.

AS: You see pictures of the radio?

LS: Yes. So that was then, and the television wasn't until [*after*] I was married, 1947, when I got my first TV.

AS: Oh, when you were married. Now, when you were in school, did you have any plans for when you finished? Were you thinking of doing anything?

LS: Well, I took a commercial course because one course was home economics, which is cooking and sewing, and we had that at [*James Madison*] Morton [*Junior High School*], which was nice. I liked that. But, I couldn't see any job in that, you know? And ... so, I said to my mother – she didn't care what we did – so I says, 'Well, I am going to take commercial course because I want to work in an office.' I couldn't take a college course, because I knew I wasn't going to college. So, I had short hand, typewriting, everything to do with commercial.

JR: That's what my mother took.

LS: Yeah, in classes [*they*] used to show us how to answer the phone, and talk. So, when I graduated [*in June, 1938, from B.M.C. Durfee High School*], I wanted an office job. There weren't the office jobs. I think they were paying $12 a week for office. And but, there weren't, you had to go to Thibodeau [*Business*] College [*Inc., 130 South Main Street, Fall River*].... Thibodeau College, you had classes. You had to go one year and they would find you a job. Well, I couldn't afford that. So, my brother went a couple of months, with his newspaper money, but he wanted a car, so he quit, which was the worst thing. He ended up in the mill. So, um, I start looking for a job in a sewing shop. My sister [*Mary Lillian*] had transferred from Paroma Draperies [*Inc.*] up to [*the*] Globe [*section of Fall River*]. She was working in a better dress shop [*Cape Cod Dress Company, women's silk dress manufacturer, 987 Broadway, Fall River*]. She was very good at sewing; I don't know if I remember her taking any lessons, maybe just what she had in school. So, um, [*when*] she was working up there in the Paroma Draperies, she made $9 a week. I don't know what she made up at the Globe, because she made the fronts of the dresses, which was the hardest part. And then, she graduated to the [*position*] floor lady, so she taught the ones coming in.

AS: So, she was the supervisor?

LS: Yes, she was a supervisor, but there was more than one. But when you were working you had to holler; my voice is loud because of that. You had to holler over the power machines, row after row of power machines. And you had [*to holler when you*] needed a needle or needed thread, and they would have bins on the side where they bring you the dresses partly put together, or parts that you were going to assemble. So, she wasn't my boss; I called her 'Boss.' She worked with the better [*dress*], the front, and the girls who made the fronts, to teach them how to do it. So, I started there. She got me a job in there. I started making shoulder pads, the flat ones, and belts. And then I went to put ribbon on the bottom of the hems, all the hems had ribbons that went to a seam binding, and went to another girl on a machine, where she made the hems. And I also did, finally, they would teach me – not my sister, though, I had another floor lady – the sides, closing the sides of the dresses. So, I worked there from September, 1938, or maybe it was August, to when I went to [*Santa Maria*] California, when my husband [*Francis Silveria Soitos*] was in the service [*United States Army, enlisted January 16, 1941, discharged October 8, 1945*]. That was 1943. So I never went back. [*Later, when*] I went back [*to visit*], the floor lady was still there. She said, 'Why ain't you come back?' Because everyone had gone to the war [*World War II*]. I said I was going to look for office work in Taunton.

AS: Do you remember your first day when you went into the mills? Do you remember what that was like? Were you nervous?

LS: Well, my first job, when [*my sister*] got me a job, wasn't sewing, it was on a table. They had ... the whole floor was Cape Cod Dress. They didn't do any cutting or anything [*because*] that all came from New York [*City*] by truck, [*and*] if the truck didn't get there in the morning, we didn't have any work. We would have to sit around. Or, if you lived in Fall River, you could go home, and then they would call you. But, you didn't get paid if you went home. I already lived in Taunton. So, anyway, um, I worked, um, they had loops ... belt loops, they used to make them with a seam. So they had a hook, a long hook. You put the hook in, catch the end, and pull it through. Gosh, did I have it tough. What the girl next to me, she had done that. She was like a whiz. Finally, I guess, I don't know how long I stayed on that, but that was twenty-five cents an hour. For $10 a week. And that is what I got for sewing. I don't know how long.

AS: What time did you go to work in the morning?

LS: Well, I was already living in Taunton, see, when I got the job in September. See, I graduated in June, [*1938*], from [*B.M.C.*] Durfee [*High School*], so, all summer, I had been looking for work. So, we went in the morning. My brother, Joe ... he worked in Fall River, and my sister, of course, worked in Fall River. And then, we brought two girls that lived down the road and they worked in the same shop, on the table. And so, that is how I got my …

AS: So, you left early? You must have.

LS: Oh yes, I came at eight [*o'clock a.m.*] to work – to start working. And we got through, it was at four, I think. Four o'clock, and we had an hour for lunch.

AS: And could you wear anything? Did you have to wear anything special? You would wear whatever you wanted?

LS: Wear whatever you wanted with no problem. You never had any breaks, the only time was when you could get to go, and you could go to the toilet and back. And that was it. We had a lunch time.

AS: Did you bring your lunch? A lunch bin?

LS: Oh yeah, we would bring our lunch.

JR: How long did you have for lunch?

LS: I don't know if it was a half hour. I think it was an hour we had for lunch. But then if the work stopped, and say they didn't have any more work to give you, you punched out. You didn't get paid. So then, you had to stay there until, like my sister might have had work and I wouldn't. Well, she had to work. She always worked a full week. I don't know what she made for a pay, but it was more than she made at Paroma Draperies, which in 1932 was $9 a week. I remember my mother saying that she depended on her, you know? And my brother, he wasn't married either. So, that is what happened there. I know I went to Har-Lee's [*Har-Lee Manufacturing Company, dress manufacturers, 425*] … Pleasant Street, [*Fall River*]; they were hiring. So, I went there in the summer [*of 1938*], and went in the morning when they went to work. I went with them, and up Pleasant Street. Stood in line, from 7:30 [*a.m.*], I think it was, and I didn't get through that line and get into the office to get an interview until 12:00 [*noon*]. And I don't know, I can picture her there, but I don't know her name. She says, 'Where you worked? What is your experience?' I said, 'I don't have any, but I went to [*Bradford*] Durfee Textile School [*64 Durfee Street, Fall River*] at night to learn how to run the power machines.' Because you had to learn how to thread them. And my mother's was a treadle [*sewing machine*], you know, that you pull back and forth, at home…. Anyway, she says, 'You don't have any experience?' I said, 'None.' She says, 'Oh, we are only hiring girls with experience.' I said, 'How can you get experience if no one will give you a chance? I know how to run the machine.' She said, 'I'm sorry.' That was it. So, after that, my sister got me a job, because she could see I wasn't going to get a job.

JR: Now those power machines, you had to press them up against your leg? Wasn't that it?

LS: No, let me see how they worked. Each power machine … I think, must have had a starter, but they were hooked to the wall, with a main power switch. And the floor lady would go up to the power switch for each aisle, so these power machines were [*on*] both sides, [*and*] you faced the girl who was working them. I don't know how many rows. And then, we say eight [*o'clock a.m.*] we started, and I think it was twelve, we would stop for lunch. She had to go to that box and pull the switches.

JR: Okay, very good.

LS: That would shut off the power. But, we must have run our individual machines ourselves. Because if you were too slow ... you wouldn't keep the job. So I can't remember. It wasn't the foot, it must have been the knee. But, I don't remember that.

AS: Do you remember anything? Does the mill have a certain smell? Or could you smell oil or anything?

LS: No, that must have been an old textile mill, I would say [*Laurel Lake Mills, closed, 1931*]. I think we were on the third floor and had to walk up three flights of stairs. No elevators or anything.

JR: So, were you paid by the dozen?

LS: No, this was not piecework, it was by the hour. And when I started there, I remember it was twenty-five cents an hour, an hour for lunch, I think, and you got $10 for forty hours. $10 a week. So, that's what you get if you were lucky enough to work the full week; sometimes we wouldn't. Maybe the job that I was doing, they didn't have any work ready from the other girls – the ones who did the waist, then the girls who joined the skirts, and then, there would be the collars. The sleeves, all different rows did that. Then, they put them all together by a symbol, with a piece of paper, and it had the size and the style of the dress and everything, so you would match the fold and match them up to give them to the ... and then they collected them, the dresses, or whatever part you were doing, and passed them on. And when they were completely assembled, they went to the presses, which were rows of pressers. I think all the women there, they had those big ...

AS: That you pull down, the pressers?

LS: Yeah, and they had tables of women also that did handwork. Sew the snaps on, sew the buttons on, whatever needed to be done to complete the dress. Then, they were put on racks after they were pressed, and they would ship to New York [*City*]. Everything went to New York. They, uh, the cut parts. We had a man in our place, that was his job, on the table. When that work came from New York, he had [*to*] assemble the parts.

AS: Like the patterns?

LS: Yeah, he didn't have to do cutting. He assembled the sleeves, and into bundles, because each girl ...

JR: Oh, he tied them.

LS: Yeah, yeah, he used to put them …

AS: Were there many men in the mills? It sounds like mostly women that were there.
LS: There were all women sewing.

AS: No men were sewers?

LS: That man, I remember, and sometimes, when I was waiting for my sister, I would help him. He would say, 'Do you want to help me?' Because he would always work over. And I would go over and he would show me where to place these things. And then, he was the one, the mechanic, if the machine broke down. And the boss … he was the boss of everybody [*Jack Kolen, manager*]. You know?

AS: The top?

LS: Yeah, he was mostly over where the presses were.

JR: Do you think he was tough? Was he a good boss?

LS: I don't know, I never had anything to do with him, but he used to watch the girls who had to sew the snaps on, because they had to be fast, you know? And sew the buttons. They didn't have machines to do that. I can't think of what his name was.

AS: You never saw the owner or heard anything about the mills? He never came to visit?

LS: I didn't even know who owned the mills. I imagined that the company must have rented that floor. Because I think down below there was a grocery store [*Worlds Super Market, 967 Broadway, Fall River*]. Way over. And down below us, on those other floors, I don't know what was there.

AS: Now, what mill was this? Sagamore [*Manufacturing Company*], that you are talking about or the one up the Flint [*section of Fall River*]?

LS: Up the Flint. No, not the Flint, [*the*] Globe [*section of Fall River*]. The dress [*manufacturer*] was Cape Cod [*Dress Company*]. They were supposed to be better dresses because they were rayon. They [H*ar-Lee Manufacturing Company*] made cheaper dresses, they were cotton.

LS: My son [*Stephen Francis Soitos*], a couple of years ago, said to me, 'Ma, let's go to Fall River; I want to see where you lived.' I says, 'Where I lived is gone.' [*He said,*] 'Oh, let's go.' So, I said, 'Okay.' We got in the car … and [*in Fall River*] … we had to go down Davol Street and cut over. And I'm telling him how to go, ya' know. I knew some section where that was all built over. So we got over on, uh, Lindsey Street, and then was Norfolk Street … And then we got on, ah ... is that Wellington Street?

AS: Yeah, yeah.

LS: And then we went down Weetamoe Street … and that's where the mills are [*Sagamore Manufacturing Company, 1822 North Main Street, Fall River*]. See, my grandmother [*Mrs. Manuel Isidorio Sr., née Filomena Souza*] lived down there [*in the Sagamore Mills Block on Sagamore Street*]. They used to have, uh, car houses … not long tenements, but I remember going down there to bring something from my mother. Uh … that's where they were when they came [*from the Azores in 1883*], I guess. [*The family resided on Sagamore Street from circa 1907 to 1932.*] That must have been all knocked down. [*The structures on Sagamore Street were razed circa 1933.*] They went on [*57*] Langley Street [*in 1933*]. Ah, see … I was young. I had to be awful young because that's when [*my grandfather*] was still [*living*]; he hadn't gotten burned [*to death*] yet. He got burned [*on August 22,*] 1926, so don't forget, I was uh, in 1926, I was four years old.

AS: So that would have been your grandfather.

LS: Yeah.

AS: How did the fire start? Did they ever…?

LS: Well, he had a little farm there and a shed for tools and … [*Manuel Isidorio, Sr. owned six lots of land on Brayton Point Road, Somerset, Massachusetts, and what was described contemporaneously as 'a tiny house … a garden, and … an orchard.'*]

AS: Over in Somerset?

LS: He had a cot to lay on when he was sleeping. He used to walk from Fall River to [*Somerset*] … planting potatoes. He had a lot of grapevines … his friends used to come and help him … tie the grapevines and everything. And so, uh, it seems that … he worked all day there, and at night he must have laid down on the cot … to sleep and he probably had had beer or wine – wine probably in those days, they made their own wine – and he must've fallen asleep smoking.

AS: Cigarette?

LS: There was a house next door [*Manuel Pimental Valero, Sr., 1969 Brayton Point Road*] but they didn't notice [*the flames*] until [*five o'clock*] in the morning. So, of course … that was in 1926, and he was only, what, fifty? [*He was fifty-five years old.*]

AS: So, so he would have been your father's father?

LS: Yes, and I didn't even ever see him. I don't recall, well, I don't remember him. I think … they said it might have [*been*] due to alcohol. But I never remember seeing him. But I do remember seeing my grandmother. She used to come up and she'd get mad because we couldn't understand Portuguese. And, oh, she was … she didn't learn English. But we were supposed to learn Portuguese, but my father never spoke

Portuguese to us; my mother knew a little bit, I don't know how, from the people coming to the store, I guess.

AS: What nationality was your mother?

LS: Her father [*James Emmett*] was English because he came from [*Mossley,*] Lancashire, England, [*in 1884*] and her mother [*née Marie 'Mary' Desmarais*] was [*of*] French-Canadian [*descent, born in Port Henry, Essex County, New York*], so she spoke French. Her and her sisters, they get together…

AS: Did you learn any French from her?

LS: French, they all spoke French. She had three sisters [*Mrs. Antone D. Medeiros, née Elizabeth Emmett; Mrs. William Irving, née Mary Emmett, later Mrs. William McGovern; and Mrs. Joseph V. Nelson, née Minnie Emmett*] and one brother [*George Joseph Emmett*]. Two sisters [*Elizabeth and Minnie*] lived here [*in Taunton*] and the other sister [*Mary*] lived in Boston … and the boy … after World War I … he married [*Eva Grace Vargas*] and went to live in Trenton, New Jersey. I never saw him.

JR: You had a lot of relatives.

LS: Oh, my goodness. What about us, with eight children?

AS: Now, how about going back to the mill? Do you remember what you took for lunch? What, what type of things did you take?

LS: Up to, uh ... when I worked?

AS: When you worked.

LS: Usually it was cold cuts. My mother would make the sandwiches for us in the morning, 'ya know, what we would take, my sister [*Mary Lillian, and me,*] we never went to a restaurant to eat. No.

AS: No. So you took a … sandwich or….

LS: Whatever. But the prices were reasonable. When I look in the paper! Prices are so unreasonable.

AS: Would you take water? Would you take anything to drink … did they sell anything at the mill?

LS: No, no I can't remember what we had to drink, must have been water. We had soda [*but*] I don't remember drinking soda, I'll tell 'ya, but … you know, you think of these things and you say, 'Well, gee, we lived through it.' Right?

AS: And you did fine.

JR: One time, you were telling me that you brought lunches to the mill.

LS: Yeah, that's when ... ah ... my sister, the oldest one [*Mary Lillian*] and me, I remember that. My [*great*] aunt, my mother's aunt [*Mrs. George Graves, Sr., née Rosalie Desmarais*], had [*several*] children ... [*Rose; Mary; John; Moise 'Moses'; George, Jr.; Joseph Francois 'Francis'; Clara; Caroline; Mary Louisa; Lillian*] but they weren't all working at the same time in the mills, but most [*of*] the girls were, I think. So, they had to have a hot meal for, for lunch – this is in the summer time – and she lived not too far from us [*the Graves family resided in a tenement at 1 Monte Street, Fall River, from circa 1931 to 1962; prior to that, they resided at 192 Leonard Street, Fall River*]. Oh, she had a table went from here to here to the kitchen. She baked pies; she did everything. They had this [*sectional*] lunch pail, the bottom, [*an*] enamel pail with a handle, and she'd have the name [*of*] who it was [*for*] – Louise or Mary, or whoever it was – and she put in the bottom the coffee; I don't think they had much with tea, I think it was mostly coffee. She put that in the bottom, that was hot, and then a little [*tray*] – I wish I had one – she'd put it in, that [*section*] would have the mashed potatoes and the meat or whatever that she had cooked, and then on the top [*they*] had the dessert ... I would think mostly pie. My mother only made pies, my mother wasn't good at cakes but she was good at pies. And then it had the cover, and my sister and I would each take at least two; they gave us ten cents a week and we'd go down to the mill ... luckily, I think they were all in the same mill. And they would meet us; we'd go in and ... the noise ... that's why my voice is so loud, 'ya know. My mother's was loud, too. My daughter [*Mrs. William Joseph Aloisa, née Francine Anne Soitos*] says, 'Ma, you talk too loud'.

AS: Now, was there a union – any type of a union in the mill in those days, or...?

LS: When I went to work there I didn't know they had a union, um, because they didn't say you have to join the union or anything. And ... but then I found out that after I was working there a while, uh, the union – the girls with the union, I guess – must have complained or something, so they reduced the hours, the forty hours to thirty-five hours, but the same pay.

AS: So they, so they made...

LS: So, they really didn't gain anything. So then, [*a*] New York [*City*] dress shop had a strike – New York, the same union. So, then they wanted us at the Cape Cod Dress [*Company*] to go on strike – which it had nothing to do with us – for support of them. Well, my mother needed the money. My sister ... she says to me, 'We're not going to go walk outside on the sidewalk and not get any pay; pay for gas to come here.' So, she says, 'We're not going to go on strike.' 'Cause it wasn't helping us. Well, they might have had fifteen out of the whole shop that did this – morning, noontime, night. Some of them came from Taunton.

AS: Carried the signs?

LS: Just walking back and forth, in support of the ... shops in New York. So, ah, we stayed working.

AS: How about when you went it; did they yell anything at you?

LS: Oh, yeah, they were really upset. My sister didn't care. She was a union member but I wasn't, 'cause I hadn't joined the union yet. I don't know why, I don't know if you had to work a certain amount of time, but anyway, first thing you know ... it got settled ... [*and*] they came back to work. Well, they were mad, 'ya know, because they lost maybe three or four weeks of work.

AS: You never get that back.

LS: So, as soon as they got back in I lost my job because I didn't go out on strike. My sister didn't, but I did. I lost my job. So I said to my sister, 'What am I going to do now?' And, uh, so I went down, um ... now, this was Globe Four Corners [*section of Fall River*] and the mill was here. I don't know what street that was that goes down to the water or whatever [*Globe Street*].

LS: Well, way down the end and to the right, I remember, was more mills. So, I went down there, looking for a job and they had a sewing shop there [*Monarch Textile Corporation, Inc., 206 Globe Mills Avenue, Fall River*] but you know what they made? They made chenille spreads and the [*bath*]robes. Do you remember the chenille robes, that had the design, 'ya know?

JR: I sure do.

LS: Of course, I had experience working on power machines, so I got hired right away. I don't remember the pay there, isn't that funny, I don't remember. And my cousin [*Mildred Irene Medeiros*] that lived here [*in Taunton*], she'd never worked in a sewing shop, so I got her a job [*at Monarch Textile Corporation, Inc.*]. So she worked, I don't know if we worked piece work, I think we worked piece work because we used to race. You know what chenille was? Well, it was different than a sewing job on dresses because the yarn came through from up above, and as you sewed the design you got the sewing stitch on one side, but underneath it cut it. How it did it, don't ask me. And the girl next to me, she was a whiz; I don't know how long she worked there, but I remember that. And the robes – I didn't work on spreads, but robes – had big skirts and you started in the middle with a pinwheel and it went round and round. I don't remember, I don't remember how many weeks, or how much money I made there. My cousin stayed; they called me back to the Cape Cod Dress afterwards and I joined the union, I guess they let me join the union. And then I worked there until I went to California; my husband [*Francis S. Soitos*] wanted me to go to California 'cause he was in the service.

AS: Now how did you meet your husband? Where did you meet him?

LS: Right when we moved to [*892 Somerset Avenue,*] Taunton. I never had a boyfriend, I'll tell 'ya, never – not in high school or … he was a neighbor across the street, and they used to come over in the neighborhood. We played croquet, of course, that was a big thing … when we moved onto the street. Five girls, they used to say 'the house with five beautiful girls,' and we'd laugh. Then … one of the neighbors had a croquet set in the yard, so that was a popular place every night, so we'd go there, and I used to talk to him, but it was nothing. They had a general store at the end of the street where we lived. He lived on the other street and I lived on this street. And my mother always had to get something at the store for next day's meal. It wasn't a supermarket, it was … a little meat market/grocery store. So we'd go in, my sister and I, go every night, we'd walk down. There was this fella, gang of fellows there from the neighborhood and he was one of them, but I never paid attention to the fella and now, first thing you know, he asked me if I wanted to go take a walk with him at night. So that started it off.

AS: And how old were you at that time?

LS: Ah, well, I was graduated from [*B.M.C. Durfee*] high school, so … I would say it was at the end of '39, so I was just eighteen. And he was, too, because he graduated Taunton High [*Class of 1938*]. So anyway, it was just a normal thing, walking – nowhere else. And then, the first real date was, um, I was over to my [*Medeiros*] cousins' across the street [*at 883 Somerset Avenue*], she [*her cousin Mildred*] and I trying to decide what we were going to do for the night – no carnivals around or anything. I heard a horn blowing at my house across the street – my mother had gone out to a bingo game with her sisters – and I looked out. I went over, I says 'What do you want? What are you looking for?' He says, 'I'm looking for you. Do you want to go over to the Raynham Auto Drive Theatre [*Route 138, Boston-Taunton Turnpike*] tonight? It's opening up tonight [*Gala opening Thursday, October 5, 1939*].' And I had just finished telling my cousin, 'Oh, would I love to go to that Raynham Auto Drive Theatre…. It's opening up tonight,' and she says, 'You can wish again 'cause you'll never go.' I come back and told her … And so I said [*'Yes'*] so we went; he took me [*in*] his father's old Chevrolet and then we went across the street – the big milk bottle that's still up on Route 138 [*Frates Dairy Milk Bottle, 785 Broadway, Raynham, Massachusetts*]. We had a cone of ice cream; that was my first date.

JR: Oh … thirty-five cents a person, no charge for your car. So he could take you to the movies for seventy cents.

LS: Yeah, and then he took me for ice cream; he must have spent his … spending money because he didn't have money. His mother [*née Mary R. Silva*] and father [A*ntone Silveira Soitos Sr.*], too, were poor.

JR: And it was October, 1939.

AS: And look at this, it says: 'Dress as you like! Smoke and relax as you please in the privacy of your own car.'

LS: Now, do I save things, or not?

AS: You certainly do. Now you were saying something about your name. We were saying how unusual Ledora is. Who did you say you were named after?

LS: My mother was a spinner. She went to work ... in the mills ... when she was, uh, twelve [*circa 1901*]; she had to leave school, she only went as far as fourth grade, I think, she told me. [*Based on the location of the Emmett residence, she likely attended Lindsey Street Primary School, grades one through three, and Borden Grammar School, Brownell Street, corner High Street, Fall River, grade four*]. And she went to learn to be a spinner ... that's what she did, all the time she worked in the mills. And she had a young girl that started there; she was a doffer [*an operative who removed full bobbins, spools, or caps from the machines and replaced them with empty ones*]. She ... cleaned the spindle for my mother, and all the others, not only my mother.

AS: Now how old were you when you married?

LS: When I got married [*in Taunton on April 18, 1942*], I was twenty and my husband was twenty-one, but he was in the Army over a year. See, he wanted to get married; he was afraid he was going overseas.

AS: Now how many children did you have, Ledora? How many children did you have?

LS: Two [*Stephen, born 1947, and Francine, born 1951*].

JR: Soitos? What's the background of your husband, the Soitos? We were trying to figure that out.

LS: Background? His father [*Antone Silveira Soitos, Sr.*] came from Faial [*Ilha do Faial, Azores*], Portugal [*in 1916*]; sixteen years old. [*His parents, Joseph Silveira Soitos and his wife, née Enacia Andrade*] ... had thirteen children.... They couldn't afford it, so, [*at*] sixteen, they sent him over here to his aunt in Dighton [*Massachusetts*] to work on a farm. But my mother-in-law [*née Mary R. Silva*] lived here [*in Taunton*].

JR: I want to get that background. You say he's from Faial? How does that name come up, because that's an interesting name.

LS: The name got spelled wrong here [*when he arrived in the United States*]. It [*his papers*] said S-O-I-T-O-S – but his brother, Souto. His brother came after him and it's S-O-U-T-O. But they never had any birth certificates.

AS: No, they didn't.

LS: So, it ended up when they said it, I guess. He [*my father-in-law*] didn't know any English or anything, he just had his name on his thing. He was sixteen, he can't speak a word of English.... His aunt and uncle were sponsoring him, so, uh, that's, that's how he got here.

JR: We want to jump back a little bit to, um, your, uh, date night ... at the movies.

AS: You must have gotten home late?

LS: Yeah, my mother was not home. My mother was not strict, believe me. I was stricter with my kids than what she was with us.

AS: And your father had already died.

LS: Yeah, and she had her two sisters here [*in Taunton*] and there was somebody they knew with a car that could take them to Rhode Island somewhere ... to a bingo game.

JR: So you met your husband ... and after that first date, what happened?

LS: Well, then I didn't see him, he didn't make any overtures for over a month, so I said, 'Oh, God, that's it, no more.' Then, he met me – he only lived on the other street, see – so if you went to the store ... but, evidently, he must have been staying away from me. But then, all of a sudden, he came over and we started dating. That was it, that was it, so then he had to go in the service. He had joined the National Guard 'cause there were no jobs. He was trying to get a job after high school; he graduated the commercial course ... from Taunton High. So, he joined the National Guards; that was before I ...was going with him. Wanted to join the Navy, but they said he was too heavy for the Navy, they wouldn't take him. The war [*World War II*] wasn't on yet. So, uh, he joined National Guards just to get the extra money. Well, [*President*] Franklin [*Delano*] Roosevelt put the National Guards to go to camp for a year and he went to Camp Edwards [*Barnstable County, Massachusetts*]. His outfit [*was*] all Taunton boys. They stayed altogether, all through the war, and not one got killed. [*Francis S. Soitos saw action in the battles of Normandy, Ardennes, and Central Europe; he was awarded the Bronze Star.*]

AS: That's amazing.

LS: Wasn't that? One got hurt – the cook – with his eye, but he came home. That's amazing. They never got bombed; it would have been terrible.

AS: So you remember, living through that, the war?

LS: So, then, we weren't married yet ... we were going out together. His father had this old Chevrolet. I never knew there was a Cape Cod. We went to Camp Edwards; his father drove, mother and the two sisters [*Anna M. Soitos and Eileen Soitos, later Mrs. Ennsencio Coelho*]. He had two sisters and a brother, but the brother [*Antone Silveira Soitos Jr.*] didn't come with us. And ... so we went to Camp Edwards to see him. So we went there and then [*again on*] December 7, 1941, we went there all day with him – went out to eat and everything – and then left, came home about seven o'clock at night. Got into [*his*] mother's house and [*his*] brother was listening to the radio – they had a radio – and he says, 'Ma ... the Japanese bombed Pearl Harbor.' 'Where [*is*] Pearl Harbor?' 'Hawaii'. 'Where's Hawaii?' I says. He ... starts saying Roosevelt was on [*the radio*] then, so we listened, and about maybe an hour or two later, in comes

Francis, my [*future*] husband; they'd just heard it. All that time we were on Camp Edwards, they never heard it. They let them all come home if they could get a ride, so ... home he came. And he stayed the night and then went back the next day. So, uh ... he stayed there, of course, then...

AS: Then they got sent...

LS: Roosevelt says [*enlisted men*] can't get out. He was supposed to get out in January, already had one year. They said nope, you have to stay in; there's going to be war. So he did. His outfit came to Plymouth, [*Massachusetts,*] which was nice; they built bunkers and ... guarded the coast. So, while he was in Plymouth – I don't know how long he was there – he came home one night [*and*] said 'Uh, let's get married.' I says, 'I can't get married.' He says, "What do you mean?' 'I don't have any money. I have twenty five dollars in the bank.' He says, 'Well, I've got money; my mother saved my money that I sent home to her to use.' Instead, she saved it for him. I says, 'Oh, no. I can't. My mother will be upset.'

AS: You said you were how old? You were only twenty?

LS: Twenty. My mother will be upset because five already inside of three years got married. Five in my family. I would've been the sixth. I said, 'Oh, no. My mother would be upset.'

AS: She'd lose your pay?

LS: No, no, but I was going to live there, 'cause I wasn't going to follow him around, or do anything ... he was in Plymouth. So I said, 'You'll have to tell her that you want to get married. I'm not telling her.'

AS: Did he give you a ring?

LS: Yeah ... I had the ring the year before.

AS: Did he get sent away?

LS: In three weeks we got married.

AS: So did you have a traditional [*wedding*], did you have a dress like your sister had?

LS: We went to church [*Sacred Heart Church, 29 First Street, Taunton*], of course. Bought my dress and then I had my veil, and I bought an outfit with the money I had; my mother had let me kept those three weeks' pay. We got married and then we had breakfast at my house. And then we ... went to Fall River; I wanted the pictures at [*Mrs. Anna E.*] Jette's [*Studio, 225 South Main Street, Fall River*] 'cause that's where my sister had her pictures, and we went to the Chinese Restaurant down on Main Street there [*Eagle Restaurant, 33 North Main Street, Fall River*] ... all of us, the wedding party.... You know how much the meal was? A dollar a meal. Full meal – a dollar a meal. He paid for everything, he was so anxious to get married. Well, my mother couldn't pay for it, I couldn't pay for it.

AS: And then he got sent to California, did you say?

LS: Oh, no, not right away. We went to New York [*City*] for our honeymoon, for three days. Then, I went to Plymouth for the rest of the week that I took off from work. A year I worked, and he stayed there in Plymouth for awhile ... he was armored, field artillery. That's a big tank. He start going first down south, then he ended up in the desert in California, then he ended up right on the coast. I figured he was going to go to the Pacific ... that was in 1943. So, uh, he says, 'I'm probably going to be here about three weeks. I want you to come out by train to visit.' I says, 'I can't. I can't go out there to visit by train.' He's on the phone, and he says, "Yeah, because there's two other fellows, and their wives, they're talking their wives into coming, so the three of you can come.' Four days to go across to California from [*Taunton*]; four days it took us. We changed trains in Chicago [*Illinois*] and got a Pullman [*car*]. Went from here, twenty-one years old.

AS: Did you have the money for that? He sent you, you had enough money to pay for the ticket?

LS: Well, for that year, see, I was getting an allotment for being married, which was the best. So, I could still pay my mother room and board, the same as she was getting [*before I married*]. She didn't lose anything, and I had that whole extra that I was saving. But we went there April 1 ... 1943. We had a nice depot here, to get our train tickets and our reservations. The conductor says, 'Where are you three girls going? You're going to California?' We said, 'Yeah, we're going to go visit our husbands.' He says, 'You might know, it's April Fool's Day.' We start laughing. We thought it was a big joke, and we went. It was quite an adventure. We didn't have any trouble. I think what impressed me the most [*was*] when the conductor came through and said, 'Los Angeles, next stop.' So, uh, we were getting our suitcases; we slept in a Pullman. You remember Pullmans?

JR: Yes, I do.

LS: Well we had one. I slept on the top because I was the smallest. And that was ... women and men that was staying in that Pullman.

JR: All women?

LS: No, it was soldiers, sailors. So, that's how safe it was. We had a main washing room here, and then we had the ladies' room to change, and they had the men's room, and then you had a dining room to go eat. And our Pullman would turn into two coach seats to sit in during the day. And ... when the Pullman porter says, 'Next stop is Los Angeles,' but he didn't say how long, we jumped up, start getting [*ready*] and we're standing there, and he says, 'It'll be a while yet.' What impressed me was the orange groves. Oh, they were so beautiful ... beautiful orange groves, all the way, and everybody was remarking about them, all these soldiers, sailors. I don't think you saw one civilian person on that train. We got off in Los Angeles. Then, we had to take a train – an old rickety train – to Lompoc [*California*], which was the closest to where they had found rooms for us, and we got on that train at night and we got to Lompoc and then from Lompoc we had to take a bus into Santa Maria [*California*], which was a little town, [*a*] farmer's town, but they had a Greyhound bus terminal. And that's where they were waiting for us. Well, he [*my husband*] sent one fellow – he couldn't come to Los Angeles – he sent this other fellow [*whose*] wife was with us ... to Los Angeles to meet us at the trains to tell us what to do.... We had rooms that a woman [*Mrs. Jamieson*] rented out [*at 609 West Mill Street*] ... to the servicemen. She had a ... Cape Cod house, so there was three bedrooms upstairs plus the hallway was a sitting room, and a bar, and she let us have kitchen privileges for breakfast, but the rest [*of our meals*] we had to eat out. But, they went back to their camp which was twenty-two miles [*away*]. [*Ledora remained in California for ten months, and arrived back in Taunton on February 2, 1943.*]

AS: Do you remember the name of the camp? What camp it was?

LS: Yup, Camp Cooke [*United States Army Armored Training Camp, Santa Barbara County, California*]. It was about twenty-two miles from Santa Maria.

AS: This has been wonderful. You have so many amazing memories.

LS: Well, my mother had a lot of stories. We used to ask her about Fall River. Well, I'm so glad you came.

AS: We thank you so much.

PHOTO GALLERY

9.1 Ledora's paternal grandparents, Manuel Isidorio, Sr., and his wife, née Filomena Souza (standing) as attendants at the wedding of an unidentified couple, circa 1910. *"I don't remember him. But I do remember my grandmother ... she used to come up and she'd get mad because we didn't understand Portuguese."*

9.2 Ledora's maternal grandparents, James Emmett and his wife, née Marie 'Mary' Desmarais, about the time of their marriage in 1887. *"James Emmett was English because he came from Lancashire, England ...* [my grandmother] *was French-Canadian, so she spoke French."*

9.3 The Emmett family, posing in front of their residence at 227 Brightman Street, Fall River, Massachusetts, 1908. Standing, left to right: Ledora's uncle, George Joseph Emmett; her grandfather, James Emmett; her mother, Anna Emmett; her aunt, Elizabeth Emmett; her grandmother, née Marie Desmarais; her aunt, Mary Emmett. Standing on porch: her aunt, Minnie Emmett. *"French. They all spoke French."*

9.4 Ledora's father, Manuel Isidorio, Jr., as a young man. *"I remember my father standing ... when we'd get ready to get up to go to school, with our clothes in front of the oven door."*

9.5 Ledora's mother, Anna Emmett, at seventeen years old, posing with a parasol in a novelty photograph, 1906; the pen work decoration on the envelope, likely done by Anna, was a popular art form during the period. *"My mother was a spinner. She went to work ... in the mills ... when she was twelve; she had to leave school."*

9.6 The typewriting room of Thibodeau Business College, Inc., 130 South Main Street, Fall River, Massachusetts, circa 1930. *"You had to go to Thibodeau College, you had classes. You had to go for one year and they would find you a job. Well. I couldn't afford that."*

9.7 Lindsey Street, Fall River, Massachusetts, in the 1930s. Monte Street, where the Isidorio family resided, intersects Lindsey Street; this view is characteristic of the neighborhood in which Ledora spent her youth. *"We had a good time in the neighborhood."*

9.8 Bradford Durfee Textile School, 64 Durfee, Street, Fall River, Massachusetts; Ledora enrolled here in the 1930s. *"I went to Durfee Textile School at night to learn how to run the power machines."*

9.9 Heroux & Son, grocery store, 177 Brightman Street, Fall River, around the time of its grand opening in 1932; this store was the scene of an exciting moment in Ledora's childhood, which she fondly remembered eighty-three years later. *"And for opening night they were giving away a radio. A little table-top radio. And you put your name in. So, all the kids and we went in, and we put our name in, put it in the box. They were going to draw it on Saturday night, who could win the radio. So, anyway, we all went down, the kids. All went down to the store to see who was going to win the radio. Well ... one of my friends, went up and they asked her to pull the name. Ledora Isidorio."*

9.10 Truesdale Hospital Inc., 1820 Highland Avenue, Fall River, Massachusetts, in the 1930s; Ledora's father died here, leaving his wife a widow with eight children. *"But then he got sick and died. He died on January 30, 1933. He died in Truesdale."*

9.11 The Weetamoe Yacht Club, 2 Monte Street, Fall River, Massachusetts, 1920s; from 1935 to 1938 Ledora's family resided in the six-tenement house depicted at the right. *"And we lived, when we finally moved a second time, we moved in the six-tenement house* [at 1 Monte Street, Fall River, Massachusetts], *which was on the banks of the Taunton River, and down below was the Weetamoe Yacht Club."*

9.12 "The Fall River Gang" posing on the shore of the Taunton River, Fall River. Massachusetts, June 10, 1938; the Weetamoe Yacht Club, which was in Ledora's backyard, can be seen at the left. *"It was the Taunton River, but we didn't care, that was where we did our swimming. That's true, everything that was in that beach, we brought down there from our house."*

9.13 Ledora's mother, Anna Isidorio, née Emmett, in 1938, the year the family moved to 892 Somerset Avenue, Taunton, Massachusetts. *"My mother was not strict, believe me. I was stricter with my kids than she was with us."*

9.14 The former Laurel Lake Mills, corner Broadway and Globe Street, Fall River, Massachusetts, 1935; the building housed Cape Cod Dress Company, where Ledora was first employed in 1938. *"And when I started there, I remember, it was twenty-five cents an hour ... you got $10 for forty hours. $10 a week."*

9.15 Ledora in the yard of the Isidorio family residence at 892 Somerset Avenue, Taunton, Massachusetts, 1939. *"Five girls. They used to say, 'The house with five beautiful girls,' and we'd laugh."*

9.16 "Cape Cod Dress Friends," 1941; the young women were Ledora's co-workers at Cape Cod Dress Company, 987 Broadway, Fall River, Massachusetts. Ledora is seated, front left. *"Well, my first job,* [my sister] *got me a job."*

9.17 "The Sewing Machine Girls," 1941; the young women were Ledora's co-workers at Cape Cod Dress Company, 987 Broadway, Fall River, Massachusetts. Ledora is standing, center. *"We were on the third floor and had to walk up three flight of stairs. No elevators or anything."*

9.18 "Cape Cod Dress Friends," 1941; the young women were Ledora's co-workers at Cape Cod Dress Company, 987 Broadway, Fall River, Massachusetts. Ledora is second from the left. *"You never had any breaks."*

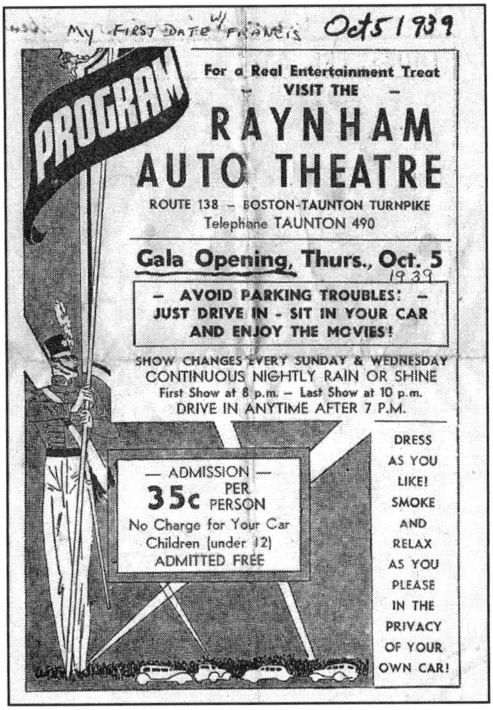

9.19 Gala Opening program, Raynham Auto Drive Theatre, Route 138, Boston-Taunton Turnpike, October 5, 1939; Ledora captioned the program "My first date w/Francis." *"I'm looking for you. Do you want to go over to the Raynham Auto Drive Theatre tonight? It's opening night."*

9.20 Interior of an unidentified sewing shop in Fall River, Massachusetts, 1930s; the scene is typical of what Ledora experienced at Cape Cod Dress Company. *"Each power machine ... I think, must have had a starter, but they were hooked to the wall, with a main power switch. And the floor lady would go up to the power switch for each aisle, so these power machines were* [on] *both sides,* [and] *you faced the girl who was working them."*

9.21 Interior of the lunch room of an unidentified sewing shop in Fall River, Massachusetts, 1930s; the scene is typical of what Ledora experienced at Cape Cod Dress Company. *"The only time* [you got a break] *was when you ... could go to the toilet and back. And that was it. We had a lunch time."*

9.22 Mr. & Mrs. Francis Silveira Soitos, April 18, 1942. *"You'll have to tell* [my mother] *that you want to get married. I'm not telling her."*

9.23 Ledora's husband, Francis Silveira Soitos, during World War II. *"His outfit* [was] *all Taunton boys; they stayed together, all through the war, and not one got killed."*

9.24 Ledora (Isidorio) Soitos, 1944.

9.25 "The Main Street, Santa Maria," California, June 1944; Ledora resided in Santa Maria for ten months in 1942 and 1943, while her husband, Francis, was stationed at Camp Cooke, a United States Army Armored Training Camp, before he was sent overseas during World War II. *"What impressed me was the orange groves. Oh, they were so beautiful … beautiful orange groves, all the way."*

TEN:

MICHALINA "RUTH" SOUCY, NÉE STASIOWSKI

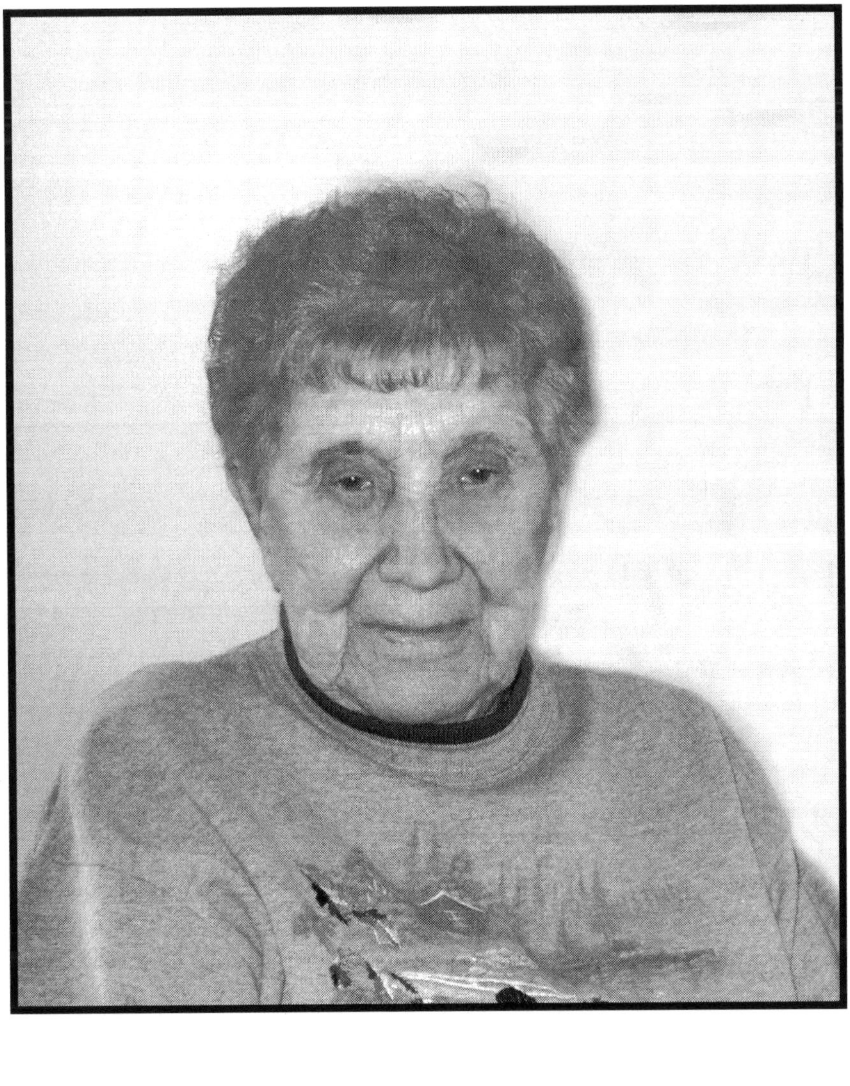

Personal Statistics

Name: Michalina "Ruth" Stasiowski
(Mrs. Joseph Napoleon Roger Soucy)

Date of Birth: December 18, 1921

Place of Birth: Fall River, Massachusetts

Date of Death: January 31, 2017

Father: Stefan Stasiowski (1881-1956)

Mother: Katarzyna "Catherine" Kaszowska (1881-1956)

Siblings:
Stefania "Stella" Stasiowski (1902-1992)
---(Mrs. Thomas Francis Cummings, Jr.)
Eugenia "Jean" Stasiowski (1902-1999)
---(Mrs. Stephen Stasiowski)
Władysław "Walter" Stasiowski (1904-1996)
Emilia "Mildred" Stasiowski (1906-1996)
---(Mrs. Eugene J. Ivers)
Bolesław "William" Stasiowski (1908-1988)
Frederick "Fred" Stasiowski (1910-1998)
Albin "Albert" Stasiowski (1912-1995)
Emil "Elmer" Stasiowski (1915-1986)
Czesław "Chester" aka "Tommy" Stasiowski (1919-2007)

Spouse: Joseph Napoleon Roger Soucy (1920-2011)

Date of Marriage: : May 3, 1947

Employment history:
S.S. Kresge Company, Fall River
Joseph Chromow & Co., Fall River
Linjay Manufacturing Corporation, Fall River
Rustic Pub, Swansea, Massachusetts

EDITED TRANSCRIPT

Interview with Mrs. Joseph Napoleon Roger Soucy, née Michalina "Ruth" Stasiowski

Interviewer: (WM) William A. Moniz

Interviewee: (RS) Michelina "Ruth" (Stasiowski) Soucy

Additional Commentary: (JR) Joyce B. Rodrigues, Fall River Historical Society

Date of Interview: June 19, 2015

Location: Somerset Ridge Center, Somerset, Massachusetts

Summary by Joyce B. Rodrigues:

Michalina "Ruth" Stasiowski Soucy was born in Fall River on December 18, 1921.

Ruth's story tells the history of Polish immigration and the rise and fall of the textile industry in the Globe Village, the south end of Fall River.

The Globe Village:

Polish immigrants, fleeing hunger, epidemics, and political oppression, came to Fall River around 1882. They, along with a number of Slavs, Ukrainians, Orthodox Russians, and East European Jews, settled in the Globe Village where there was work in the many cotton mills. The church was the center of the Polish immigrant community. The Globe Village, then as now, was known for its Polish social clubs, businesses, schools, and cultural events.

Ruth's father, Stefan Stasiowski, immigrated to the United States from Galicia, Poland, in 1897 at the age of sixteen. He settled in the Globe Village and worked as a weaver in the King Philip Mills.

Ruth's mother, Katarzyna "Catherine" Kaszowska, immigrated to the United States in 1890 from Wysoka, Bohemia, an area located on the border of Poland and the Czech Republic; she settled with her family in the Globe Village. Catherine worked as a sizer in the cotton mills, (i.e., applying a protective finish to yarn to reduce breakage).

Stefan and Catherine met in Fall River and married in 1901 at the Blessed Virgin Polish National Catholic Church, the city's first Polish church, established in 1898.

Growing up Stasiowski:

There were ten children in the Stasiowski family. Ruth, the youngest, was doted on by her six brothers. The family owned their own home on lower Globe Street, a well maintained six-family triple-decker.

Ruth's view of growing up during the Great Depression was that she "had the best of it." With her older brothers and sisters contributing to the support of the household, Ruth was able to take dance lessons, had a bicycle, went to the movies, and shopped with her mother at R.A. McWhirr Company department store and Cherry & Webb Company, a ladies' specialty store. She took the commercial course at B.M.C. Durfee High School and graduated in 1939, the only one of her family to complete high school.

From her home, Ruth could see the Fall River Line steamers passing down the Taunton River on their way to New York City. She recalls seeing President Franklin D. Roosevelt in 1936 when the president and his family came to Fall River for the funeral of FDR's political advisor and secretary, Louis McHenry Howe.

While in high school, Ruth worked part-time "downtown", for twenty-five cents an hour at S.S. Kresge Company five-and-dime store. After graduation, office jobs were scarce. Many south end mills had already closed.

Ruth started working in the needletrades at Joseph Chromow & Co., Inc. (aka Lin-Jay), manufacturers of underwear and sportswear, as a floor girl, (i.e., a girl or woman in the needletrades who runs errands and does odd jobs around the shop). She worked at Chromow's for thirty-four years, from the age of sixteen to fifty, progressing from floor girl to floor lady (supervisor).

Ruth's narration clearly describes her years as a supervisor, the impact of the union (ILGWU) on the workers, and how she, as a floor lady and representative of management, strove to be fair to workers. Because Ruth was a non-union employee, she retired with income from Social Security and a company pension plan. In her retirement years, she worked briefly as a bookkeeper for a well-known area restaurant.

Ruth married Roger Soucy, her high school sweetheart, in 1947. They had no children.

Note: This interview has been slightly edited for continuity and readability; in order to preserve the integrity of the conversation, the phraseology remains that of the interviewer and interviewee. Italicized information in square brackets has been added for the purposes of clarification and context.

WM: Today we are interviewing Mrs. Ruth Soucy about her career and employment and otherwise. Ruth, tell us about your early childhood and your family.

RS: My early childhood? Okay, I come from a family of ten [*Stefania "Stella" Stasiowski; Eugenia "Jean" Stasiowski; Władysław "Walter" Stasiowski; Emilia "Mildred" Stasiowski; Bolesław "William" Stasiowski; Frederick "Fred" Stasiowski; Albin "Albert" Stasiowski; Emil "Elmer" Stasiowski; and Czesław "Chester" Stasiowski*]. I [*Michalina "Ruth" Stasiowski*] am the youngest; they're all gone except me. I've only got nieces and nephews left and some of them are already gone, and here I am, and what else can I say? I had a very good childhood being the tenth – the last of the bunch, I could say. I had six brothers that looked over me, and I guess I was the one that had the best of all of it, because the older ones started to work, and I was the baby, and they – what my parents [*Stefan Stasiowski, and his wife, née Catherine Kaszowska*] couldn't give me, they gave me. I took dance lessons. I was the one that was able to graduate from [*B.M.C. Durfee*] High School [*in 1939*], and what else can I say?

WM: You were born in Fall River, Ruth?

RS: Huh?

WM: You were born in Fall River?

RS: Oh, yes.

WM: In?

RS: [*On December 18,*] 1921.

WM: Now your parents, uh, were Polish background? Polish, your parents?

RS: Polish, yes.

WM: What was your maiden name?

RS: Stasiowski.

WM: Tell me about your parents. Tell me about their background.

RS: Huh?

WM: Your parents, what were they like?

RS: Well, they come from, uh, Poland.

WM: First generation?

RS: Uh, the first ... yup, they were the first ones to come over here, and my Dad could speak English. [*Ruth's father immigrated in 1897; her mother, in 1890.*] In fact, during the epidemic of the flu [*Influenza Pandemic, 1918 – 1919*], he was one of 'em that went with the doctors to the ... Polish families because they couldn't talk [*English*], they couldn't tell the doctor what was wrong, so my father was like an interpreter for the doctor. And we all survived it.

WM: Where did your parents work, Ruth?

RS: My, my mom, I don't ever believe she worked. My dad was a weaver in a mill, which was horrible, 'cause I went to bring him a lunch one day and I went in that weave room; that was horrible – the noise.

WM: Which mill did he work in, Ruth? Do you know? Which mill?

RS: He worked [*as a weaver*] in the King Philip [*Mills, 372 Kilburn Street, Fall River*] … I'll tell you, [*there was*] the main building of King Philip and then there was like a little one in the back. Well, that was the weave room, because I remember bringing his supper there one night. I was brought up at the Globe [*Village section of Fall River, in the southern part of the city*].

WM: I was going to ask you that. Where did you live in the Globe? Which street?

RS: [*At 76*] Globe Street.

WM: Right on Globe Street?

RS: Right at the bottom almost at Bay [*Street*]. That is why we were always at the [*Taunton*] River, the Mount Hope Bay, the boats and everything else.

WM: You were telling me earlier about the Fall River Line. You used to …

[*The Fall River Line of steamships, in operation from 1847 to 1937, sailed from Fall River to New York City, with a stop in Newport, Rhode Island; the ships were famous for their luxurious interior accommodations.*]

RS: Oh, yeah, that was beautiful.

WM: You used to row out to the boats, did you?

RS: Ah, we used to go out for the waves [*made by the wake of the passing ship*], it was the picture to see it going by. These kids don't know nothing today.

WM: It's all changed.

RS: They have so much in life.

WM: Were you a [*Roman*] Catholic? Catholic religion?

RS: Yes, oh yes.

WM: Which parish did you belong to?

RS: I belonged to St. Patrick's [*Church, 1598 South Main Street, Fall River*]. Well, I'll tell you my dad had a fight with, with Father [*Reverend Hugo Emanuel*] Dylla [*at the*

Church of St. Stanislaus, 38 Rockland Street, Fall River,] and he stayed, but us kids, he put us in with St. Patrick's parish.

WM: Where did you go to school, Ruth?

RS: First, from the, um, we used to call it kindergarten – we played in sand boxes. We went, I went to [*Jerome Dwelly*] School [*at 59*] Foote Street; of course, that is all gone.
WM: Yup.

RS: That was from pre-primary to sixth grade. Then I had to go to Fowler School, [*286 Sprague Street, Fall River*] – that was seventh to eighth grade. Then from eighth grade to [*B.M.C.*] Durfee [*High School,*] until I graduated [*in 1939*].

WM: You were one of ten children, right?

RS: Yup.

WM: And you were the last.

RS: I'm the last one.

WM: Tell us a little bit about your siblings. Your brothers and sisters, what were they like?

RS: Well, I had twin sisters [*Stefania "Stella" Stasiowski, later Mrs. Thomas Francis Cummings Jr.; and Eugenia "Jean" Stasiowski, later Mrs. Stephen Stasiowski*]. They were the oldest, and 'course, they both worked; one in the King Philip Mill[*s*], one worked in the Firestone [*Rubber & Latex Products Company, 172 Ferry Street, Fall River*]. The one that worked in the Firestone had a better job because it wasn't as messy as working in a card room in the King Phillip Mill[*s*]. Now my brother Walter [*Władysław Stasiowski*] worked ... at Firestone; he worked a midnight shift. Brother Bill [*Bolesław "William" Stasiowski*] worked in Firestone until it burned down [*on October 11, 1941*]; then he was sent out to, out to Boston, [*Massachusetts,*] to work in one of the mills out there. My brother Fred [*Frederick Stasiowski*] – he was the one that was the go getter. He worked ... he worked [*as a doffer in a cotton mill, and as a collector and salesman for Ideal Radio and Furniture Company, 292 Pleasant Street, Fall River*] and he had his own ... by the end of his career he owned his own furniture store, Stacy's Furniture [*Company, 1140*] Bedford Street, [*Fall River*]. And brother Elmer [*Emil "Elmer" Stasiowski*] worked for the [*Fall River*] Gas [*Works*] Company, [*155 North Main Street*]. Brother Al [*Albin "Albert" Stasiowski*] worked for the Gas Company. My brother Tommy, [*Czesław "Chester" Stasiowski*] well, he worked here and there.

WM: You told me you were born in 1921, so you would have been a teenager during the [*Great*] Depression.

RS: Oh, I went right through with the Depression.

WM: Tell us about, what was it like growing up during the Depression?

RS: Like I told you. I didn't – I've seen so when no one had anything to eat. Kids would be going along the roads and, you know, like an apple core, they would pick it up and take the last little bits of it to eat. There was no freebies them days. Nobody gave you nothing for nothing; it was horrible, it was horrible. Like I say, I went through it, but I didn't miss any[*thing*] because the family being so big, the elders worked, and they helped to donate to the family and we had – I was lucky, I was one of the lucky ones. But I seen the kids – and when we went to school, we weren't dressed like the kids today. I remember being in high school, you had a cardigan. One day you wore it buttoned all the way up, the next day you wore the buttons in the back. No, it was tough, it was tough; you never had too much. And food was horrible. There was a lot of hungry kids, let me tell you.

WM: But your family, because you had older siblings who were working…

RS: That's right, that is what helped my parents, and then they bought a house [*in 1921*] because I was coming, and you know, where you gonna rent a house for ten kids? [*Prior to 1921, the Stasiowski family resided in Fall River at: 118 Wilcox Street, circa 1902; 106 Wilcox Street, circa 1903; 203 Tripp Street, circa 1904; 406 Montaup Street, circa 1905 - 1908; 360 Montaup Street, circa 1909 - 1916; and 279 Montaup Street circa 1917 -1921.*]

WM: So, where was the, where was the house that they bought?

RS: On [*76*] Globe Street, right opposite Foote Street.

WM: Okay.

RS: It was a beautiful, six-tenement house. In fact, I lived there until I moved to Swansea [*in 1963*]. There was, like, six rooms in the front, four rooms in the back tenements. I can't … yeah, we managed the family, but like I, I'm telling you, it was horrible. It was that – and jobs, when I got [*my first*] job … I worked for twenty-five cents an hour … yeah, I worked for twenty-five cents an hour. I [*worked at*] Kresge's Five-and-Ten [*S. S. Kresge Company, department store, 71 to 87 South Main Street, Fall River*]. After high school, on a Friday, we went to work at Kresge's until ten o'clock then – that's when the stores were open on a Friday night, they weren't open like they are today – and then on Saturday we worked all day 'til ten o'clock at night. Got twenty-five cents an hour, that was a lot of money!

WM: Was that your first job out of high school?

RS: Yeah … I was in high school at the time … that was a little part-time job.

WM: What did you do for, what did you do for Kresge's? What was the nature of your job?

RS: My nature of job, I … can't really describe it. Because [*later*] when I started to work [*in the sewing shops*], they called it a floor girl; fifty cents an hour. I graduated from twenty-five to fifty cents. Uh, I started as a floor girl and … if a girl needed a bobbin of thread, I would get it for her, or if they needed, needed work, I would tell the floor lady that they were running out. And they were on piecework, and you, if you want slave labor, there it is.

WM: Now where was this?

RS: This was in all sewing shops. Not only one.

WM: Not at Kresge's though, this was after Kresge's.

RS: No, if you got hired for piecework, you had a machine that was going like this, constantly.

WM: What was your first job full time job?

RS: That was it when I got out of high school. I went to work in a sewing factory.

WM: Which one?

RS: Chromow's [*Joseph Chromow & Co., underwear manufacturers, 987 Broadway, Fall River; later, underwear and sportswear, 951 Broadway,*] he was the, uh, [*the president and treasurer of the company.*] I was like a floor girl. I would get the thread for the girls and I had to make sure they worked. Then I graduated to a little better [*position,*] and, then, I finally got my little, little own department where they used to put the buttons on and sew, and they examined the garment, they folded it, and it was shipped out. And then I was, I was on, I was on salary; from fifty cents an hour to salary.

WM: How long did it take you to do that? How many years?

RS: How many years? Um, I, I, stay there all my life, since I was sixteen. Well, Chromow, he died [*in 1954*]. He sent, no, he sold the business to … the cutter … and a [*Hyman Horvitz*], he was like a salesman [*he was formerly a broker*]. He sold the business to these two. They kept it … up the Flint [*section of the city*] there, I don't know the name of the mill [*the former Wampanoag Mills, 420 Quequechan Street, Fall River*]. Then, my boss and the other one, they decided to open up down north [*as Linjay Manufacturing Corporation*], where all the doctors are [*now*]. On the first floor, we were on that …

WM: That's [*the former*] Narragansett Mills [*1567 North Main Street, Fall River.*]

RS: And that is where I ended it; at fifty, I quit.

WM: At age fifty? That was your last job?

RS: They can have it.

WM: Good for you.

JR: Now what, I have to go back a second, and where was the Chromow factory?

RS: Yeah, Mr. Chromow, it was on Broadway, the Globe [*Four*] Corners. You know the [*former Laurel Lake*] Mills [*951 Broadway, Fall River,*] on the Globe Corners? The gas station [*Winiarski Service Station, 964 Broadway*] was here, the mill was on Broadway.

WM: Globe Mills.

RS: Broadway, in the circus grounds.

WM: That's Globe Mills.

RS: We used to call it the Circus Grounds.

WM: Right, exactly, and that is where it was at first.

RS: Yup.

WM: And then it moved? It moved to the Flint, you say?

RS: They, I don't know, we were on the top floor. I don't know if they got evicted or what – they moved to [*420*] Quequechan Street, [*Fall River*]. We were on Quequechan Street, where … you know, the Fall River Knitting Mills, [*Inc.*] and all them were.

JR: Right.

RS: The front part. Then these two bosses, these two bosses [*Hyman Horvitz and Eugene Joseph Rutkowski*] decided to own, to buy, to buy them out. And we started down in Narraganset Mills, down north.

WM: Tell us a little bit more about the bosses. What were they like?

RS: Huh?

WM: Your bosses, what were they like? Did you get along with them?

RS: Well, I got along with them because I could con them. Awful to say, but …

WM: What do you mean by that? What do you mean 'con them?' How did you con them?

RS: I would be nice to them then I'd be a …

JR: Bitch?

RS: Bitch.

JR: Okay.

WM: Okay.

JR: You want to give us an example?

RS: Because I was for the girls. I wasn't for the bosses, but they thought I was for them.

WM: Do you have any specific instances that you would like to tell us about?

RS: On the sewing part, just that they worked like slaves and got no credit. It was terrible. You couldn't imagine. There would be a pile of work like this.

JR: What were they making? Were these dresses?

RS: We were making … different kinds of things. We were making night gowns, and pajamas, and dusters, and then on another section we were making nylon panties. So, it was like two different – and Mr. [*Hyman Horvitz*] was the salesman [*and treasurer*], and [*Eugene Joseph*] Rutkowski was the boss that stayed there. He was a hellion to the girls. And then union – I wouldn't give you two cents for the union. I am not a union person. I never was and I will never would … they did absolutely nothing for these girls except take their dues every week.

WM: Tell us more about that. That was the International Ladies Garment Workers Union?

RS: Yes.

WM: ILGWU [*Local 178, 304 South Main Street, Fall River*], yeah. And what do they do?

RS: What did they do? Nothing for the girls. Nothing.

WM: If the girls …

RS: The girls had … what you would call a shop stewardess. If you had a complaint, you would talk to her. The shop stewardess would talk to the boss, then if they fought, the union would come in. So the union come in; so instead of going to the … shop stewardess to talk to her to find out what the problem was, they would go to the boss. Then all of a sudden everything is all fixed, and you see them coming out with nightgowns and …

WM: In other words, what you are saying is they were on the take, right?

RS: Not on the take, but they would settle it between themselves and the girls got nothing. No credit out of it; they got nothing.

WM: How much were the dues in those days, do you remember?

RS: Well, I remember some was fifty cents.

WM: Was that a month?

RS: Fifty cents a week.

WM: A week?

JR: That is a lot of money.

WM: What year would that have been? In the '30s?

RS: That was in the'30s, yeah, [*late*] '30s and '40s, then it went up, it kept going up. But I don't … I lost track of it when they gave me that job, and a lot of girls wouldn't talk. A lot of girls were afraid to talk to me, thinking I would, but they should have known better.

WM: Well, you were, what was your title, Ruth? What was your title? Were you a floorlady?

RS: Uh, I was, uh, well, it would've been a supervisor.

WM: Supervisor.

RS: Supervisor.

WM: And you had a department?

RS: Yeah.

WM: How big was your department? How many employees did you have?

RS: Well, I had, let me see … I had a certain section. I had the, the girls that put … they put buttons and they [*made*] button holes, and grippers [*zippers*]. You know the grippers, when the grippers come out? And then I had all the girls' tables where they examine the garment, took the thread out, [*and*] made sure everything was all right, [*that*] the seams and everything were put together.

WM: So, they were inspectors.

RS: And then it was brought over to another table where the girls would fold them, because at that time everything was folded – pressed and folded – and then it went into the shipping department. Then the shipping department filled out the orders and shipped it out. Yeah, it was tough. All them girls, they worked hard.

WM: What were the hours?

RS: Huh?

WM: The hours, what were the work hours?

RS: Them hours were from eight in the morning – eight in the morning 'til five at night when we first started. It was an eight-hour day.

WM: What did you get for lunch? How much time?

RS: Eight-hour day for five days.

WM: Half an hour for lunch?

RS: Yup.

JR: How about breaks in the factory to go to the restroom? Because I've often heard that it was pretty difficult to leave your station to go to the restroom.

RS: Yeah, well, they'd hate to leave it because the next girl would be waiting, while you finished, to go, to the next girl, and that was where all the fights would go. But they had to go to the rest room; that they had to do. They had to let them go. But don't worry, they more or less watched if you stayed there too long or to have a cigarette, or anything.

JR: Timing it.

RS: I never timed my girls, they could go and stay there. All I figured is they are losing, they are on piecework. If they stay in there an hour, they weren't working that hour, or fifteen minutes, or if they went in fifteen minutes, they come out and they started to work, of course, they are going to make more than the girl that stayed in there half an hour having a smoke or something. The girls, they … when it really, really, got bad was when the Portuguese people come in to sew. It was hard to talk to them, but they could always knew their money, that they knew right from the beginning. They were hard workers – I will say, they were hard workers, and they really ruined it for a lot of us, because, you see, we never had air condition in the mills. So, if it was a hot, hot day, after a certain degree [*on the thermometer*], if the girls wanted to go home, they could shut the factory down and go home. But when the Portuguese people come in, the boss would say, "If anybody wants to stay and work" – they are willing to work, of course, they were willing to work; we had to stay there with them. But, you see, they wouldn't shut the whole place down, they stayed and they worked, and we had to stay.

WM: So you stayed, too?

RS: We had to.

WM: That was the old Department Of Labor And Industries; they had a rule about humidity and heat in those days.

RS: It was tough in that hot, and the windows never opened because the mills were so old. You couldn't open them windows for nothing.

WM: Now, you had breaks, though, scheduled breaks.

RS: Oh, yeah, they did have breaks. They had so long in the morning and so long – I think it was ten or fifteen minutes in the morning, ten or fifteen minutes in the afternoon.

WM: Did you have vending machines in the, vending machines?

RS: No.

WM: Everybody brought their lunch?

RS: They were the things [*that were*] were coming. No, they didn't.

WM: Everybody brought their lunch?

RS: Although, we did have a coffee [*machine*] … but they had to pay for their own coffee.

JR: No cafeterias to get it, huh?

RS: You brought your own sandwiches or go out.

WM: So, now you say, you, uh, you retired early.

RS: Huh?

WM: You retired early at age fifty.

RS: Yeah, I had a good husband [*Joseph Napoleon Roger Soucy, called 'Roger'*].

WM: Tell us about your husband. We haven't talked about him.

RS: My husband … I met in high school.

JR: Oh, wonderful, a Durfee romance!

RS: Well, no it wasn't. He was 'R.S.' and I was 'R.S.', so we always sat in homeroom in front or in back of each other, and we would kid with one another, like, how you kid when kids in high school. We had classes together on some, because, you know, you had classes with them; other classes, you didn't. So, both, he graduated and I graduated the same year, [*in 1939*], and like I say, Depression. His dad [*Joseph Napoleon Soucy*] was a foreman or something in one of the mills [*he was a second hand in the Shawmut Mills, 638 Quequechan Street, Fall River*], and he got him a job to work in a mill. He worked there one week and said to his father, he said 'Dad, this isn't for me.' So his father says, 'Well, it's up to you, you know.' His father could say it. He says, 'I am going to join the service,' so he [*enlisted, May 8, 1940, in the United States Army National Guard,*] and his ... buddies went to join the service. At that time you could say where you wanted to go. Well, these three boys were going to go to Hawaii.

JR: Oh, wait a minute. That sounds dangerous.

RS: One of them didn't pass the exam, he had tuberculosis and he didn't know it, [*and*] the other one was shipped God-knows-where. My husband stayed around this area; I think he went to Portland, Maine [*Fort McKinley, Great Diamond Island, Portland Maine Harbor*]. And, uh, he stayed in Portland, Maine. At that time, when you went in the army, you didn't have a school, you was put right in with the regular army, so his first night that he spent in the army was in a jail because there was no room for him in the barracks. So, he come home.... He come home, and he had, like, a – I don't know whether it was a weekend or his ten days that they usually got a year, and, uh, he found out that all his buddies were either married or they had steady girlfriends. So, he was sitting in the house like a log. So, his mother [*Mrs. Joseph Napoleon Soucy, the widowed Mrs. Henri Vaillancourt, née Amelia Beauchemin*] says to him, 'Why don't you call some girl that you went to school with? You know? And see, maybe she isn't going steady or anything. Go out with her.' So, he called me ... and we are talking, and everything, [*and*] he says, he asked me if I was going steady. I said, 'No.' I says I was going out with different ones. So he says, 'Sure.' He asks me if he could come down. I says, 'Of course you can come down, Roger.' He says, well, he says, 'You know, ask your mother if it's alright if I come in uniform.' I said, 'Ask my mother? You got to be kidding.' He says, 'Yes ... Yes, my civilian clothes don't fit me 'cause I outgrew them,' because he went in as a kid. And so he come down, and that's how it started.

WM: What year was that?

RS: Um, oh, let me see. 1939, 1940, '41, something like that.

JR: This was before [*the Japanese attack on*] Pearl Harbor [*on December 7, 1941*]?

RS: Oh, yes.

JR: Now, you had a telephone. He could call you, and he had a telephone.

RS: Oh, he, he used to call from the barracks. He used to call me. No, no, he was stationed in Portland, Maine.

JR: Did you, did you, have telephones in your home?

RS: Oh, we had telephones, yeah. Well, one telephone, 'ya know. And uh, so, he come down and that's how it started. And, when he came down again, he would call me and I would say, 'Sure, come down.' But I was going out with another one. But I told the other one, if he ever come down, I would go out with him first, because I felt sorry because he was in the service.

WM: So how did it progress from there? When did you get engaged?

RS: Well, we started to go out and it just boomeranged, I guess. It boomeranged. And, uh, he stayed in Portland, Maine, for a while, until they opened up Camp Edwards [*United States Army National Guard Training Camp, Barnstable County, Massachusetts, dedicated in 1938*]. He was in pup tents in Camp Edwards; spent one night there, one night there, when the barracks were being built. And, then ... that was when [*World*] War [*II*] was declared. Then, he was sent to Boston [*where*] they were on top of Schraft's Candy Factory, [*Sullivan Square, Charlestown, Massachusetts*]; they were protecting the harbor, Boston Harbor. They spent that Christmas in that – that was on the beach – in the sand, in pup tents. They never had no barracks; no nothing there. They were sleeping in pup tents on the beach in the winter. Oh, they had it tough.

WM: So when did you get engaged?

RS: When did I get engaged? Before he went over, before he went overseas – no, it was after. I kept writing to him, but I was writing to this other fellow [*'Billy'*], too, and when they both landed – now, Roger was in the United States – Billy, he got drafted, and they shipped him to England. And when the World War, when it started, the two [*allied troops*] from the United States and England, they all formed into one convoy and they were in the invasion of, uh ...

JR: France?

RS: Of that North Africa. [*Operation Touch, the Anglo-American occupation of Morocco and Algeria, commenced November 8, 1942*].

WM: North Africa.

RS: So, when I got a letter from this one, and I got a letter from this one, and all they could say [*was that they were*] somewhere in North Africa. They couldn't tell you where they were or anything. If you got a letter, sometimes you didn't even know what it was, everything was cut out.

WM: That was the censors. [*Military Intelligence, Unites States Postal Censorship*].

RS: Censors, yeah. So, he stayed over. He was over there three years and some months.

WM: When did he come back?

RS: Huh?

WM: When did he come back?

RS: Three years and some months later.

WM: What year?

JR: Forty-five? 1945?

RS: Yeah, had to be. Let me see, I got married [*on May 3, 1947*], I got married at twenty-four and he was twenty-five. So....

WM: 1945. Yeah, that was the year [*war*] ended [*in Europe*].

RS: And they didn't want to ship him back, but he told them, he says, 'If you don't, I'm going to call, talk, write to my Congressman." You had to come back by points, and he had way over the points, but they wouldn't send him home. He was in charge of this big rest area out in, uh ... Italy, and uh, when the boys were going to be shipped home they brought them in there, gave them a rest and everything else, and shipped them through there.

WM: You said earlier that ... you said earlier that he was a good husband. What did he do for a living when he came back?

RS: When he come back? When he come back, he worked for the [*United States*] Navy – he was an accountant in the Navy.

JR: In Newport?

RS: Yeah. [*Naval Station Newport, Newport/Middletown, Rhode Island*].

JR: Oh, very good.

RS: And he finished his twenty years as a, in [*the*] Reserves. Went in as a private; come back as a Major, got out as a Major.

WM: Really? An officer? Wow.

RS: He got his first promotion when he was working with [*General Dwight David 'Ike'*] Eisenhower, [*Supreme Commander of Allied Forces in Europe*]. When he was in Italy – it was a funny thing because they wanted someone, they had the whole unit out – and you know, there was a story, if you were in the service, you know, you don't know nothing, you don't know a thing, you don't know how to do anything either, you just don't know. So, they wanted somebody that could speak French and write in French; so, nobody was saying [*anything*], nobody answered. So, I guess they checked, so, he got picked. He was with the 68th Coast Artillery [*anti-aircraft artillery brigade*]; them poor guys went on, [*but*] he stayed in Italy. He was in the same office as Eisenhower. Every morning, Eisenhower tapped 'ya, tapped 'ya on the back and said, 'Good morning' to you. He [*my husband*] said he was a regular Joe.

JR: So he could speak and read ... French?

RS: Oh yes, he went to Prevost [*Parochial*] Grammar School, [*431 Eastern Avenue, Fall River*].

JR: Okay.

RS: So, he knew how to speak French.

WM: Where did you live when you were married? Where did you live?

RS: Where did I live? [*At 76*] Globe Street.

WM: When you were married?

RS: I lived in one of my Father's tenements; four bucks a week. My father wanted – we all did, all of us kids lived in the tenement – my father wanted to raise the rents; taxes were going up – my mother wanted to kill him. Four dollars a week. Oh, it was cute. Four-room apartment. I had it fixed cute.

WM: You, ah, you lived on Globe Street, and ah ...

RS: All my life, like I told you. Until I moved [*in 1963*].

WM: To Swansea. But you continued to work, though, you retired around 1970, '71.

WM: Tell us more about your career. Where did you [*work*] towards the tail end of your career? Did you stay with the same company?

RS: I stayed. Well, it changed over to their names. What the heck was it? What was it? Linjay [*Manufacturing Corporation*], Linjay.

JR: Oh, I've heard that, I've heard that name.

RS: Lynn was, ah, the other boss's daughter's name, and Jay was, uh, [*Eugene Joseph*] Rutkowski's name, [*his*] son's name. So they bought Linjay. The two kids' – Lynn and Jay – it was cute. Yeah.

WM: At age fifty, after you retired, what did you do?

RS: Well, I had my car. I'd go to the beach. Go out for breakfast. And I was at this little restaurant, and do you remember the Rustic Pub [*G.A.R. Highway, Swansea, Massachusetts*].

WM: I do.

RS: Well, Russell [*Winslow, Jr.*], the son was there, in this little restaurant that we used to go for coffee and that, and we was talking and everything else, and he was talking, and I said, 'Ah, don't give me that bull, Russell. I'll tell you one thing. If I went to be interviewed at that restaurant, do you think you would hire me at my age instead of a young kid?' He said, 'Of course, if you're qualified.' I said, 'You're full of bull.' He says, 'Yes, well, okay, seeing you're so smart ... we're looking for somebody in the office to ... book banquets, and to show the place out; tell them what we've got to offer and everything. It's a nice little job.' He says, he says, ah, 'Why don't you come down and get interviewed; see if my father [*Russell Winslow, Sr.*] will hire you, seeing you're so smart.' So, I was with my neighbor, huh, and, she's sitting at the table, and everything. He called me and he's interviewing me; I got the damn job.

JR: And how old were you then?

RS: Well, let me see, I was in my fifties. Oh, Christ. Well, I was up there, well, I wasn't in my sixties. I had to be in either my late fifties, or in early fifties, something around there.

WM: How long did you have that job?

RS: Oh, for quite a while, and I liked it. I was having a ball. It wasn't a full-time job. I'd go in around ten o'clock, 'ya know. If he had any problem, he'd ask me to take care of it for him, over the phone and that, so – he was, he was a good boss to work for.... Then, he asked me to work New Year's Eve. 'Ya know, the son ruined that place when he got bands upstairs.

WM: I remember that.

RS: 'Ya know, there was like an alcove up there, if you remember. I went with one of my friends one Saturday to have dinner. I went in next Monday, I says to Mr. Winslow, 'Mr. Winslow,' I says – He says, 'How did you enjoy it Saturday night?' I said, 'I didn't.' He said, 'What do you mean, you didn't?' I says, 'We couldn't even hear ourselves talk with that thing upstairs.' I said, 'That's going to be the ruination of your restaurant whether you know it or not.' And it was. And a nice restaurant like this, 'cause it was a first class restaurant.

WM: It was; it was at one time.

RS: It really was nice. He built that all by himself. He worked hard, that man.

WM: So, you retired again?

RS: Yeah, retired again.

JR: I just have to jump back a little bit because somewhere in there, there was Social Security.

RS: Oh, I was on Social Security.

JR: Tell us about a union pension.

RS: I wasn't in the union, so I never got no pension from the union. I got a pension from my job. He had something set up for us.

WM: Oh, he did?

RS: Oh, yeah.

WM: Well, that was unusual.

RS: And it didn't cost us a penny. He put it all in.

WM: Was that profit sharing?

RS: Huh?

WM: Profit sharing?

RS: I don't know how it was. He says, 'Don't worry.' We had to sign, of course, and all that. He says, 'You'll be taken care of. I know you're not a union member, 'ya know, where you'll get a small pension.

WM: That's unusual for that time.

RS: Yeah. Oh, yeah, and it was nice, it was a pretty good pension.

JR: So, do you remember when Franklin Roosevelt came in with Social Security?

RS: I don't even remember that. When was it?

JR: It was about 1935. [*Social Security Act, August 14, 1935*].

WM: You would have been a teenager then.

RS: I was a teenager. I didn't give a damn about Social Security, all I was interested in was having fun.

WM: Teenagers don't today, either.

RS: No, I remember when his.... Who was it that got buried in [*Oak Grove Cemetery*] that worked for Roosevelt?

WM: Louie, Louie Howe [*Louis McHenry Howe*].

RS: Because I hopped over a darn, uh, fence there, you know that, ah....

WM: A granite wall?

RS: Yeah, hopped over that wall, to see. Well, I wanted to see [*Louis McHenry Howe's funeral, on April 22, 1936*]. Hey, if I was going to go all the way from Globe Street, all the way to ... the [*Oak Grove*] Cemetery, I want to see something. [*Howe died at Bethesda Naval Hospital in Washington D.C., on April 18, 1936; his remains lay in state at the White House before being transferred to Fall River for burial.*]

RS: Yeah, I forgot his name.

WM: Louie Howe.

JR: My father told me that his wife [*née Grace Hartley, a Fall River native,*] was the postmistress.

RS: Yes, for years, and years, and years, and years.

WM: The first female postmistress, I think, in the United States. [*Mrs. Louis McHenry Howe was appointed as Fall River postmistress by President Franklin Delano Roosevelt in 1936.*]

RS: But that's when we had a big post office in the center. [*In 1931, the imposing Custom House and Post Office building in Fall River, constructed in 1875-1880 at 55 Bedford Street, corner of Second Street, was razed, and replaced with a modern structure, which opened for business on July 18, 1932. Advocates of the new building claimed it made for more efficient use of office space.*]

WM: Well, Roosevelt came to that, that; Roosevelt came to that funeral.

RS: Oh, yeah, that's why we all wanted to go [*to the funeral*]. We wanted to see the President. We didn't care that they were going to put him in a hole. Who cares? [*President Roosevelt attended the funeral accompanied by his wife, née Anna Eleanor Roosevelt, his sons, James Roosevelt, and Elliott Roosevelt, and his daughter, Mrs. Curtis Bean Dall, née Anna Eleanor Roosevelt.*]

JR: Yeah, he was, um, a political – the assistant to the President.

WM: Chief of Staff.

JR: Chief of Staff. [*Close friend and chief personal advisor to the president, Howe was lauded as 'The man who made Roosevelt.'*]

RS: He was quite the man. Everybody liked him.... And it wasn't, it wasn't because of him – they all felt bad ... but a lot of people would have gone anyhow, to see it, but it was because the President was coming down, and you know, who saw a President around here? They never bothered coming around here.

JR: That was a big thing. That was big.

RS: Yeah, that was a big thing.

WM: Did you have any children, Ruth?

RS: No, I was one of the unlucky ones. I had to have a hysterectomy when I was twenty-nine [*years old*].

WM: Wow, that's young.

JR: Yeah, that was unusual. That was, that was [*a*] difficult operation.

RS: I stayed in the hospital three weeks. Now, they do it in a day and now you're out.

WM: Where did you have that done – in Fall River?

RS: In Truesdale Hospital [*Inc., 1820 Highland Avenue, Fall River*]. I had a double uterus [*Uterus didelphys*].

JR: Oh, my goodness.

RS: The doctor told my husband that one out of a million girls are born with a double uterus. My, my ovaries were like two, black as two men's fists. Well, at that age, we never had doctors to go to. They would touch you here, and there, and that was it, a regular doctor. Well, you're alright.

WM: That would have been 1940, roughly 1940?

RS: I wasn't married too long, and I even told my husband, 'I can't have children. If you want to split, go,' 'cause I felt sorry for him, because he loved kids. I did. We always had our nieces and nephews.

JR: Well, that's what I was going to say. You probably had a lot of nieces and nephews, with all your sisters and brothers.

RS: Oh, only eleven....

WM: Your husband. When did he pass away?

RS: What is it? Three years ago, [*in 2011,*] at ninety.

JR: Were you still at home with him at that time?

RS: I was home after he died. I'm just here [*Somerset Ridge Center, physical therapy clinic, 455 Brayton Avenue, Somerset, Massachusetts*] a year, because I fell and broke my knee.

WM: At age – you're ninety-five? Ninety…?

RS: No, I'm ninety-three [*years old*]. And [*my husband*] would've been ninety-four.

JR: You were, you were keeping a house up until about, a year ago….

RS: Yeah, I was in my own house [*in Swansea*], yeah.

WM: As you look back at things, at age ninety-four, what would you have done differently if you had it to do over again?

RS: If I had to do it over again, gee, I don't know. Like I told you, I was one of the lucky ones that had a good, good life, all because of brothers and sisters, which were able to do a lot and give me a lot. And I don't know if, at that time, I ever appreciated it. But, no, no, they were all very, very good to me, my brothers and sisters, I will say. That's why I went to all their funerals.

WM: Otherwise, you wouldn't have gone?

RS: No.

JR: That's wonderful.

RS: Hey listen, out of ten kids, to say you stayed together, that was something. Because it's not the kids, because if there were any problems in, say – it wasn't the brothers and sister – it was always the in-laws. This in-law didn't like this in-law. So what did the brothers have to do? They had to stick up for their wives, or the girls had to stick up for their husbands, so, 'ya know, it was tough. But I was friendly with, I was friendly with them all. I could call any one of them up and say, 'Hey, I need help.'

WM: What else would you like to tell us? Do you have any advice for the young people today?

RS: The young people today? Get out and enjoy themselves. Do what they want to do and don't wait 'til they get older because it never comes. It's true because you say, well, I remember saying it to my husband. 'Oh, let's not do it now. When we retire, we've got plenty of time, we'll do it.' We were lucky, we did have plenty of time. But others don't. He lived to ninety and I lived, I was eighty-nine when he passed away. So that was….

JR: Did you do any traveling with him?

RS: Oh, yeah, we used to travel. Yeah. But always to historical places. We were the type, we didn't like the showy, we wanted to see things.

WM: Well, you've had an interesting life.

RS: Oh, yeah. I did.

JR: I want to jump back a little bit to, ah … some of the years when you were growing up. I'm just kind of curious, how did you heat your home? I know when I grew up with my grandmother, she had a coal stove.

RS: Yeah, a coal stove. You had one coal stove and it would be in the kitchen because it would be one of these black ones where you could cook on the top…. You'd buy coal and wood; you'd get it by tons, coal by tons. There'd be a horse and wagon, at first, and they'd put the coal in a chute from your basement window into the cellar. And you'd have wood to start it. I never had to do it, but …

JR: Your brothers did, maybe?

RS: Oh, yeah, of course, they wouldn't let my father do it when they got old enough.

WM: Well, you were the youngest one.

RS: Yeah, I was the youngest one. Then, as soon as gas came in, well, they [*family members*] were working for the [*Fall River*] Gas [*Works*] Company, so we got it right away ….

JR: Did your mother teach you how to cook?

RS: I did not cook. My husband did the cooking.

JR: Oh, oh.

RS: Oh, he was a good cook; I did the baking, I could bake very good. And I made the golabki [*a traditional Polish cabbage roll*]. But, the baking I did, right from scratch. Not from the box, right from scratch. See, when I bought my house [*on Old Warren Road, in Swansea, Massachusetts*], the house next door [*350 Old Warren Road*] … had a nice garden – he was a Portuguese man [*Bento Gomes*] – he had a nice garden. When the [*Wampanoag*] Golf Course came in, the golfers used to go into his garden, so he decided to put a fence along, and he put a chicken wire fence. And I got a brand new house, and a chicken wire fence around, [*and he*] painted the posts yellow. So, so we're reading the Sunday paper, and Roger says to me, 'Ruth, we're going to go to Warwick, [*Rhode Island*] today. We're going to take a ride to Warwick'. I said, 'What for?' 'They've got blueberry bushes for ninety-nine cents; count the posts.' I counted the posts. We planted a blueberry bush right in front of every post … we planted blueberry bushes. They're still there; some of them died. It was horrible. Yellow; I almost died when I seen him painting it. Hey, it was his property – he could do what he wanted.

JR: I just have another couple of questions, because we didn't touch on these. Did you drive a car? Did you learn how to drive a car?

RS: Oh, I was driving, yeah.

JR: Did your parents have a car?

RS: Well, my parents didn't have a car. My brother, Walter [*Władysław Stasiowski*] had a car, then the older boys got cars. But my Dad never had cars; they walked.

JR: Trollies? And you took trollies?

RS: Oh, they were nice. The open trollies. I remember them.

WM: Now you would remember the electric trollies, right? You don't remember the horse drawn trollies?

RS: No, no, no, the electric ones. I remember the old ones from Jerome Dwelly School, [*59 Foote Street, Fall River*]. We'd have our picnics all the way, and then trolley cars, all the way to Lincoln Park.

WM: I was going to ask you if you went to Lincoln Park.

RS: These kids don't have nothing like that. 'Ya know, what have they got to remember – that I was on a computer all day?!

WM: I know, I know. The trolley companies actually built Lincoln Park.

JR: Now, I want to bring you back to the days on Main Street, when you went downtown shopping.

RS: Beautiful. That's where you met your friends; you talked and that. You'd go in these stores. The sales ladies were so polite, very helpful.

JR: And well-dressed.

RS: Huh?

JR: And the sales ladies were well-dressed.

RS: Oh, yes. In McWhirr's [*R.A. McWhirr Company, department store, 165 – 193 South Main Street, Fall River*], they were dressed a certain way; I forgot whether it was, skirts, with the name tag. Then, you went upstairs to the other level where the kids' clothes were. It was beautiful, and the old thing, where you put the money in and it would go ... do you remember that? [*The store was equipped with a pneumatic tube system*].

WM: Did you ever sit on Santa Claus's lap at McWhirr's?

RS: No, no.

JR: I did. I have, I have pictures of me with Santa Claus in McWhirr's. [*A beloved Fall River tradition*].

RS: See that.

JR: And, how about your favorite stores. What was the favorite stores downtown?

RS: Cherry & Webb [*Company, ladies' and misses' ready-to-wear clothing, 139 – 149 South Main Street, Fall River*]. That was, that was 'the' store ... you'd go to these little stores, and I never believed in them little stores. My mother always traded, the girls [*her sisters*] always got their clothes in Cherry & Webb; the boys always got them, in ... what was it?

WM: The Hub?

RS: The Hub. Yup. [*The Hub Clothing Company, 162 Pleasant Street, Fall River*]. That was the place; they got their clothes there, and up to, Christ, I think when they were getting married, they would go there; just automatic, since they were so used to it since they were kids. My mother, Cherry & Webb's. I remember, she felt so – because my husband, well, he was my boyfriend – 'cause my boyfriend was going overseas,' and she felt so sorry for me, she says, 'Mildred, [*the interviewees sister, Mrs. Eugene J. Ivers, née Emilia "Mildred" Stasiowski*] why don't you go and buy her a fur coat? Make her feel better.' Fur coat; I didn't want no fur coat.

JR: Did you get a fur coat?

RS: I had to get it.

JR: In Cherry & Webb, I bet. They had a fur salon.

RS: Of course. Of course, Cherry & Webb. You wouldn't go anywhere else. When I was getting married [*in 1947*], Nelson [*Reed*] Cherry [*treasurer, Cherry & Webb Company*] was the one. When I got my gown, he was – when I was trying on wedding gowns, Nelson Cherry, he was right there. And Miss [*Piche*]? Remember Miss [*Piche*] from the hats [*department*]? [*Marie Anna Piche, later Mrs. Roland S. Fontaine, was the buyer for the Millinery Department at Cherry & Webb Company.*]

JR: Yup.

RS: They had a veil there, a long, long veil that was going to be in one of the trade shows, and Nelson Cherry said, 'No, that's for Ruth. That's for her, for her gown. You don't put that in the style show.' I had Nelson Cherry ...

JR: Wow. I don't know anybody that had Nelson Cherry working on their wedding. That's something.

RS: Well, that's because my mother had four of us, and everything, everything was bought there.

WM: That's good business, for sure.

RS: Business.

WM: You know what I wanted to ask; I forgot to ask. You lived down the Globe. Do you remember the Park Theatre, [*1425 South Main Street, Fall River*]? The Park Show?

RS: Of course, I used to go there.

WM: Tell us about it.

RS: Twenty-five cents to get in. I knew 'Marquee' Gosciminski [*likely Chester J. Gosciminski, who was employed as a projectionist at the Park Theatre from 1931 to 1947*]. He and my girlfriend – 'Marquee' was keen on his station, so we used to go; 'Marquee' used to get us into the show for nothing. Well, we used to go to Park Show, that's something, for dishes [*so-called 'Dish Night'*].

JR: Oh, yeah.

RS: One day you'd get a cup, one week you'd get a cup, next day you'd get a plate, and you'd get a whole set of dishes.

JR: Well, if you had ten children, you could all get a plate and a cup.

RS: Oh, no, they didn't all go to the show. I used to go with my mom. The others were kinda older then. I was the youngest; I would go with my mother. We would walk up Globe Street and go to the show, and my mother thought it was great because she didn't know any better. Sorry to say, but it's true.

JR: Were you crazy about the movie stars?

RS: Huh?

JR: Did you like the movie stars?

RS: In them days, yes. They were movie stars. Not today. They're not actors and actresses today. They're scum – the way they dress. No, no. There's no need of that.

JR: You like the glamour. You liked the glamour of that period of time.

RS: Oh, yes. I liked the shows that they had, and everything else. Even on TV now – what is there on TV? Nothing. You know what I watch? The Portuguese Channel.

WM: Really?

RS: I see nice parades, I see beautiful women dressed in nice costumes. Very religious, of course, but that goes beyond [*saying*]. You got to give 'em credit. Beautiful.

WM: The Globe. Was the Ukrainian Club [*Ukrainian National Home, restaurant, 482 Globe Street, Fall River*] active then? Do you remember the Ukrainian Club?

RS: Oh, the Uke Club? Oh, the food.

JR: The food, yes.

WM: Did you go there?

RS: Oh, all the time. I knew, I knew … the cook. He graduated from eighth grade with me. The big, fat cook.

WM: I remember him, sure. How about the Polish [*National*] Home, [*872 Globe Street, Fall River*]?

RS: The Polish Home didn't have much. My father had shares in it. Nothing ever come out of it…. That burned down and they got nothing. Not a thing.

WM: You know what's still around, down in the Globe? Still there, down the Globe is Hartley's Pork Pies [*1729 South Main Street, Fall River*]. Still there. Do you remember that? It's a hundred years old. [*The business was established by Thomas Hartley as a bakery in 1900.*]

JR: Hartley's, Hartley's Pork Pies. [*The pies are a Fall River tradition, considered a delicacy by many.*]

RS: Oh, I knew, I knew 'Porky,' [*John Russell Hartley.*] He wanted to take me to the [*B.M.C. Durfee High School senior*] prom and I wouldn't go with him because he was too short.

WM: His name was 'Porky.' What else, what else would his nickname be? [*According to the 1939 edition of* The Durfee Record, *he was also called 'Russ.'*]

JR: I'm just going to jump back a minute to high school. Did you take the commercial course, or …

RS: Yes.

JR: So you thought you were going to go into …

RS: Well, I'll tell you what. During World War II, my brother got me – my brother Al [*Albin "Albert" Stasiowski*] worked at Quonset Point [*Quonset Naval Air Station, North Kingstown, Rhode Island*]; not at Quonset Point – in one of the islands. He got me an application to work in Newport [*Naval Station Newport*]. I filled out the application and everything else, and I told my boss that I was gonna leave, and I was going to work, and he said, 'No, you can't leave.' 'What do you mean I can't leave?' He says, 'You know, if you leave,' he says, 'you won't be able to work for, I don't know how long.' I says, 'Why'? He says, 'Well, if you know, we're making nurses' uniforms for the [*United States*] Government, and we're working for the Government, so you cannot leave unless you stay out of work for so long. Then you can go to your job.'

JR: Ah, he had something over your head.

RS: So, I says to my brother Al, 'Al, forget it.'

JR: I'm thinking that, being a supervisor, there had to be a lot of stress for you because I think the owners wanted a lot of production. And did they hold you responsible?

RS: Oh, yes, we had to report to them why production was going down; why [*in*] this operation there's so much trouble going on. 'Why? Because of you people, for Chrissakes. You want, you want – these girls are working like slaves, and you want more?'

JR: Did you often feel that you were in the middle, [*that*] you were caught in the middle between them and the employees?

RS: Well, uh, uh, I was pretty – the employees knew I was with them; I think in a way, they knew.

JR: I think we're going to be wrapping it up a little bit. Is there anything you think we may have forgotten? Anything you want to tell us?

RS: Well, you people were kind of interested in our work and like I told you I worked for twenty-five cents in Kresge's, and then I graduated to fifty cents.

JR: And when you finished, when you retired, how much were you making?

RS: I was on a salary.

JR: Ah, all right. You're not going to tell us what it was. Okay, I won't ask.

RS: You wouldn't believe it.

WM: One question I had – as a supervisor, did you do any hiring?

RS: No, I didn't do any hiring, but I did the firing.

WM: They made you fire.

RS: The dirty jobs, you did. The good jobs, they did.

WM: Interesting.

RS: But, I, I really got along – the Portuguese girls, the Portuguese women, I really got along with them. There was some way....

JR: Okay, we're going to, we're going to wrap it up now. Thank you very much, Ruth, because we've learned a lot. We have learned a lot, a lot of detail. It's been really a pleasure to meet you.

WM: Great interview. Thank you.

PHOTO GALLERY

10.1 Ruth's father, Stefan Stasiowski, and her mother, née Katarzyna Kazowska, on their wedding day, October 19, 1901; at the time of their marriage, the groom was employed as a weaver in a cotton mill, and the bride as a "sizer" in the sizing department. *"Well, they came from …Poland."*

10.2 Michalina "Ruth" Stasiowski at age two, 1923. *"I had a very good childhood, being the tenth – the last of the bunch I could say."*

10.3 Interior of the King Philip Mills, 372 Kilburn Street, Fall River, Massachusetts, circa 1920. *"My Dad worked in the King Philip … which was horrible, 'cause I went to bring him a lunch one day, and I went in that weave room; that was horrible – the noise."*

10.4 Ruth posing in ballet costume, 1928; the photographs were taken by Gay Art Galleries, 44 North Main Street, Fall River, Massachusetts, the city's leading studio. *"I guess I was the one that had the best of all of it because the older ones started to work and I was the baby and they – what my parents couldn't give me, they gave me."*

10.5 St. Patrick's Catholic Church, 1598 South Main Street, Fall River, Massachusetts, as it appeared the year after its completion in 1889. *"I belonged to St. Patrick's ... my Dad had a fight with Father Dylla* [at St. Stanislaus Church] *and he stayed, but us kids, he put us in with St. Patrick's parish."*

10.6 The Fowler School, 286 Sprague Street, Fall River, Massachusetts, 1920s. *"And* [then] *I had to go to Fowler School."*

10.7 Ruth when a girl, early 1930s. *"I was one of the lucky ones that had a good, good life. And I don't know if, at that time, I ever appreciated it."*

10.8 Fall River Line Steamer *Commonwealth*, en route to New York City, 1930s; called 'The Giantess of the Sound,' she was launched in 1907 and carried 2000 passengers. *"Oh, yeah, that was beautiful. Ah, we used to go out for the waves, it was a picture to see it going by."*

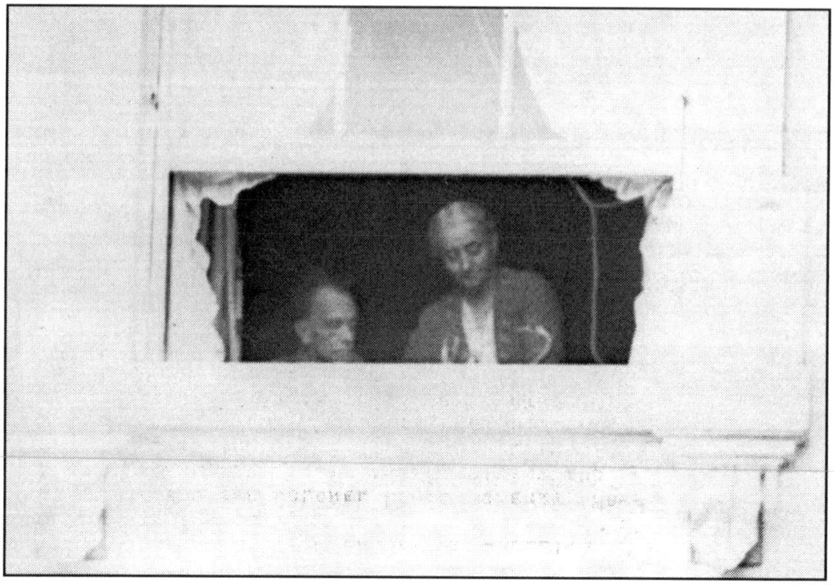

10.9 Louis McHenry Howe and his wife, née Grace Hartley, 'Viewing the Easter-egg rolling from a second story window of the White House, April 22, 1935'; the photograph was taken exactly one year to the day before his burial in Oak Grove Cemetery, Fall River, Massachusetts. Howe was a close friend and chief 'personal advisor' to President Franklin Delano Roosevelt, lauded as 'the man who made Roosevelt.' *"Yeah* [I] *hopped over that wall to see* [the funeral] *... We wanted to see the President. We didn't care that they were going to put him in a hole. Who cares? And it wasn't because of – they all felt bad, but ... the President was coming down, and, you know, who saw a President around here?"*

10.10 The Hub Clothing Company, 162 Pleasant Street, Fall River, Massachusetts, 1928; the store was one of the leading men's shops in the city. *"The* [boys] *always got their clothes there. That was the place."*

10.11 Ruth's father and brothers outside the family residence, 76 Globe Street, Fall River, Massachusetts, circa 1937. Standing, left to right: Stefan Stasiowski; his sons: Czesław "Chester" aka "Tommy" Stasiowski; Emil "Elmer" Stasiowski; Albin "Albert" Stasiowski; Frederick "Fred" Stasiowski; Bolesław "William" Stasiowski; Władysław "Walter" Stasiowski. *"I had six brothers that looked over me."*

10.12 B.M.C. Durfee High School, Fall River, Massachusetts, circa 1940. *"I graduated in 1939."*

10.13 Ruth posing with her father, Stefan Stasiowski, early 1940s; the photograph was taken in the yard of the family residence, 76 Globe Street, Fall River, Massachusetts. *"My dad* [came] *over here from Poland and . . . could speak English. In fact, during the epidemic of the flu, he was one of 'em that went with the doctors to the . . . Polish families because they couldn't talk* [English], *they couldn't tell the doctor what was wrong, so my father was like an interpreter for the doctor."*

10.14 Ruth during her junior year at B.M.C. Durfee High School, Fall River, Massachusetts, 1937-1938; she is holding her high school pennant. *"I was the one that was able to graduate from high school."*

10.15 Ruth during her junior year at B.M.C. Durfee High School, Fall River, Massachusetts, 1937-1938; she is standing in the yard of the Stasiowski family residence, 76 Globe Street, Fall River, Massachusetts. *"It was a beautiful six tenement house. In fact, I lived there until I moved to Swansea."*

10.16 South Main Street, Fall River, Massachusetts, 1940s; S. S. Kresge Company, department store, on the corner of Pocasset Street. *"I worked at Kresge's five-and-ten. I worked for twenty-five cents an hour ... yeah. That was a lot of money!"*

10.17 A window display at S. S. Kresge Company, department store, 71 to 87 South Main Street, Fall River, Massachusetts, circa 1930. *"After high school on a Friday we went to work at Kresge's until ten o'clock ten ... and then on Saturday we worked all day 'til ten o'clock at night."*

10.18 Ruth, as she appeared in the 1939 edition of *The Durfee Record;* the youngest of a family of ten children, she was the only Stasiowski sibling to graduate high school. *"I took the* [commercial course]*."*

10.19 Ruth's future husband, Joseph Napoleon Roger Soucy, called "Roger," as he appeared in the 1939 edition of *The Durfee Record;* a fellow classmate, they were both members of the Commercial Club. *"My husband ... I met in high school. He was an 'R.S.' and I was an "R.S.', so we always sat in homeroom in front or in back of each other, and we would kid with one another ... like when kids in high school."*

10.20 John Russell Hartley, as he appeared in the 1939 edition of *The Durfee Record;* he was Ruth's classmate, called by the diminutive 'Porky,' or 'Russ.' *"Oh, I knew 'Porky.' He wanted to take me to the senior prom and I wouldn't go with him because he was too short."*

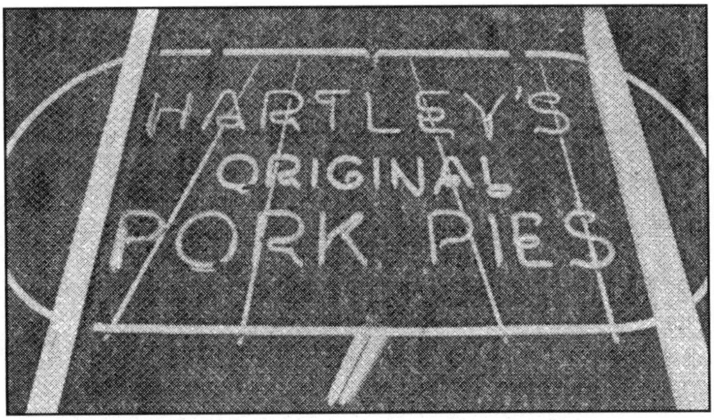

10.21 Neon sign display, Hartley's Pork Pies, 1729 South Main Street, Fall River, Massachusetts; the pies are a Fall River tradition. *"[Oh,] Hartley's, Hartley's Pork Pies."*

10.22 Ruth's mother, Mrs. Stefan Stasiowski, née Katarzyna Kaszowska. *"She felt so sorry for me 'cause … my boyfriend was going overseas. She says, 'Why don't you go and buy her a fur coat? Make her feel better?'"*

10.23 Firestone Rubber & Latex Products Company, 172 Ferry Street, Fall River, Massachusetts; the plant was destroyed by fire on October 11, 1941, taking with it 15,850 tons of rubber at a loss of $12,000,000. *"Brother Bill worked in Firestone until it burned down."*

10.24 R.A. McWhirr Company, department store, 165 – 193 South Main Street, Fall River, Massachusetts, 1940s; the establishment was the city's most beloved department store. *"You'd go in these stores. The sales ladies were well dressed. Oh, yes. In McWhirr's they were dressed a certain way … it was beautiful."*

10.25 Interior of the vacant Laurel Lake Mill, Broadway, Fall River, Massachusetts, 1935; the photograph is one of a series taken to advertise the city's surfeit of available factory space to out-of-town manufacturers. Ruth was employed at Joseph Chromow & Co., underwear and sportswear manufacturers that later occupied this space. *"Mr. Chromow, it was on Broadway, the Globe. You know the mills on the Globe* [Four] *Corners?"*

10.26 A group of bicyclists made up of Ruth's co-workers from Joseph Chromow & Co., underwear and sportswear manufacturers, 987 (later 951) Broadway, Fall River, Massachusetts, early 1940s. Ruth is the second girl from the left. *"I started as a floor girl. I graduated from twenty-five cents to fifty-cents an hour."*

10.27 A group of Ruth's co-workers from Joseph Chromow & Co., underwear and sportswear manufacturers, 987 (later 951) Broadway, Fall River, Massachusetts, early 1940s. Ruth is the second girl from the left in the front row.*"That was when I got out of high school. I went to work in a sewing factory."*

10.28 Cherry & Webb Company, ladies' and misses' ready-to-wear clothing, 139 – 149 South Main Street, Fall River, Massachusetts, 1940s. *"My mother always traded, the girls always got their clothes in Cherry & Webb. That was 'the' store ... you wouldn't go anywhere else."*

Soucy-Stasiowski

United in marriage this morning at 8 in St. Patrick's Church were Miss Ruth Stasiowski, daughter of Mr. and Mrs. Stefan Stasiowski of 76 Globe Street, and Roger Soucy, son of Mr. and Mrs. Joseph Soucy of 80 Jepson Street. Rev. John E. Boyd officiated.

Attending the couple were Mrs. Irene Vezina, sister of the bridegroom, of New Bedford, and Albert Stasiowski, brother of the bride.

The bride wore a candlelight ivory satin gown with a shirred colonial bodice, silk marquisette yoke edged with a satin bertha and seed pearl trimming, and a full skirt en train. She wore a long French illusion veil and carried lilies of the valley and orchids.

The matron of honor was gowned in yellow moire with matching mitts and apple green picture hat. She carried a bouquet of bronze snapdragon with yellow marguerites.

Receptions were held at the home of the bride and at Luke's Lodge. The couple left for New York, Montreal and Quebec on their honeymoon, the bride wearing a grey suit with pink and grey accessories and mink furs.

Both are alumni of B. M. C. Durfee High School. Mrs. Soucy is employed by Joseph Chromow. Her husband, a World War II veteran, is employed by Braley's Creamery, Inc.

10.29 Ruth's wedding announcement from the *Fall River Herald News*, May 3, 1947. *"The bride wore a candlelight ivory satin gown ...."*

10.30 A postcard depicting Luke's Lodge, Stafford Road, Tiverton, Rhode Island; Ruth's wedding reception was held at this establishment. *"I got married on May 3, 1947."*

LUKE'S LODGE, STAFFORD ROAD, TIVERTON, R. I.

10.31 A photograph taken during Ruth's wedding reception, held at Luke's Lodge, Stafford Road, Tiverton, Rhode Island; the couple were married on May 3, 1947. Left to right: The groom's sister, Mrs. Roland Vezina, née Irene Soucy; the groom; the bride; the bride's brother, Albin "Albert" Stasiowski. *"When I was getting married, Nelson* [Reed] *Cherry was the one. When I got my gown ... when I was trying on gowns, he was right there. They had a veil there, a long, long veil that was going to be in one of the trade shows, and* [he] *said, 'No, that's for Ruth. That's for her, for her gown.'"*

10.32 Truesdale Hospital Inc., 1820 Highland Avenue, Fall River. *"I stayed in the hospital three weeks. Now they do it in a day and you're out."*

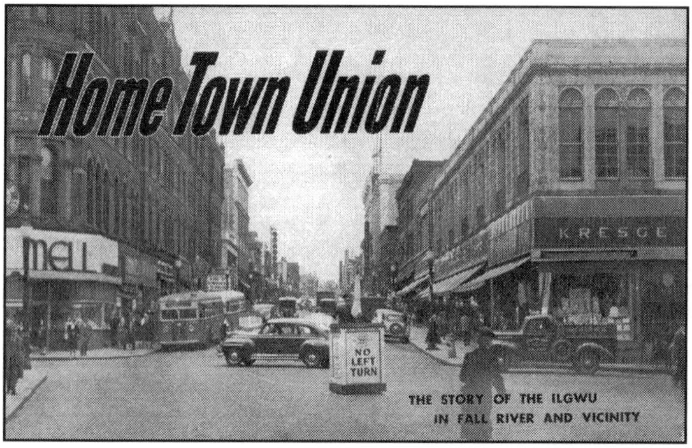

10.33 Front cover illustration from the International Ladies Garment Workers' Union *Home Town Union* booklet, 1948; this publication was distributed to workers "in Fall River and vicinity." *"And the union – I wouldn't give you ten cents for the union. I am not a union person. I never was, and I never would* [be]*."*

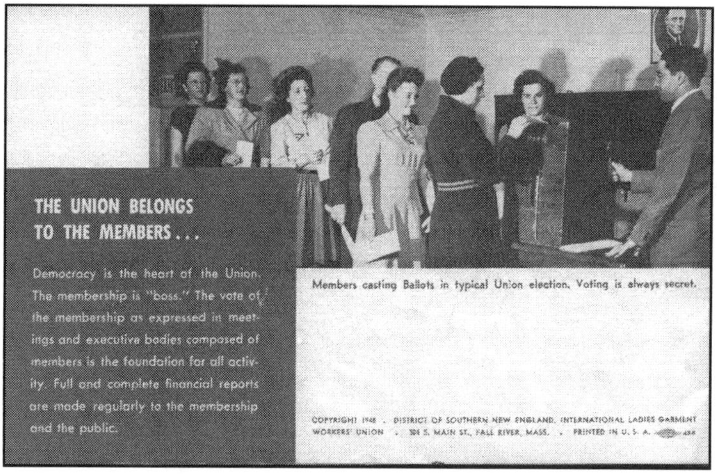

10.34 Back cover illustration from the International Ladies Garment Workers' *Union Home Town Union* booklet, 1948; this publication was distributed to workers "in Fall River and vicinity." *"They did absolutely nothing for these girls except take their dues every week."*

10.35 The Wampanoag Mills, 420 Quequechan Street, Fall River, Massachusetts, circa early twentieth century; Ruth was employed in this building in the 1950s, when it housed Joseph Chromow & Co., underwear and sportswear manufacturers. *"And then I finally had my own little, little department where they used to put the buttons on and sew, and they examined the garment, they folded it, and it was shipped out."*

10.36 The Narragansett Mills, 1567 North Main Street, Fall River, Massachusetts, early 20th century; Ruth retired in 1971 from Linjay Manufacturing Corporation, which was located in this building. *"And that's where I ended it; at fifty, I quit. They can have it."*

10.37 The Ukrainian National Home restaurant, affectionately called 'The Uke,' 482 Globe Street, Fall River, Massachusetts, 1970s; the building was originally constructed as the offices of the Laurel Lake Mill. Ruth's first factory job, as a 'floor girl," was at Joseph Chromow Company, underwear and sportswear manufacturers, located around the corner on Broadway, in the former Laurel Lake Mill. *"Oh, the Uke Club? Oh, the food."*

PLYMOUTH SPORTSWEAR COMPANY, INC.

Plymouth Sportswear Company, Inc., was founded in Fall River, Massachusetts, circa 1940 by Arnold Gerard (1889-1959), a man of Russian birth who had immigrated to the United States with his parents and siblings in 1906. A resident of Brooklyn, New York, he had been employed in the garment trade since his youth, first in the manufacture of cloaks, then as a contractor of children's dresses, and later a dress tailor; his wife, née Sophie A. Altschuler (1889-1983), also a Russian immigrant residing in Brooklyn, had also been employed as an operator manufacturing ladies' waists. The couple were married in Manhattan in 1910, and were the parents of three children: Pauline (1913-1920), Irving (1914-1978), and Sylvia (1920-1981).

Gerard relocated with his family to Fall River, circa 1939, and began Plymouth Sportswear. The firm was a manufacturer of ladies' and boys' sportswear, and was first located at the "rear 289 Pleasant [Street], 5th Fl[oor]" in Union Mill No. 1. Gerard, president of the company, was joined by his son, Irving, who served as a shipping clerk, and his daughter, Sylvia, who held the position of office clerk. In 1946, the business relocated to 18 Pocasset Street in Fall River. It was at this time that Arnold Gerard surrendered the presidency of the company to his son, assuming instead the position of treasurer. Sylvia was then named plant manager. A family outfit, Arnold's wife, Sophie, was also employed as the director of boy's sportswear.

By 1951, the firm was listed in the *Directory of Massachusetts Manufacturers*, published by the Massachusetts Department of Commerce and Labor, with the classification "Code 8", indicating that the establishment employed a work force of between fifty to ninety-nine production workers.

By 1957, Irving Gerard was no longer associated with the business in Fall River, and his father assumed the positions of both president and treasurer. He was still actively employed at the time of his death on September 11, 1959. The company continued in operation under the direction of, first, Sophie Gerard, and later her daughter, Sylvia, until it dissolved circa 1962.

Photographs illustrating the day-to-day activities in Fall River's garment factories are surprisingly rare. The following series of images depicting Plymouth Sportswear Company, Inc., dating to 1940, are contained in the collection of the Fall River Historical Society, Charlton Library of Fall River History.

PS.1 Arnold Gerard (wearing necktie), president, Plymouth Sportswear Company, Inc., Fall River, Massachusetts, posing with a group of his employees, 1940.

PS.2 Mrs. Arnold Gerard, née Sophie Altschuler, "director of boy's sportswear," Plymouth Sportswear Company, Inc., Fall River, Massachusetts, serving as hostess at an employees' party in celebration of Franklin Delano Roosevelt's reelection to his third term as president, November, 1940. Prominently displayed in a place of honor behind the elaborately decorated cake is a photograph of President Roosevelt.

PS.3 Sylvia Gerard cuts the cake at an employees' party in celebration of Franklin Delano Roosevelt's reelection to his third term as president, November, 1940, at Plymouth Sportswear Company, Inc., Fall River, Massachusetts. Among the group of employees assembled behind the table are her father, Arnold Gerard, and her mother, née Sophie Altschuler.

PS.4 An employee of Plymouth Sportswear Company, Inc., Fall River, Massachusetts, posing in the cutting department, 1940.

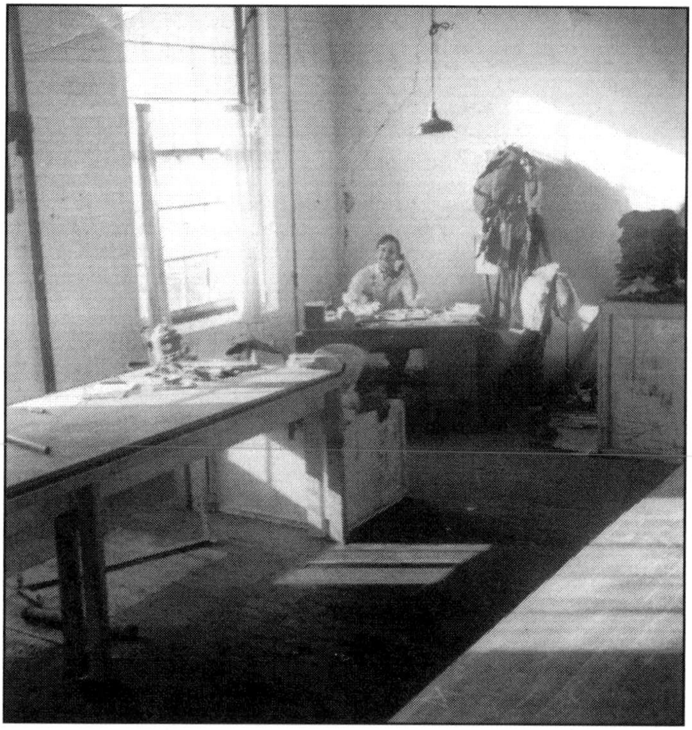

PS.5 Irving Gerard, shipping clerk, Plymouth Sportswear Company, Inc., Fall River, Massachusetts, posing at his desk, 1940.

PS.6 Sylvia Gerard, office clerk, Plymouth Sportswear Company, Inc., Fall River, Massachusetts, posing at her desk, 1940.

PS.7 A view from Plymouth Sportswear Company, Inc., Fall River, Massachusetts, fifth floor, rear, of Union Mill No. 1, 1940.

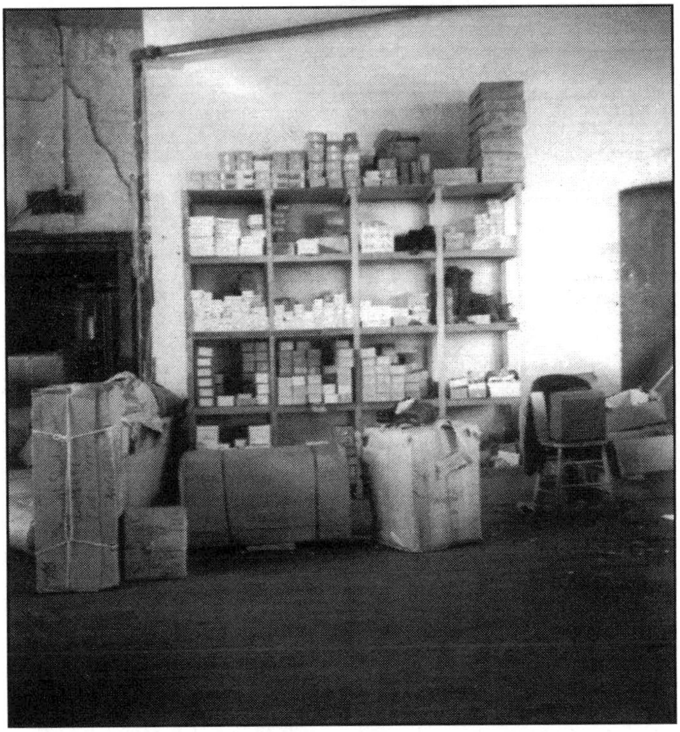

PS.8 The receiving and supply department, Plymouth Sportswear Company, Inc., Fall River, Massachusetts, 1940.

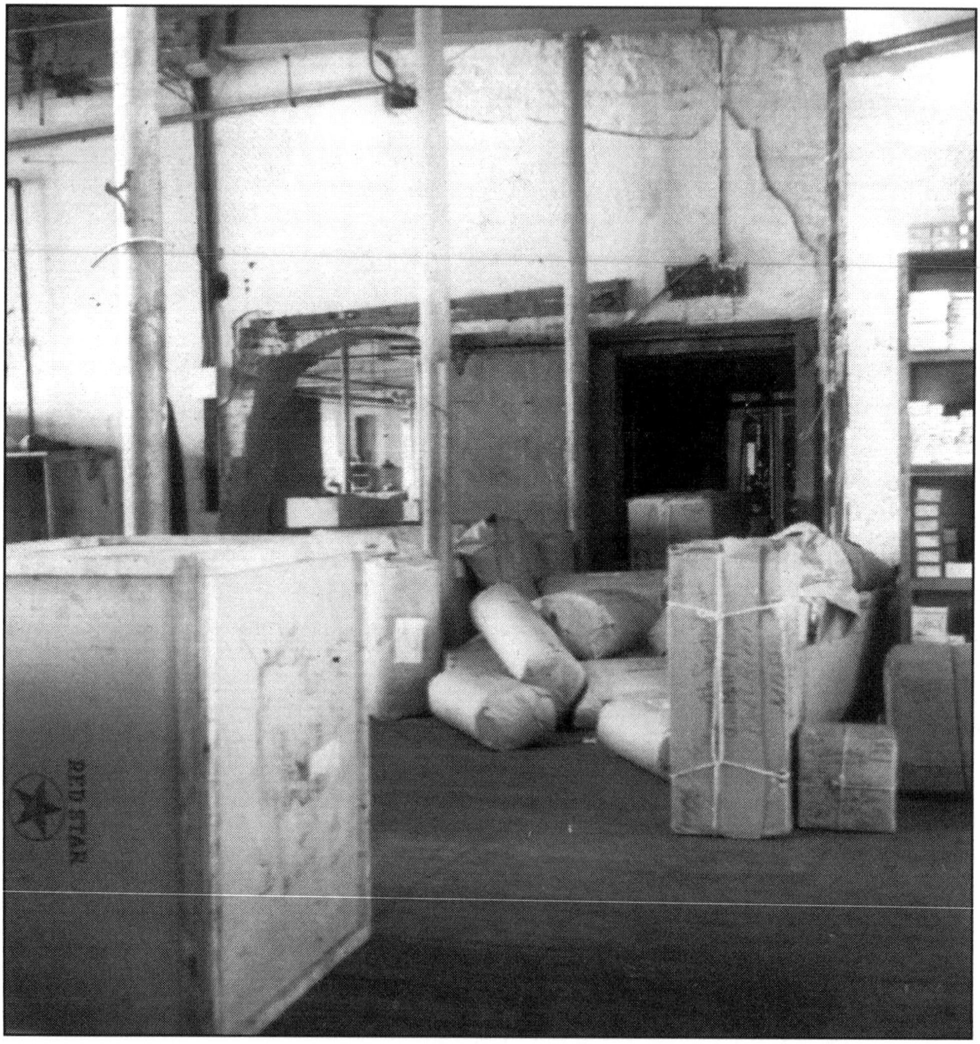

PS.9 The receiving and supply department, Plymouth Sportswear Company, Inc., Fall River, Massachusetts, 1940.

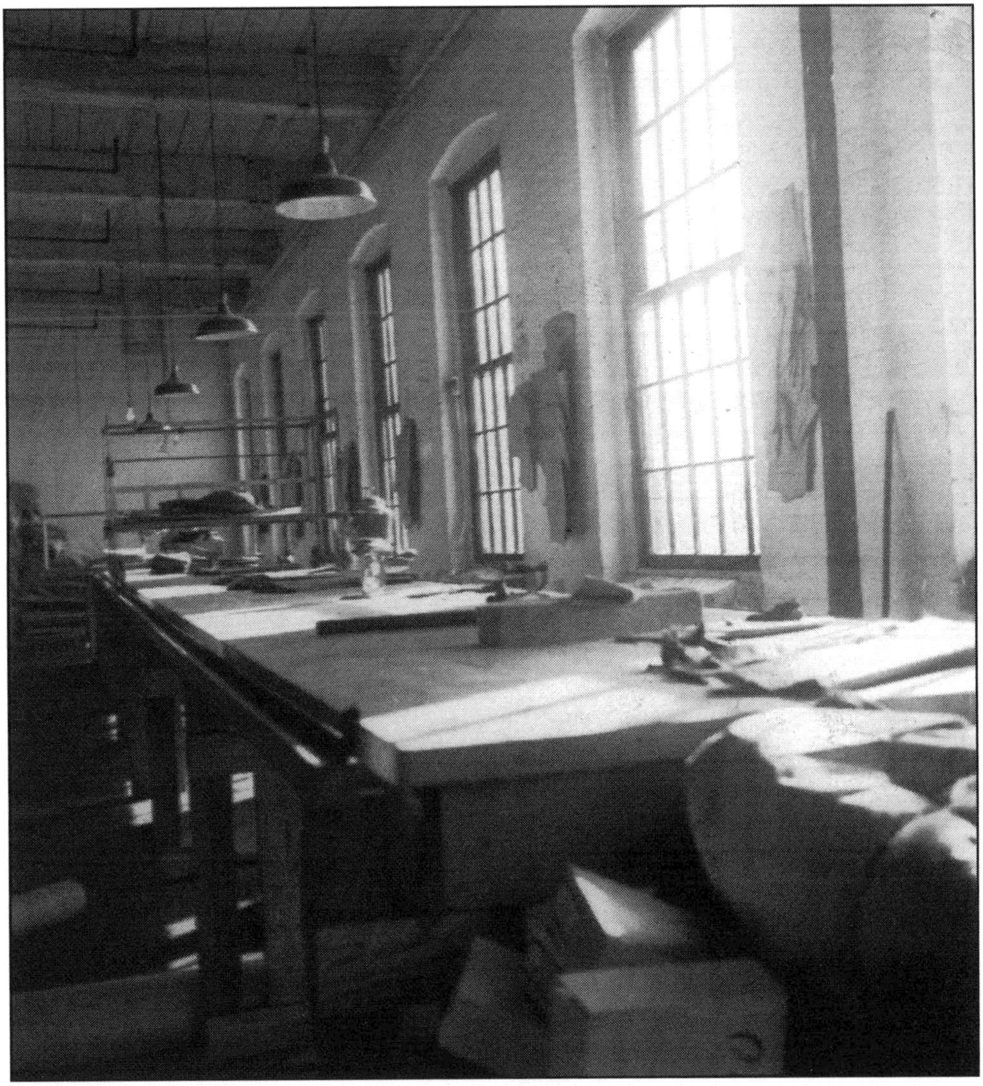

PS.10 The cutting department, Plymouth Sportswear Company, Inc., Fall River, Massachusetts, 1940.

PS.11 The factory floor, Plymouth Sportswear Company, Inc., Fall River, Massachusetts, 1940.

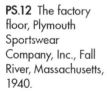

PS.12 The factory floor, Plymouth Sportswear Company, Inc., Fall River, Massachusetts, 1940.

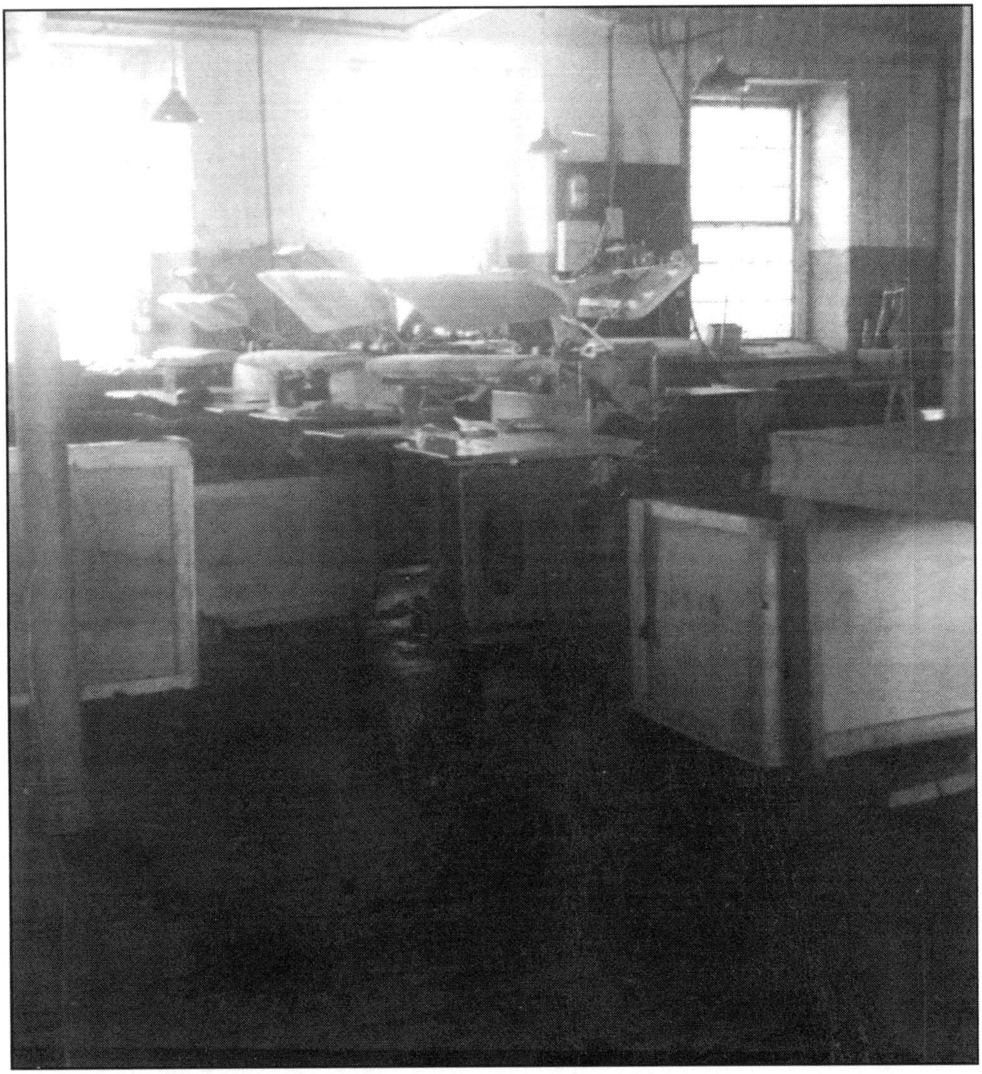

PS.13 The pressing department, Plymouth Sportswear Company, Inc., Fall River, Massachusetts, 1940.

ACKNOWLEDGEMENTS

This project would not have been possible without the kind support and help of the many individuals and organizations listed below:

Mass Humanities:

The original online exhibit, *Women at Work*, the inspiration for this volume, was funded, in part, by Mass Humanities, which receives support from the Massachusetts Cultural Council, and is an affiliate of the National Endowment for the Humanities.

The Fall River Historical Society gratefully acknowledges the following for their generous assistance and encouragement:

Pleun Bouricius, Director of Grants & Programs
Melissa Wheaton, Grant Administrator/Administrative Assistant

Special Thanks:

The Fall River Historical Society is deeply indebted to Joyce B. Rodrigues, who expertly served as grant writer and project coordinator for *Women at Work*. Thanks to her steadfastness, the life experiences of the women profiled in this exhibit are preserved for posterity. Thank you, Joyce!

Fall River Historical Society:

Historical Research/Development:
Michael Martins, Curator
Dennis A. Binette, Assistant Curator

Research Assistants:
Caroline Aubin
Jay J. Lambert
Constance C. Mendes
Jane Mello
David J. Roseberry

Marketing:
Jayne Darcy

Women at Work Project Team:

Grant Writer/Project Coordinator:
Joyce B. Rodrigues

Advisory Team:
Paula Costa Cullen
Robert Kitchen
Robert G. Nolan
Albertina R. Pacheco
Philip T. Silvia, Jr., PhD
Keith Thibault

Lead Interviewer:
Joyce B. Rodrigues

Interviewers:
John J. Conforti, Jr.
George D. Kelly
Constance C. Mendes
William A. Moniz
Ann Rockett-Sperling

Transcriptionists:
Deborah Mello
Nancy Teasdale

Photographic Services/ImageRestoration:
Swan Imaging, Inc., Somerset, Massachusetts
Bill Crombie
Sue Crombie

Webmaster:
Stefani Koorey, PhD

Brown University:
John Nicholas Brown Center for Public Humanities and Cultural Heritage
Anne M. Valk, PhD, Deputy Director
Sarah Yahm, PhD, Candidate in American Studies

Interviewees' Family Members and Caregivers:
Alan P. Abdallah
Pat Abdallah
Dennis Abdow
Sandra Abdow
Steven D. Abdow
Francine A. (Soitos) Aloisa
Paul J. Amaral
Norma Rose Brandt
Joanne M. (Correira) Cadieux
Ruth A. (Soucy) Ferreira
Dorothy "Dolly" Ann (Terceira) Hardy

- Arlene B. Harnett
- Carol Jostka
- Shirley (Abdow) Messie
- Claire M. (Petrin) Norfolk
- Lori (Almeida) Pereira
- Irene V. (Arruda) Rigby
- Gary Stasiowski
- Doris E. (Rochefort) Bernier Thibault

Residential Facilities:

- Catholic Memorial Home:
  - Thomas Healy, Administrator
  - Mary Jean Storino, Therapeutic Activities Director

- Somerset Ridge Center:
  - Jeff Govoni, Administrator
  - Ann Marie Anunciacao, Activities Director

Cemeteries:

- Notre Dame Cemetery, Fall River
- St. Patrick's Cemetery, Fall River

City Clerks:

- Fall River City Clerk's Office:
  - Alison Bouchard, City Clerk
  - Inês Leite, Assistant City Clerk
  - Cathy Augiar
  - Cathy Howard
  - Mary Rezendes
  - Gloria Souza

- City Clerk's Office, New Bedford, Massachusetts

- City Clerk's Office, Somerset, Massachusetts

Thanks to:

- Sister Elizabeth A. Conyers, F.M.M.
- Ben Cooper
- Mary Jo Cordeiro
- Jean Dias
- Franciscan Missionaries of Mary
- Peter Green
- Robert Green
- Klear-Vu Corporation
- Peter Koury
- Patricia (Green) Lovet
- Marilyn (Cherry) Martin

Marilyn Marvel
Wilkinson B. Marvel
Milady Murphy
Old Colony History Museum, Taunton, Massachusetts
Albertina Pacheco
Betty Prescott
Kathleen Rockett
Janis (Sopkin) Rothman
Sheila Salvo
Denise Smith
Bernard A. G. Taradash
Temple Beth-El, Fall River
    Judy Morgenstern
Harvey I. Trieff
Judith E. Trieff
Andrea (Brenner) Williams
Wayne Wood
Georgette Yamin

Libraries:
In Massachusetts:
    Boston Public Library
    Fall River Public Library
    Lawrence Public Library
    New Bedford Public Library
    Somerset Public Library
        Bonnie D. Mendes, Director
    Swansea Public Library
    Taunton Public Library
    Westport Public Library

In New York:
    Franklin Delano Roosevelt Presidential Library and Museum, Hyde Park
    Gloversville Public Library

In Rhode Island:
    East Providence Public Library
    Providence Public Library

Media:
The Anchor
    Kenneth J. Souza

Fall River Herald News
    Deborah Allard
    Marc Munroe Dion

ACKNOWLEDGEMENTS

The Fall River Spirit
William A. Moniz

W.S.A.R.
Kathleen Castro

REFERENCES

Interviews:

ABDALLAH, Constance Joan (Waskiewicz) and Abdallah, Alphonse Kalil, by Constance C. Mendes, Swansea, MA, May 27, 2015.

ABDOW, Olivia Raposo (Terceira), by John J. Conforti, Catholic Memorial Home, December 10, 2014.

ALMEIDA, Delores (Silvia), by Joyce B. Rodrigues, Somerset Ridge Center, June 10, 2015.

AMARAL, Hortencia "Ester" Pacheco Ribeiro, by Joyce B. Rodrigues, Fall River Historical Society, November 12, 2014.

CORREIRA, Mary Vincent (Arruda), by Joyce B. Rodrigues, Westport, MA, October 17, 2015.

DESCHENES, Marie Lillian, by Joyce B. Rodrigues, Fall River, MA, August 22 and 29, 2015.

HARNETT, Marita Frances (Vokes), by John J. Conforti, Catholic Memorial Home, December 3, 2014.

ROCHEFORT, Marie Eva (Gagnon), by Ann Rockett-Sperling, Fall River, MA, July 29, 2015.

SOITOS, Ledora (Isidorio), by Ann Rockett-Sperling, Taunton, MA, June 3, 2015.

SOUCY, Michalina "Ruth" (Stasiowski), by William A. Moniz, Somerset Ridge Center, June 19, 2015.

Newspapers:

Fall River Herald News, Microfilm Collection, The Charlton Library of Fall River History, Fall River Historical Society.

Fall River Herald News, Reference and Special Collections, the Fall River Public Library, at: fallriverlibrary.org/reference.html.

Oral history guidelines:

Interviewing Guidelines, UCLA's Oral History Program, at: oralhistory.library.ucla.edu/interviewGuidelines.html

Mercier, Laurie and Madeline Buckendorf, *Using Oral History in Community History Projects,* Oral History Association Pamphlet Series #4, 2010, at: oralhistory.org/publications/pamphlet-series/.

Principles for Oral History and Best Practices for Oral History, Oral History Association, 2009, at: oralhistory.org/about/principles-and-practices/ and: oralhistory.org/wp-content/uploads/2009/10/OHA_principles_standards.pdf.

Oral history collections:

American Memory, Library of Congress, at: memory.loc.gov/ammem/awhhtml/index.html.

Shifting Gears, Digital Oral History at the Center for Lowell History, The University of Massachusetts Lowell, at: library.uml.edu/clh/OH/SHIFT/OH1.htm.

Voices of Labor Oral History Project, Southern Labor Archives, Special Collections Department, Pullen Library, Georgia State University, at: library.gsu.edu/spcoll/Labor/voices/VoLprogram.htm.

Oral History Projects, Archives and Special Collections, Claire T. Carney Library, UMASS Dartmouth, at: lib.umassd.edu/archives/oral-history-projects.

Published sources:

Ashton, Barbara. *Of Men and Money and the Fall River National Bank, 1825-1975.* Fall River: Privately printed, 1975.

Belanger, Marc N. *A Guide to Fall River's Mills and Other Industrial Sites.* Taunton: Marc N. Belanger, 2013.

Bendure, Zelma & Pfeiffer, Gladys. *America's Fabrics: Origin and History, Manufacture, Characteristics and Uses.* New York: The Macmillan Company, 1947.

Blewett, Mary H. *The Last Generation: Work and Life in the Textile Mills of Lowell, Massachusetts, 1910-1960.* Amherst: University of Massachusetts Press, 1990.

Blewett, Mary H. *Constant Turmoil: The Politics of Industrial Life in Nineteenth-Century New England.* Amherst: University of Massachusetts Press, 2000.

Brand, Donald Robert. *Corporatism and the Rule of Law: A Study of the National Recovery Administration.* Ithaca: Cornell University Press, 1988.

Burkhart, Janice (Ed.). *Baptisms of Saint Anne Catholic Church, Fall River, Massachusetts, 1869-1996*, Vols. 1–4. Pawtucket: American-French Genealogical Society, 1999.

Burkhart, Janice (Ed.). *Marriages of Saint Anne Catholic Church, Fall River, Massachusetts, 1869-1996*, Vols. 1–4. Pawtucket: American-French Genealogical Society, 1999.

Burkhart, Janice, and Letourneau, Goetz (Eds.). *Marriages of St. Matthew's Catholic Church, Fall River, Massachusetts, 1888-1986.* Pawtucket: American-French Genealogical Society, 1987.

Burkhart, Janice (Ed.). *Marriages of Blessed Sacrament Catholic Church, Fall River, Massachusetts, 1892-1995.* Pawtucket: American-French Genealogical Society, 1996.

Burkhart, Janice (Ed.). *Marriages of St. Jean-Baptiste Catholic Church, Fall River, Massachusetts, 1901-1996.* Pawtucket: American-French Genealogical Society, 2000.

REFERENCES

Burkhart, Janice (Ed.). *Marriages of St. Roch Catholic Church, Fall River, Massachusetts, 1899-1982*. Pawtucket: American-French Genealogical Society, 2002.

Burkhart, Janice (Ed.). *Baptisms of St. Roch Catholic Church, Fall River, Massachusetts, 1899-1982*. Pawtucket: American-French Genealogical Society, 2003.

Burkhart, Janice (Ed.). *Baptisms of Immaculate Conception Catholic Church, Fall River, Massachusetts, 1882-2010*. Pawtucket: American-French Genealogical Society, 2012.

Burkhart, Janice (Ed.). *Baptisms of Blessed Sacrament Catholic Church, Fall River, Massachusetts, 1892-1995*. Pawtucket: American-French Genealogical Society, 2007.

Burkhart, Janice (Ed.). *Baptisms of Notre-Dame de Lourdes Catholic Church, Fall River, Massachusetts, 1874-2001*, Vols. 1–4. Pawtucket: American-French Genealogical Society, 2005.

Burkhart, Janice (Ed.). *Marriages of Notre-Dame de Lourdes Catholic Church, Fall River, Massachusetts, 1874-2001*, Vols. 1–4. Pawtucket: American-French Genealogical Society, 2005.

Charlton, Earle Perry, II & Winius, George. *The Charlton Story: Earle Perry Charlton 1863-1930*. New York: Peter Lang, 2001.

Conforti, John J. *Fall River's First Italians: 1872-1914*. Fall River: Privately printed, 1975.

Cumbler, John T. *Working-Class Community in Industrial America: Work, Leisure, and Struggle in Two Industrial Cities, 1880-1930*. Westport: Greenwood Press, 1979.

Department of Commerce, Bureau of the Census, Bulletin 112, *Mortality Statistics 1911*, Washington: Government Printing Office, 1913, p. 14, at: http://www.cdc.gov/nchs/data/vsushistorical/mortstatbl_1911.pdf.

A Directory of Massachusetts Manufacturers Employing Fifty or More Production Workers 1951 – The Commonwealth of Massachusetts – Prepared by Division of Statistics, Massachusetts Department of Labor and Industries, Boston, at archive.org/details/directoryofmassa951mass.

Dunwell, Steve. *The Run of the Mill: A Pictorial Narrative of the Expansion, Dominion, Decline and Enduring Impact of the New England Textile Industry*. Boston: David R. Godine, 1978.

Fall River City Document No. 79, 1925. Fall River: Gagnon Printing Co., 1925.

Fenner, Henry M. *History of Fall River*. New York: F. T. Smiley Publishing Company, 1906.

Gagnon, Louis J. *Le Guide Francais de Fall River, Mass. 1909-1910*. Fall River: L.J. Gagnon, 1910.

Garment Worker: Har-Lee Edition, ILGWU. Publications: 5780 PUBS, Kheel Center for Labor-Management Documentation and Archives, Martin P. Catherwood Library, Cornell University, at: rmc.library.cornell.edu/EAD/htmldocs/KCL05780pubs.html.

Georgianna, Daniel. *The Strike of '28*. New Bedford: Spinner Publications, Inc., 1993.

Hard, William and Rheta Childe Dorr. "The Women's Invasion: Fall River an Outpost on the Edge of the Future." *Everybody's Magazine*, XIX (November, 1908) pp. 579-591.

Hartford, William F. *Where is Our Responsibility? Unions and Economic Change in the New England Textile Industry, 1870-1960.* Amherst: The University of Massachusetts Press, 1996.

Higgins, Alfred & LaVault, Rudolph I. *A Comprehensive Dictionary of Textile Terms.* Fall River: Dover Press, 1948.

Himmelberg, Robert F. *The Origins of the National Recovery Administration: Business, Government, and the Trade Association Issue, 1921–1933*. New York: Fordham University Press, 1993.

Lambert, Jeannette J. *Fall River's Apparel Industry, 1920-1986*. Paper submitted to Bristol Community College, 1988.

Lief, Alfred *The Firestone Story*. New York: Whittlesey House, 1951.

Maiocco, Carmen J. *The Narrows*. Fall River Cultural Council, 1992.

Maiocco, Carmen J. *Up the Flint*. Fall River Cultural Council, 1996.

Maiocco, Carmen J. *The Granite Block: Downtown Fall River in the mid-twentieth century*. Fall River Cultural Council, 1999.

Markowitz, and David Rosner. *Slaves of the Depression: Workers' Letters about Life on the Job*. Ithaca: Cornell University Press, 1987.

Martins, Michael & Binette, Dennis A. *Parallel Lives: A Social History of Lizzie Borden and Her Fall River*. Fall River: Fall River Historical Society, 2010.

Moniz, Evelyn. *My Story: A Memoir*. Boston: ILGWU-UNITE, 2011, available here.

Nichols, Henry W. & Broomhead, William H. *Standard Cotton Cloths and Their Construction*. Fall River: Dover Press, 1927.

Nienburg, Bertha M. *Reemployment of New England women in private industry*. Washington: U.S. Government Printing Office, 1936.

Opus 70. Fall River: Bishop Connolly High School, 1970.

Parish, W. H. *Artwork of Fall River, Massachusetts*. New York: The W.H. Parish Publishing Company, 1897.

Phillips, Arthur Sherman. *The Phillips History of Fall River, Fascicle I*. Fall River: Dover Press, 1944.

Phillips, Arthur Sherman. *The Phillips History of Fall River, Fascicle II*. Fall River: Dover Press, 1945.

Phillips, Arthur Sherman. *The Phillips History of Fall River, Fascicle III*. Fall River: Dover Press, 1946.

Pickin, Mary Brooks. *The Fashion Dictionary*. New York: Funk & Wagnall's, 1959.

Pictures of the Worst Fire in Fall River's History. New Bedford: Reynolds Printing Co., 1928, at: sailsinc.org/durfee/fire.pdf.

Salmond, John A. *The General Textile Strike of 1934: From Maine to Alabama*. Columbia: University of Missouri Press, 2002.

Silvia, Philip T., PhD. *Victorian Vistas: Fall River, 1865-1885, as viewed through its newspaper accounts*. Fall River: R.E. Smith Printing Co., 1987.

Silvia, Philip T., PhD. *Victorian Vistas: Fall River, 1886-1900, as viewed through its newspaper accounts*. Fall River: R.E. Smith Printing Co., 1988.

Silvia, Philip T., PhD. *Victorian Vistas: Fall River, 1900-1911, as viewed through its newspaper accounts*. Fall River: R.E. Smith Printing Co., 1992.

Smith, Thomas Russell. *The Cotton Textile Industry of Fall River, Massachusetts: A Case Study of Industrial Localization*. New York: King's Crown Press, 1944.

Stiles, Lela. *The Man Behind Roosevelt*. New York: The World Publishing Company, 1954.

The 1939 Durfee Record. Fall River: The Senior Class of B.M.C. Durfee High School, 1939.

City Directories:

Directory of Dighton, Rehoboth, Seekonk, Somerset & Swansea, Massachusetts, 1955. Newport, RI: Eastern Publishing Company.

Directory of Dighton, Rehoboth, Seekonk, Somerset & Swansea, Massachusetts, 1963-1964. Newport, RI: Eastern Publishing Company.

The Fall River City Directory, 1921 – 1938. Boston: R.L. Polk Co., Publishers.

The Fall River City Directory, 1981 – 1990. Malden: R.L. Polk Co., Publishers.

The Fall River City Directory, 1994 – 1997. Taylor, MI: R.L. Polk Co., Publishers.

The Fall River City Directory, 1939 – 1980. Boston: Sampson & Murdoch Co.

Miscellaneous:

Fall River Church Files (various): The Charlton Library of Fall River History, Fall River Historical Society.

Fall River School Files (various): The Charlton Library of Fall River History, Fall River Historical Society.

Newspapers:

The Berkshire Eagle, Pittsfield, Massachusetts

Fall River Daily Globe, microfilm collection, Charlton Library of Fall River History, Fall River Historical Society.

Florence Morning News, Florence, South Carolina

The New York Times

Photographs & Images:

Private family collections.

Fall River photographs (various): Collection of the Fall River Historical Society, The Charlton Library of Fall River History.

Fall River postcards (various): Collection of the Fall River Historical Society, The Charlton Library of Fall River History.

Ephemera:

International Ladies Garment Workers Union (I.L.G.W.U.):

Home Town Union: The Story of the ILGWU in Fall River and Vicinity, Fall River: International Ladies Garment Workers Union, 1948. Collection of the Fall River Historical Society, The Charlton Library of Fall River History.

Testimonial Banquet to the International Ladies Garment Workers Union by Har-Lee Members, Local 178 - ILGWU, Fall River: Har-Lee Banquet Committee, 1941. Collection of the Fall River Historical Society, The Charlton Library of Fall River History.

Textile Workers Union of America (C.I.O.):

Agreement By and Between Fall River Textile Manufacturers Association and Textile Workers Union of America (C.I.O.), Fall River: Fall River Textile Manufacturers Association, 1943. Collection of the Fall River Historical Society, The Charlton Library of Fall River History.

Fall River ... A Brighter To-Morrow, Fall River: Fall River Educational Department of Textile Workers Union of America, C.I.O., circa 1945. Collection of the Fall River Historical Society, The Charlton Library of Fall River History.

INDEX

by Stefani Koorey, PhD

Entries are arranged in letter-by-letter order, using the *Chicago Manual of Style, 16th Edition*. References to page numbers for illustrations are indicated by numerals in bold type.

All females are listed by their last known surname, followed in parentheses by married name, with cross-references provided from maiden name for ease of location. In places where maiden surnames are unknown, first names are provided. All placenames, including streets, companies, churches, and schools, are located in Fall River, Massachusetts, unless specifically noted. Bold numerals indicate illustrations. Bold names indicate the subject of the oral histories that make up this book.

B

NOTES

NOTES

NOTES